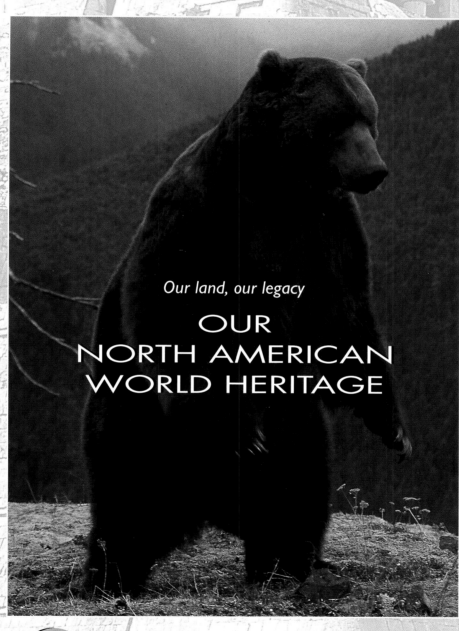

*Our land, our legacy*

# OUR
# NORTH AMERICAN
# WORLD HERITAGE

WORLD HERITAGE PUBLISHING

INAH

Editorial
**RAÍCES**

*Our land, our legacy*

# OUR
# NORTH AMERICAN
# WORLD HERITAGE

First published 1997 by Harper-MacRae & Associates, Inc., Instituto Nacional Antropologia e Historia (INAH) and Editorial Raices.

Harper-MacRae & Associates, Inc.
PO Box 18125
Columbus OH 43218-8125 USA
Facsimile 614-488 1452
Telephone 1-800-2611943 and 614-488 6458

Produced by: Harper-MacRae Publishing Pty Limited
6 - 8 Patonga Drive, Patonga, Australia 2256

Project Co-ordination: Robert Osborne, Kay Osborne.

Writing: **US and Canadian natural sites:** William Lines; **US and Canadian cultural sites:** Maree Reid; **Mexican sites:** Marney Dunn; **Cahokia Mounds:** William R. Iseminger; **Sian Ka'an:** Juan E Bezaury Creel, Executive Director and Secretary, Amigos de Sian Ka'an.

Design: Brett Cullen.

Editor: Mark Swadling.

Production Consultant : Gordon Liu
Production Assistance: Sharyn Driscoll.

The Publishers would like to give special thanks to the following individuals and organizations for their invaluable assistance: Dr Jim Thorsell, Head - Natural Heritage Program, IUCN - The World Conservation Union; Anthony Duffy; UNESCO - World Heritage Centre, Paris, France; IUCN - The World Conservation Union, Gland, Switzerland; WCMC - The World Conservation Monitoring Centre, Cambridge, England; ICOMOS, Paris, France; Parcs Canada of the Department of Canadian Heritage, Montreal, Canada; US National Parks Service, Washington, DC, USA.

Publisher's Cataloging in Publication
(Prepared by Quality Books Inc.)

Our land, our legacy: Our North American World Heritage.
p. cm.
ISBN: 1-57769-004-4
Includes index.

1. Cultural property, Protection of - North America. 2. Historic sites - North America. I. Swadling, Mark, ed. II. Title: Our North American World Heritage
CC135.087 1996          909
                    QBI96-40444

Pre-press Production: Fancy Graphic Production Ltd , Hong Kong.

Printed in Hong Kong by Inter Scan Limited on acid free paper produced from new growth plantation forest.

PAGE ONE   *Grizzly bear*
PAGE ONE BACKGROUND   *The Castillo, Chichen Itza*
PREVIOUS PAGE   *Willow Lake and Wrangell Mountains*
THIS PAGE   *White-tailed deer*
OPPOSITE   *Mountain bluebird*

# CONTENTS

# PREFACE

The World Heritage Convention, with 146 signatories as of May 1996, is undoubtedly one of the most successful international heritage conservation instruments in the world. Adopted by the General Conference of UNESCO in 1972, the Convention seeks to foster the conservation of outstanding natural and cultural properties in a spirit of international cooperation. It responds to the increasing threats to cultural and natural heritage caused by poverty in many countries, neglect, and in some countries, by unconsidered economic growth and development. State Parties are encouraged to identify, protect and present cultural and natural heritage for future generations.

Canada, Mexico and the United States have been active partners in the field of World Heritage conservation for many years. The United States played a fundamentally important role in the development of the Convention. Promoted by conservationists in the United States in the late 1960s, it was their idea of a World Heritage Trust that led to the development of this Convention, that not only aims to protect the most outstanding natural areas, but also places of unique historical, archaeological, architectural and cultural value.

As the first step in the World Heritage conservation process, cultural and natural properties of 'outstanding universal value' that are deserving of protection are identified and included on the World Heritage List. Of the 469 properties currently inscribed on the List, forty four are located in Canada, Mexico and the United States. These properties include some of the finest examples of natural and cultural heritage in the world. The sovereignty of the State Parties on whose territory these World Heritage properties are situated, is in no way threatened or compromised by World Heritage listing, and existing individual and national property rights are maintained.

Some of the world's most spectacular and well-known archaeological sites are located in Mexico. The vast urban and religious centers of Teotihuacán, Oaxaca, Palenque, Xochimilco, El Tajín and Chichén Itzá are all testimony to the pre-Hispanic peopling of the region. They are joined on the World Heritage List by the prehistoric rock paintings of the Sierra de San Francisco in Baja California with their depictions of people, and animals such as fish, reptiles and birds. The Historic Center of Pueblo, Zacatecas, Guananajuato and the monasteries of Morelia and Popocatépetl show the influence of Spanish colonialism in the form of magnificent urban and religious architecture. Sian Ka'an, a UNESCO Biosphere Reserve located on the east coast of the Yucatán Peninsula, includes richly diverse tropical forests, coral reefs, mangroves and marshes, while the Whale Sanctuary of Vizcaino is not only an important reproduction and wintering site for grey and blue whales, seals and sea lions, but also provides lagoon sanctuaries for four species of endangered marine turtles.

In Alberta, Canada, some of the most important discoveries of dinosaur fossils, more than 75 million years old, have been protected at Dinosaur Provincial Park. In New Mexico in the United States, the vast network of huge caves at Carlsbad Caverns National Park with its profuse, diverse and beautiful mineral formations has also recently been included on the List, joining the earlier inclusion of Mammoth Cave National Park in Kentucky, one of the world's largest networks of limestone caves.

The magnificent national parks of Grand Canyon, Redwood, Olympic, Hawaii Volcanoes, Yosemite and the Great Smoky Mountains in the United States and the Canadian Rocky Mountains, Gros Morne, Wood Buffalo and Nahanni in Canada have all been included on the World Heritage List. These parks are home to some of the world's most dynamic scenery with spectacular wild rivers, forests and mountains of massive scale and large populations of wildlife. Canada and the United States are also home to two of the most powerful expressions of successful cross-frontier World Heritage conservation partnerships: Kluane, Wrangell-St. Elias, Glacier Bay and Tatshenshini-Alsek Parks and Glacier-Waterton International Peace Park.

One of the most important protective mechanisms of the World Heritage Convention is the List of World Heritage in Danger. If a World Heritage property is threatened, the World Heritage Committee may decide to include the property on this List with the aim of providing assistance to the State Party to conserve the property. In the United States of America two properties have been included on the List of World Heritage in Danger. Yellowstone National Park in Wyoming, celebrated as the first national park in the world was, up until recent White House intervention, threatened by a large mining project. It is still suffering the impact of mass tourism. The fragile ecology and water systems of Everglades National Park in Florida suffered the calamity of a hurricane in August 1992 and are threatened by encroaching urban development and nutrient pollution from agricultural activities. The inclusion of these two United States national parks on the List of World Heritage in Danger highlights the need for urgent attention to be given to the conservation of these properties if they are to be enjoyed and valued by future generations.

The broad range of human occupation of the North American continent from prehistoric to historic times is demonstrated by the 6,000 year old hunting site of Head Smashed-In Bison Jump Complex in Alberta, Canada; the traditional hunting and fishing village of Ninstints on Anthony Island off the west coast of Canada; and the 11th century wood and earthen houses recognized as the first tangible traces of a European presence in the Americas, at L'Anse Aux Meadows in Newfoundland. At the confluence of the Missouri and Mississippi Rivers, the site of Cahokia Mounds, a complex of mounds, palisades and dwellings, illustrates the sophisticated social, political and economic organization of pre-Columbian settlement in the southeastern United States. The prehistoric villages of Mesa Verde, with their impressive stone cliff dwellings, along with the nearly 1,000 year-old urban dwellings of Chaco Canyon, now lie abandoned in the southwest desert of the United States. Pueblo de Taos, a centuries-old adobe settlement in New Mexico, is still an active ceremonial and urban center for Pueblo Indians of the area.

The Statue of Liberty and Independence Hall, both well-known symbols of the principles of American independence, and Monticello and the University of Virginia in Charlottesville, designed and built by Thomas Jefferson in an architectural evocation of his hopes for universal freedom and democracy are also included on the World Heritage List.

The colonial history of North America is further illustrated by La Fortaleza and San Juan Historic Site in Puerto Rico, built as a strategic defence for the city and San Juan Bay. In Canada, Quebec's historic center and Lunenburg - recognized as the best example of a British colonial city in North America - are both living and functioning urban centers included on the World Heritage List.

The beauty, majesty and scientific values of the extraordinary diversity of North American cultural and natural heritage presented in this book have been recognized as being of 'outstanding universal value'. I encourage you all to participate in the challenge of conserving this great wealth of natural and cultural heritage in the North American region.

Bernd von Droste
Director
UNESCO World Heritage Center

OPPOSITE *Cactus Saquaro*

# FOREWORD

Some works of nature and of humankind are irreplaceable. In the north of the American continent, our three nations share the custody and safeguard of sites of the cultural and natural heritage of humankind. The diversity of living creatures, the unique adaptations of species to their environment and the manifestations of cultures are the fundamental part of the rich heritage which we should preserve for future generations of men and women.

Hence, this book 'Our North American World Heritage', a product of collaboration between institutions which are in charge of executing the agreements of the United Nations Convention Concerning the Protection of Cultural and Natural World Heritage should be celebrated as a significant effort on the road to the protection of this legacy.

Currently, Mexico has achieved the inscription of fourteen of nearly 500 sites included in the World Heritage List; it is the highest number amongst the Latin American countries. Twelve of them are of cultural interest and two are natural creations which are inhabited by protected plant and animal species. Our nation has always been conscious of the importance of preserving its historical roots and its cultural heritage. The images of these fourteen sites and their prompt inscription are proof of the enormous task that we Mexicans have yet to carry out in order to maintain in the best possible condition this great wealth that forms part of the treasure of the planet which is our only home.

Ma. Teresa Franco
Directora General
INAH

# INTRODUCTION

I am writing this introduction from my home in Seattle, Washington. It's early morning and the peaks of the Olympic Mountains are protruding above the fog on Puget Sound. Another beautiful day in the Pacific Northwest of North America.

Today is also a special day. It is April 22, the 26th anniversary of Earth Day. I am reminded that the most valuable lesson I have learned during my life as an environmental advocate is the importance of a 'sense of place'. Quite simply, people are more likely to take care of their 'places' - the things they know and love. This includes, of course, our families, our homes and the communities in which we live. It also includes those natural 'places' in our lives - our backyards, local parks and forests. Collectively, our 'places' are the essence of our lives. They are what makes life worth living.

I believe we must also have a global sense of place. As a part of the family of humankind, we in North America are privileged to be home to some of the world's most spectacular cultural and natural areas. This book, 'Our Land, Our Legacy, Our North American World Heritage' is a wonderful tribute to the most famous places that have been protected in Canada, Mexico and the United States of America.

However, all is not well for some of these incredible places. It was shocking in December 1995 when UNESCO's World Heritage Committee listed Yellowstone National Park - the first World Heritage site - on the List of World Heritage in Danger. Sadly, Yellowstone joins the Everglades as the only two sites in North America on the Danger List. This does not reflect well on our legacy of stewardship for these invaluable natural areas. Surely we can - and must - do better in the future.

UNESCO's World Heritage Fund program began as an idea in 1965 when Russ Train, one of America's greatest conservationists, raised it at a White House Conference on International Cooperation. The following year, IUCN - The World Conservation Union - expanded the concept at their ninth General Assembly in Lucerne, Switzerland.

It was concluded that there should be an international legal instrument under the auspices of UNESCO through which the most outstanding samples of the world's natural and built heritage would be preserved. A sort of 'Nobel Prize' or 'Hall of Fame' for the 'best of the best' places on earth. Over the next seven years, various drafts of a legal text were discussed and finally, at the Stockholm Conference on the Environment in 1972, the World Heritage Convention was sent to UNESCO for final adoption. In 1973 the United States was its first signatory country.

This book illustrates the wonderful places that have been listed under the World Heritage Convention in North America. They include nineteen of the best of North America's national parks and twenty five of the region's most exceptional cultural monuments. But the identification process is not yet over and the list must grow if all the sites of universal significance are to be included. I personally feel that there are several natural sites above the Arctic Circle that would meet the criteria, and I urge both the Canadian and United States authorities to consider making nominations from this unrepresented part of the continent. Likewise, I note that in the United States, nearly all the properties listed are under the authority of the National Parks Service. There are no World Heritage sites for a number of qualified public lands. For example, the Kalmiopsis Wilderness Area in the Siskiuyou National Forest in southern Oregon, is an obvious candidate.

Nominating a site under the convention, however, is not just a matter of identifying somewhere outstanding and putting it on a list. It is a positive political act by the governments concerned. It demonstrates that these governments - and the citizens they represent - recognize that areas thus designated are not just important within their own borders, but are in a real sense a heritage shared with the entire world. Designation confirms that the people and their governments accept the responsibility to care for these areas, on behalf of all humanity, now and in the future.

Such actions are both timely and difficult. They are timely because we have come to realize that we live in a world where all people and all of nature are interdependent. All societies must work for a peaceful, equitable and sustainable future for all world life. But it is also difficult. With over 5 billion people already living in the world, the pressures on global natural resources are great. In less than a century from now those resources will have to provide for the needs of an estimated 10 to 12 billion human individuals. The pressure on most areas of land and sea is increasing, and safeguarding even the most outstanding natural areas designated under the World Heritage Convention will require continuous effort. We see around the world many sites, some designated under the Convention and others worthy of such designation, that are in danger. We in the IUCN regularly bring these problems to the attention of the World Heritage Committee, but their powers and resources, like those of many governments, are severely limited. Mining, forest destruction, over-fishing, pollution, urban encroachment and the sheer pressure of tourism are all eroding sites which the governments concerned, and the wider world community, would like to protect.

We shall only safeguard these masterworks of humans and nature if there is genuine international cooperation, to help the governments that are custodians of these places to carry out the commitments they have entered into under the World Heritage Convention. Many lower-income countries lack the resources for monitoring and safeguarding the sites that they have named. Some lack even the capability to survey the sites that they know they would like to designate. Even in the developed countries, with much more abundant resources, national budgets often place less emphasis on protecting the environment than they should.

As the listing of Yellowstone National Park on the List of World Heritage in Danger reminds us, there are difficult challenges ahead. Those who read this book should not just treat it as a manual for armchair travel. They should see it as a challenge - and an opportunity - to help protect these areas for the benefit of current and future generations. Only with our collective willingness to adopt lifestyles that nature can sustain, with informed advocacy with our governments and with a focus on improved levels of international cooperation to safeguard the world's environment, can the objectives of the Convention be fulfilled. We have a great deal more work to do, and I urge all who read this book to commit themselves to that end.

And remember: 'Earth Day - Every Day - You Can Make A World of Difference', and by working together, we can make a different world.

Jay D. Hair, PhD
President
IUCN - The World Conservation Union

OPPOSITE   *Yellowstone River at sunrise*
NEXT PAGE   *Mt Olympus, Olympic National Park*

# THE UNITED STATES OF AMERICA

# YELLOWSTONE

## NATIONAL PARK

O F THE FORTY-EIGHT CONTIGUOUS UNITED STATES, much of what remains of wild America can be found in the rugged folds of the Rocky Mountains. Arbitrarily inscribed in the heart of this wild area are the boundaries of Yellowstone National Park. The park's 2,221,773 acres (899,818 ha) sit in the northwest corner of the state of Wyoming and overlap into Montana to the north and Idaho to the west. Yellowstone became the first site to be inscribed on the World Heritage List in 1978 - for its world famous hydrothermal features and because it is the largest wildlife preserve in the contiguous United States.

Although Yellowstone is one of the largest national parks in the continental United States, it neither endures nor inspires on its own. Fortunately, Yellowstone is surrounded by six national forests, Grand Teton National Park, and two wildlife refuges. Together these areas, containing nearly 18.8 million acres (7.2 million ha), make up the Greater Yellowstone ecosystem, one of the largest intact ecosystems in the temperate zone of the earth.

Yellowstone was America's first federally protected public park and the first national park in the world. The necessary legislation passed through Congress in 1872 with barely any opposition, mainly because the area was virtually unvisited, uninhabited and beyond the fringe of desired land. Proponents assured their colleagues that not only was the area geographically unique, but it was too high and cold to cultivate. Maintaining it as a park would do 'no harm to the material interests' of the nation.

PREVIOUS PAGE   *Elk*
TOP   *Bison*
ABOVE   *Mammoth Hot Springs, Pools and Terraces*
OPPOSITE   *Old Faithful Geyser*

From the lowest point in the park at mile-high Gardiner, Montana, to the highest peaks of the Absarokas, in the southeast corner, is a spread of nearly 6,000 feet (1,830 m). In that span, entire worlds form - from warm, dry quilts of sage to frigid sprawls of Arctic willow and woodrush.

Areas in the western portion of the park receive significant amounts of precipitation, especially snow, as moisture-laden air is pushed up by the high peaks. The southwest corner of the park receives nearly 70 inches (1,780 mm) of precipitation annually, while Gardiner receives 10 to 12 inches (250 to 300 mm), placing it just above a desert.

The rain and snowmelt gather in hundreds of lakes and ponds. Rushing streams, white with foam, cut through black-walled canyons. Placid rivers meander through meadows that, in season, blaze with wild flowers.

The park's main river, the Yellowstone, rises in the Absaroka Range and flows through the park, south to north. From the point where it emerges into a dry, desert-like basin outside of Gardiner, it has roughly 800 miles (1,280 km) to go before losing itself in the brown waters of the Missouri.

Arctic and Pacific air meet and mix over Yellowstone. The cool Arctic air keeps the average monthly temperature near the center of Yellowstone a chilly 32.8°F (0.4°C), but average does not mean consistent: the record high in the park is 103°F (39.4°C), while the record low is -66°F (-54.4°C) - a sizeable spread of 169°F (76°C).

Yellowstone's spaciousness is a stronghold for wildlife. Grizzly bear, moose, elk, bighorn, deer, antelope, wolves, coyotes and bison roam the backcountry. Hundreds of bird species frequent the park. Among them are great winged birds; the bald eagle, raven, great gray owl and trumpeter swan.

ABOVE    *Pronghorn antelope buck*
LEFT    *Bull moose in meadow, fighting for dominance*

The trumpeter is the largest wildfowl on the continent. On a diet of twenty pounds of aquatic plants a day, it may often attain a wingspan of 8 feet (2.4 m). The bird nests primarily in the Yellowstone region and in northern Canada and Alaska. By 1932 hunting and loss of habitat reduced the population of trumpeters in the Yellowstone ecosystem to less than one hundred birds. Thanks in large part to efforts by the U.S. Fish and Wildlife Service at nearby Red Rock Lakes National Wildlife Refuge, there are today over 350 individuals in the park.

Climate determines life in Yellowstone. No great herds of bison or elk would graze in the northern valleys and meadows of the central plateau if conditions had not favored the growth of grasses such as fescue and wheatgrass, and herbs like lupine, phlox and groundsel. Grizzlies might not find the area so hospitable if the land were significantly drier, as there would be no yampa, biscuit root, yarrow and whitebark pine for them to feed on. But for the small, dry pocket of blue-bunch wheatgrass, needle and thread, and junegrass growing on the lowlands at the north end of the park near Gardiner, no antelope would winter in the park at all.

Lodgepole pine is the most common tree and makes up about 80 % of Yellowstone's forests. It is tall and straight and grows in dense stands with few if any branches on its lower trunk. There are also climax forests of Engelmann spruce and subalpine fir.

The forests of the Yellowstone Rockies cannot maintain their health and vigor without fire; they are part of a land created and recreated from the ashes. In 1988 fires swept through the park and burned about 995,000 acres (403,000 ha), or 45 % of the park. The heaviest fires were in stands of aging lodgepole pine, waiting to be ignited to make way for new growth.

Wild flowers also benefitted from the fires. They grow throughout the park but are more profuse on the high and wet alpine meadows. The most common are Indian paint-brush, aster, penstemmon, lupine, mountain bluebell, monkey flower, fireweed, balsam root, glacier lily, wild geranium, harebell, blue flax and Rocky Mountain fringed gentian, the official park flower.

Most visitors to Yellowstone are attracted by the park's hydrothermal features. More than 10,000 spouting geysers, terraced hot springs, sulfurous steaming fumaroles, boiling hot pools, and bubbling mud pots, make Yellowstone the most active thermal area in the world.

This activity owes its existence to a great subterranean blister of molten rock, forever threatening to erupt. About 600,000 years ago it did erupt, lifting some 1,000 square miles (2,590 sq km) of the Rocky Mountains in a paroxysm of violent eruptions that deposited a huge pile of ash and dust over much of North America. The unsupported crust collapsed into the emptied chamber to leave a 1,200 square mile (3,100 sq km) caldera.

Later, less violent eruptions almost filled the caldera with ash and lava, blocking the ancestral Yellowstone River and creating Yellowstone Lake. However the river continued to evolve and, aided by the glaciers of three ice ages and even more by hot water and steam that softened and yellowed the caldera's rock rim, slowly carved out today's Grand Canyon of the Yellowstone that descends from the lake in two waterfalls.

Volcanism left the primal heat of the planet nearer to the surface in Yellowstone than in any other location. Water seeps down through porous rock to a depth of about 5,000 feet (1,500 m), near the molten rock. There, under pressure, it is super-heated to a temperature far above boiling. The hot water rises and emerges at the surface as either a geyser, hot spring or fumarole.

LEFT  *Lower falls of Yellowstone River*
RIGHT  *Female red-shafted flicker*

ABOVE   *Hayden's camp, United States Geological Survey, August 24, 1870.*
BELOW   *The United States Geological & Geophysical Survey of the Territories, Conducted by Hayden, en route with pack train upon the trail between the Yellowstone and East Fork Rivers, 'showing the manner in which all parties traverse these wilds'.*

Geysers are Yellowstone's most talked-about feature: awesome waterspouts such as Old Faithful, which every 1 to 2 hours climbs boiling and roaring up to 200 feet (60 m) into the sky. Others, all different, include Grotto Geyser, emerging from a white silica cave; Riverside Geyser, arching a plume of boiling water over the Firehole River; and Steamboat - the tallest in the world - with eruptions nearly twice as high as Old Faithful's but erratic, spouting at intervals of anything from four days to four years.

Amid the spectacle, beauty, and wilderness, there are growing threats. The land around Yellowstone is checker-boarded with mineral claims. More and more, gold mines, tailing dumps, settling ponds, clear-cuts and oil and gas drilling operations threaten to unravel the integrity of the Greater Yellowstone ecosystem. In 1988 the Wilderness Society placed Yellowstone Park on its list of the ten most endangered national parks in America. A delegation from the World Heritage Commission visited the area in September 1995 and concluded that Yellowstone should be placed on the List of World Heritage in Danger. Their recommendation was accepted, and now the world's first national park and one of its first World Heritage sites shares, along with Everglades National Park, the ignominious distinction of being one of two United States parks threatened with removal from the World Heritage List.

Fortunately the threat from one particularly contentious gold mine has recently been averted with an agreement struck by the White House. Set to operate a mere 2.5 miles (4 km) from Yellowstone's northeast corner, its potential to despoil the land with toxic wastes, sinkholes, unfilled shafts, and tailings would have made nonsense of any notion of a buffer around the park.

Visitor access is via one of five park entrances, where accommodation is also available: from the north at Gardiner, Montana; the west at West Yellowstone, Montana; the south at Jackson, Wyoming; the east at Cody, Wyoming; and the northeast at Cooke City, Montana. July and August are peak periods and should be avoided.

*Further Information: Yellowstone Museum and Library Association, Yellowstone National Park, WY 82190.*

*....Their size is somewhat above that of our common bullock, and their flesh of a delicious flavour, resembling and equalling that of fat beef. Their flesh which is easily procured; furnishes the savages of these vast regions the means of a wholesome and good subsistence ...The buffalo bull is one of the most formidable and frightening looking animals in the world when excited to resistance; his long shaggy mane hangs in great profusion over his neck and shoulders, and often extends quite down to the ground.*

George Catlin, 'North American Indians'

ABOVE  *Black bear*

More than 10,000 spouting geysers, terraced hot springs, sulfurous steaming fumaroles, boiling hot pools, and bubbling mud pots make Yellowstone the most active thermal area in the world.

BELOW *Morning Glory Pool*

ABOVE   *Bohemian waxwing*
BELOW   *Bobcat*
ABOVE RIGHT   *Mountain lion chasing snowshoe hare*
RIGHT   *Coyote*

ABOVE   *Trumpeter swan*
RIGHT   *Hot springs and pools in Bisquit Geyser Basin*
BELOW   *Mountain bluebird*

ABOVE   *Norris Meadow at sunrise*
RIGHT   *Indian paintbrush*
BELOW   *Timber wolf*

We reached the old wolf in time to watch a fierce green fire dying in her eyes. I realized then, and have known ever since, that there was something new to me in those eyes - something known only to her and to the mountain. I was young then, and full of trigger-itch; I thought that because fewer wolves meant more deer, that no wolves would mean hunters' paradise. But after seeing the green fire die, I sensed that neither the wolf nor the mountain agreed with such a view.

Aldo Leopold,
'A Sand County Almanac'

ABOVE *Osprey*
MAIN PICTURE *After a forest fire*

# STATUE OF LIBERTY

THE STATUE OF LIBERTY, OR LIBERTY ENLIGHTENING THE WORLD as it is formally known, is undoubtedly one the world's most recognizable monuments. Located on Liberty Island (formerly Bedloe's Island) in the upper bay of New York Harbor, the colossal statue was a gift to the United States from France to mark the friendship between the peoples of the two countries and to commemorate America's centennial. On October 28, 1886, more than ten years after the commencement of the project, the statue was dedicated by President Grover Cleveland. He told the thousands who gathered to witness the unveiling ceremony, 'We will not forget that Liberty has here made her home; nor shall her chosen altar be neglected.' Indeed, since its unveiling the statue has undergone continual improvements, culminating in a multi-million dollar restoration project completed in 1986. Though exposure to the elements has meant that the hollow figure has lost its bright copper-colored appearance, its metal exterior remains in excellent condition.

The design of the statue is rich in symbolism. The young female figure is draped in classical robes and wears a crown with seven spokes (representing the seven seas and seven continents). She holds a torch in her raised right hand and cradles in her left arm a tablet of the law inscribed with the raised Roman numerals of the date July 4, 1776 - the date of the Declaration of Independence. The broken shackles of slavery lie at her feet. From the base of its concrete pedestal to the top of its upright torch, the figure stands at 151 feet (46 m); its overall height is 305 feet (92 m).

Until the construction of the St. Paul's Building in 1899, Lady Liberty was the tallest structure in New York. Spectacular views of New York Harbor and the surrounding area can be seen from the top levels of the pedestal, or through the diadem windows in the observation platform in the statue's crown, just over 260 feet (79 m) above sea level. To the millions of immigrants who sailed past it on their way to neighboring Ellis Island, a Federal immigration station from 1892 to 1954, the gigantic statue represented the freedom and opportunity open to them in the New World. In 'The New Colossus', the best-known poem about the statue, Emma Lazarus aptly described Liberty as ' ... the Mother of Exiles'.

The construction of the mammoth statue was a supreme technical achievement. By 1875 the final form of the figure had been set in a clay model measuring about 4 feet (1.3 m). Three plaster enlarged versions followed. Once the full-scale enlargement process had been completed, the 36 foot (11 m) figure was divided into several sections; each of these sections was then enlarged to four times its size. With a conventional bronze cast rejected because of its

TOP LEFT    *Paris factory workers, beating copper to framework*
TOP RIGHT   *Face of statue prior to construction*
ABOVE    *Illustration showing internal spiral staircase*

weight and cost, an ancient construction technique known as 'repoussé' was used to form the exterior of the figure. This procedure involved hand-hammering into shape three hundred thin sheets of copper onto wooden frames which had been constructed to follow the contours of the plaster model. The sheets were then joined with copper rivets, and eventually welded onto a skeleton of four massive iron supports.

The French bridge engineer Alexandre-Gustave Eiffel, who later designed the Eiffel Tower in Paris, was responsible for constructing the framework of the statue. The 89 foot (27 m) pedestal, which stands on a 53 foot (16 m) concrete foundation, was designed

by New York architect Richard Morris Hunt, and built within the star-shaped walls of Fort Wood, a former military battery erected in the early 19th century to defend New York Harbor. After several interruptions, the pedestal was finally completed in April 1886. With a combined weight of 27,000 tons (24,545 tonnes), the pedestal and foundation remains one of the heaviest pieces of masonry ever built.

The origins of the statue can be traced to a dinner party held at the home of a French intellectual and expert on United States constitutional history, Édouard René Lefebrve de Laboulaye, near Versailles, France, in 1865, shortly after the end of the American Civil War. Though he never visited the United States, Laboulaye was a great admirer of the country's political institutions. Following dinner, the host broached the idea of presenting a gift from the people of France to the people of United States to mark the forthcoming centennial anniversary of American Independence. The proposal made an impact on one guest in particular, Fédéric-Auguste Bartholdi, a 31year-old Alsatian sculptor. When the two men discussed the project again in early 1871, Laboulaye, along with other eminent men, encouraged Bartholdi to travel to the United States to examine the possibility of erecting a monument ' ... in remembrance of the ancient friendship of France and the United States.' That same year, the young sculptor made the first of four trips to the United States where he ' ... tr[ied] especially to glorify the Republic and Liberty over there, hoping that I will one day find them back here.' After spending five months abroad, during which time he met with President Ulysses Grant, Henry Wadsworth Longfellow and others, Bartholdi returned to France to begin work. While in the United States, he chose the flat 12 acre (5 ha) Bedloe's Island (since 1956 known as Liberty Island) as the perfect site for the memorial - which he had decided would take the form of a female figure. The sculptor later admitted that Liberty's face was that of his mother's. It was soon realized that the statue would not be ready for the centennial year; in fact, fifteen years would pass before the gift would be presented to the people of the United States.

Meanwhile it had been decided that the cost of the project would be shared by the two countries. While the French people would sponsor the construction and transportation of the statue, the responsibility for building the foundation and pedestal would rest with the people of the United States. To this end, fundraising committees were set up in both countries. In France, a large portion of the cost - one million francs - was raised by public subscription. To finance the construction of the statue a variety of fundraising methods were employed: for instance, a lottery was organized, songs were written and performed, and clay replicas of the statue were sold. In June 1878, the completed head and shoulders of the statue were placed on public display in Paris. By July 1882, the total amount of money needed to complete the French end of the project was secured. Well before this, and with the approval of those who had encouraged him to travel to the United States, Bartholdi had commenced work on the statue. By June 1884, the 225 ton (204 tonne) statue was ready for shipment to its new home.

While the French people contributed generously to the building of the statue, American contributions for the construction of the pedestal were not so forthcoming. The half-hearted response from the federal government did not help matters. In fact Congress had been reluctant to accept the statue in the first place. From 1877 public appeals had been launched, but the American people's response was disappointing. The public's apathy was due, in part, to the belief that the memorial would never be finished. To allay this fear, the statue's 42 foot (13 m) right arm was displayed at the Centennial Exposition in Philadelphia in 1876, and later at Madison Square in New York City.

It was thanks largely to the intervention of publisher Joseph Pulitzer that the funds for the pedestal were eventually raised. In his paper the New York World, he berated the public for accepting the statue without ' ... our having provided even so much as a landing place for it.' Furthermore, he denounced the wealthy for failing to inject money into the project and appealed to the general public for contributions: ' ... Let us not wait for the millionaires to give this money. It is not a gift from the millionaires of France to the millionaires of America, but a gift to the whole people of France to the whole people of America.' The publishing tycoon himself contributed $1,000 to the project. In a move designed not only to raise funds but to increase the World's circulation, Pulitzer promised to publish the name of every individual who contributed to the fund to build the pedestal. Additionally, he emphasized that the gift was to the whole nation, not just New York. In time, his strategy worked. By August 1885 he had succeeded in raising $100,000 (from 121,000 readers) towards the $250,000 needed for the pedestal's construction; at the same time, the circulation of his paper had increased substantially. The rest of the money was raised through sporting events, theater performances, balls, and other activities.

To assist the cause, Emma Lazarus, an American literary figure, penned a sonnet, 'The New Colossus', which, along with works by Walt Whitman, Mark Twain and Bret Harte, appeared in a collection that was auctioned for $1,500 at an art exhibition in December 1883. In 1903, her poem was inscribed on a bronze plaque and placed inside the pedestal. The plaque reads in part:

> Give me your tired, your poor,
> Your huddled masses yearning to breathe free,
> The wretched refuse of your teeming shore.
> Send these, the homeless, tempest-tost to me,
> I lift my lamp beside the golden door!

In Paris, on July 4, 1884, the statue was presented to the United States ambassador to France. Disassembled and packed into 214 boxes, Liberty arrived in New York City a year later. While it would take months for it to be reassembled, the arrival of the statue provided a much needed boost to the fundraising campaign in the United States. In April 1886, after several interruptions because of insufficient funds, the pedestal was completed. Finally, on October 28, 1886, with Bartholdi in attendance, President Grover Cleveland dedicated the monument. It was, he said, a ' ... token of the affection and consideration of the people of France.' Sadly, Laboulaye, the originator of the memorial, died in 1883 without ever seeing it finished.

The statue area was declared a national monument in 1924, and in 1937 was placed under the jurisdiction of the National Park Service. From 1901 to 1933, it had been under the administration of the War Department. Ellis Island was added to the national monument in 1965 and a museum tracing the history of United States immigration was constructed on the island and opened in 1972. The inclusion of Ellis Island brought the monument's total area to approximately 58 acres (24 ha).

By Independence Day 1986, just short of the statue's centennial, American and French craftsmen had completed a multi-million dollar restoration project. As part of the three-and-a-half year project, improvements were made to the two spiral staircases, and the statue's right arm which had been incorrectly installed in 1886 was strengthened. The badly deteriorated torch was replaced with a new torch coated in 24-carat gold leaf. The original torch is displayed in the main lobby. The Statue of Liberty was designated a World Heritage Site in October, 1984.

A ferry service, operating from 9 am to 5 pm daily with extended hours in summer, leaves for Liberty Island from Battery Park in New York and Liberty State Park in New Jersey. Those keen to climb the twenty two stories to visit the statue's crown might be faced with a 2 to 3 hour waiting time. While no admission fee is charged, donations are greatly appreciated.

*Further Information: Statue of Liberty National Monument, Liberty Island, New York, New York, 10004.*

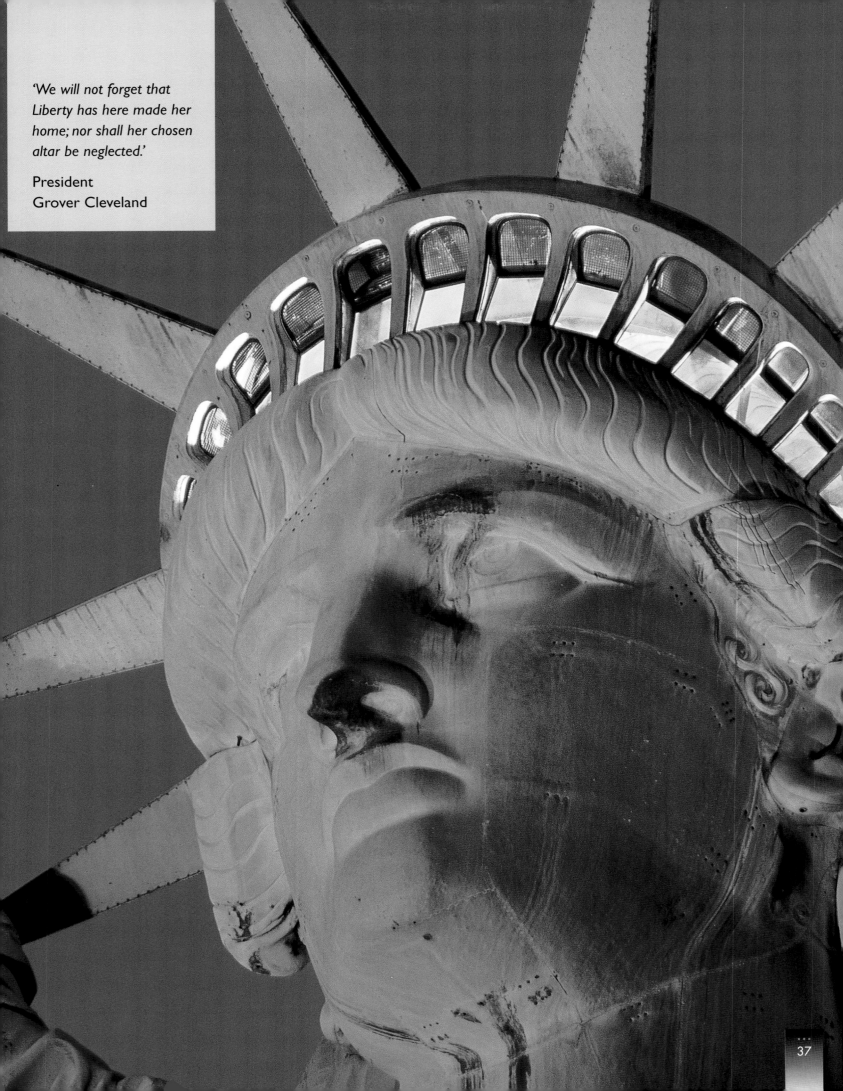

'We will not forget that Liberty has here made her home; nor shall her chosen altar be neglected.'

President
Grover Cleveland

# YOSEMITE

## NATIONAL PARK

ABOVE  *Half Dome, Merced River*
RIGHT  *El Capitan*

IN 1868 CONSERVATIONIST JOHN MUIR SET OFF ON FOOT for the Sierra Nevada mountains, 150 miles (241 km) east of San Francisco. From the eastern edge of the Central Valley '... rose the mighty Sierra, miles in height, and so gloriously colored and so radiant it seemed not clothed with light, but wholly composed of it, like the wall of some celestial city.'

Muir's destination was a glacial valley hidden behind the solid granite flank of the Sierra's predominantly forested west side. This valley and much of the area surrounding it was inscribed on the World Heritage List in 1984 as a place of outstanding universal value - for its display of exceptionally glaciated topography, and for its diverse and important array of flora and fauna that are presently in decline elsewhere in California.

Only 7 miles (11 km) long and up to 1 mile (1.6 km) broad, Yosemite Valley is actually a widened portion of the prevailing narrow canyon of the Merced River, which meanders the length of the valley from east to west.

Walling the valley are cliffs of gray granite, mountainous in height and size, varied in form, some smooth and sheer, some carved, some crowned with domes or rock spires; all separated by wooded ravines or deep shadowy canyons, threaded by streams and

cascades. Many of these landmarks - El Capitan, Half Dome, the Three Brothers, and Sentinel Rock - are known the world over.

El Capitan, standing 7,569 feet (2,307 m) above the sea, is one of the tallest unbroken cliffs in the world. Half Dome, which at 8,842 feet (2,695 m) dominates the upper end of the valley, appears to have been cut in two with some giant axe.

From the top of the cliffs, waterfalls make free leaps of such immense height as to set them apart from all others. Yosemite Falls, which even more than El Capitan and Half Dome has given Yosemite Valley its renown, is composed of a large upper fall, a small lower fall, and a connecting chain of cascades, having a combined height of nearly half a mile. The Upper Fall, at 1,430 feet (435 m), is the highest free-leaping waterfall in the world. The Lower Fall's drop of 320 feet (97 m) is twice the height of Niagara.

Beyond the valley's cliff tops, to the north and south and spreading among the crest peaks of the Sierra, lies a world of alpine lakes set in granite basins; of flower-filled meadows, ringed by conifer forests, including one of the finest virgin sugar pine stands in the world; of streams and waterfalls; spires and domes; of little rock gardens blooming with heather and pestemon, fuschia and phlox, and tiny golden violets.

Lower elevations of Yosemite National Park are covered with chaparral woodland, with bull pine and mixed coniferous forest of ponderosa pine, Douglas fir, white fir, California black oak, incense-cedars and enormous sugar pines.

Near the park's western boundary, north and south of the valley, are three groves of rare trees, the Giant Sequoia (Sequoiadendron giganteum). Covering just 417 acres (169 ha), these trees are relics of some forty species of sequoia that flourished in the Northern Hemisphere about sixty million years ago. In sheer bulk - height and girth combined - Giant Sequoia are the largest trees in the world.

Birds and mammals occur in number throughout the high country: tanager, flycatcher, grouse, quail, owl and kingfisher; deer of three subspecies; coyote, marmot, badger, chipmunk, pika, pine marten and black bear are all found. Some species have become locally extinct and others are threatened. The last grizzly bear recorded in Yosemite was killed around 1895. California bighorn sheep were re-introduced to the park from the southern Sierra and a small population remains after a decade. Peregrine falcons had disappeared but have recently started to re-establish a presence, recovering since the use of DDT (the agent found to be responsible for the thinning of their egg shells) was outlawed in the United States.

John Muir was not the first European to climb Yosemite's mountains or hike its trails. Mountain climbers started ascending various rock faces in 1860. Hiking was always a popular way of visiting places of interest, but Muir, more than anyone else, encouraged people to explore and examine and care for what they saw. He inspired others.

In 1864 the federal government ceded Yosemite Valley and the adjoining Mariposa Grove of Big Trees to the state of California '... for public use, resort, and recreation ... for all time.' This marked the beginning of government involvement in land protection, which led ultimately to the U.S. National Park system and to the protection of parks worldwide.

Important as the transfer was in establishing a precedent for government protection of wilderness, it was not entirely successful in saving Yosemite from commercial exploitation. As John Muir grew to know the region, he realized that without further control, sheep grazing and logging would eventually destroy the area that others had worked so hard to save.

Muir was not only an impassioned advocate for a conservation ethic that gained public support. He was also an effective politician, enlisting influential figures in his crusade for government protection of wild lands.

With presidents, railway magnates, and magazine editors on his side, Muir was able to build an ever larger public constituency for conservation. He influenced the establishment of five national parks in addition to Yosemite, which was created in 1890 and given back from state to federal control in 1906. Seven more changes were made to the park's boundaries between 1929 and 1984, when Yosemite was designated a World Heritage Site, with an area of 1,169 square miles (3,000 sq km), of which Yosemite Valley occupies only 4,480 acres (1,800 ha).

The natural creation of the valley began sixty million years ago when a series of upthrusts began building the Sierra Nevada Mountains. One of a number of west and southwest flowing streams, the Merced River, began trenching a broad valley. Further uplifts continued to raise the Sierra bloc, steepened the Merced's incline, and hastened its flow so that it trenched a rugged V-shaped canyon more than 1,000 feet (300 m) deep.

The final elevation of the Sierra coincided with the arrival of a colder climate that brought snow to the heights in such quantity that the summer sun was unable to melt it all. Great masses of compacted snow turned into ice and started moving. These glaciers superseded the Sierran streams as cutting and erosive agents.

Glaciers entered the Yosemite chasm at least three times. At 3,000 to 4,000 feet (900 to 1,200 m) deep, only the summits of El Capitan, Boundary Ridge, Clouds Rest, Half Dome, and Sentinel Dome stood above the frozen mass. The glacier quarried sideways, as well as downward; ground, plucked, and trimmed the jutting spurs and craggy side walls; and transformed the narrow, strongly winding river gorge into a deep, wide, and only slightly sinuous valley.

Among national parks renowned for their breathtaking scenery, no other offers such a variety of natural features in such a limited space - thundering waterfalls, immense cliffs and

ABOVE  *Mountain lion or cougar*
OPPOSITE  *Yosemite Falls*

From the eastern edge of the Central Valley 'rose the mighty Sierra, miles in height, and so gloriously colored and so radiant it seemed not clothed with light, but wholly composed of it, like the wall of some celestial city.'

John Muir

John Muir hoped the park would puncture the myth of human omniscience. He saw wilderness as a place of divine beauty and a source of great spiritual power.
He wrote of Yosemite: 'No temple made with hands can compare with Yosemite ... Every rock in its walls seems to glow with life ... as if into this mountain mansion Nature had gathered her choicest treasures.'

towering mountain peaks. These characteristics are Yosemite Valley's greatest asset and yet the source of its biggest problem.

The ideal of sanctuary and preservation - that Yosemite should represent a vignette of primitive America - has conflicted with the expectations and pleasures of a mobile, affluent society.

Right from its beginnings as a National Park, tourism has been actively encouraged in Yosemite. The concessionaires of today seek greater profits from increased visitation and advocate visitor comfort and convenience over preservation. In turn, the public has come to expect roads, hotels, stores, camp-grounds and parking lots in Yosemite Valley as a matter of course - even users of the back-country expect to find comfort and convenience in the valley. They can also find a jail and a court house.

By the time Americans came to understand the argument that Yosemite Valley had reached or exceeded its desirable limits of growth, the forces of development had themselves become entrenched as part of the Yosemite experience.

The park received 600,000 visitors a year in 1941. The Park Service looked on growth as inescapable, and prophecies of increasing visitation became self-fulfilling. Additional provisions for visitation only spurred visitation all the more. In 1954 visitation passed one million; in 1967, two million; twenty years later, over three million; in 1994, four million. The impact from this high number of visitors includes problems of sewage and garbage disposal, decline in air quality, the introduction of alien plants and animals, trampling of vegetation and loss of solitude.

If he were alive today, it would perhaps be this loss of solitude that would disturb Yosemite's founding visionary most of all. John Muir hoped the park would puncture the myth of human omniscience. He saw wilderness as a place of divine beauty and a source of great spiritual power. He wrote of Yosemite: 'No temple made with hands can compare with Yosemite ... Every rock in its walls seems to glow with life ... as if into this mountain mansion Nature had gathered her choicest treasures.'

Visitor access is via four entrances, three of which are open all year: Arch Rock Entrance, 67 miles (107 km) from Merced via El Portal; South Entrance, 59 miles (94 km) from Fresno; and North Entrance, 71 miles (114 km) from Oakdale. The fourth entrance is from the east over the Tioga Pass, and is open according to weather conditions, usually from around Memorial Day to early November. Air and bus services are available to both Fresno and Merced, where rental cars are available.

*Further Information: Superintendent, Box 577, Yosemite National Park, CA 95389.*

LEFT    *Merced River and North Dome*
BELOW    *A young marmot*

ABOVE    *Great gray owl*
RIGHT    *Coyote chasing field mouse in snow*

# INDEPENDENCE HALL

EAST WING 1735-6        STATE HOUSE STARTED IN 1732        WEST WING 1739

ARCHED PIAZZA OVER STAIRS        ARCHED PIAZZA OVER STAIRS
BLANK WALL IN REAR        BLANK WALL IN REAR

1741-9 BRICK TOWER ON SOUTH SIDE TO CONTAIN STAIRCASE - WOODEN STEEPLE, 1753

STATE HOUSE OF PENNSYLVANIA IN 1753

Designed by lawyer Andrew Hamilton and built between 1731 and 1757, the stately Georgian-style building now known as Independence Hall has quite rightly been described as '... the mecca of American history.' It is here, in the oldest part of Philadelphia, that so many momentous events associated with the founding and early growth of the United States of America took place. This historic structure is one of twenty six buildings and sites located on Independence Square.

'Independence Hall', reflected the authors of the Diary of Independence Hall ' can look back on her past with understanding, merriment and equanimity ... She has known both the heights of exaltation and grubby treatment as well. She sheltered men who strove to stabilize a colony. She adapted herself to being a gaol for war prisoners and a hospital for fever-ridden. She watched the gestation of revolt and served as midwife to the birth of a nation. She accepted the affront of being turned into a museum for curios, was tinkered at by this person and that, and long knew shabby neglect.' The addition of Independence Hall to the World Heritage List in 1979, together with the preservation efforts undertaken by the National Park Service, means that the building's future as the nation's foremost shrine to democracy is now assured.

In 1948 the 80th Congress designated Independence National Historical Park, encompassing 42 acres (17.5 ha), '... for the purpose of preserving for the American people ... certain historical structures and properties of outstanding national significance located in Philadelphia ... associated with the American Revolution and founding and growth of the United States'. Independence Hall, along

with nearby Congress Hall and Old City Hall, are owned by the city of Philadelphia but administered by the National Park Service. In 1950 the city of Philadelphia and the Secretary of the Interior entered into an agreement which ensured that '... no changes or alterations should be made in ... its buildings and grounds ... except by mutual agreement'. In January 1951 the National Park Service gained custody of Independence Hall. A major restoration of the area was completed in the 1970s. Additionally, in recent times, an open landscaped area, known as Independence Mall, has been created by the Commonwealth of Pennsylvania.

Independence Hall itself is rich in history. Originally constructed as the State House of the colonial province of Pennsylvania, it served as the principal meeting place of the legislature until 1799. Prior to the building of the State House, the Pennsylvania Assembly held its meetings in private residences or taverns. During the British occupation of Philadelphia in 1777-78, the State House was used as a barracks, and following the battle of Germantown it served as a hospital. American officers captured by the British at the battles of Brandywine and Germantown were held as prisoners of war in the building. At the end of their nine-month occupation of the city, the British, according to one observer, left the State House in '... a most filthy and sordid situation [with] the inside torn much to pieces.'

The Second Continental Congress convened on and off in Independence Hall's Assembly Room between 1775 and 1783. It was in this 40 square foot (3.7 sq m) chamber, located to the east side of the hallway, that George Washington, on June 16, 1775, accepted his appointment as commander-in-chief '... of all continental forces raised, or to be raised for the defense of American liberty.' It was here also that the Declaration of Independence was adopted and signed. The background to the signing of the document is well known. Before the Continental Congress on June 7, 1776, Richard Henry Lee of Virginia read his resolution which began: 'Resolved: That these United Colonies are, and of right ought to be, free and independent States, that they are absolved from all allegiance to the British Crown, and that all political connection between them and the State of Great Britain is, and ought to be, totally dissolved.' On the same day, John Hancock proposed '... certain resolutions respecting independency'. Soon after, a committee, consisting of Thomas Jefferson, John Adams, Benjamin Franklin, Roger Sherman, and Robert Livingston, was formed to prepare a statement arguing the case for independence. The draft, penned by Jefferson in a rented room in Jabob Graff's house, was submitted to the five-man committee and small amendments were made by Franklin and Adams.

On July 4, 1776, after a few additional changes were made, the revised version of the Declaration of Independence was adopted unanimously by Congress. A copy of the document is today housed in the Declaration Chamber. In 1778 behind the locked doors of the same room, the Articles of Confederation were signed by eight states, and in 1787, after four months of debate, the Federal Constitution was adopted and signed. The five remaining states signed at a later date.

TOP  *Assembly room*
ABOVE  *Portrait of Thomas Jefferson,* Charles Wilson Peale, 1791
OPPOSITE  *The Declaration of Independence*

After hosting such historic events, the State House retained its name and reverted to its original role of serving the state. After the national capital relocated from Philadelphia to Washington in 1800, the building became known as the Old State House. Over

# IN CONGRESS, JULY 4, 1776.

## The unanimous Declaration of the thirteen united States of America.

When in the course of human events, it becomes necessary for one people to dissolve the political bands which have connected them with another, and to assume among the powers of the earth, the separate and equal station to which the Laws of Nature and of Nature's God entitle them, a decent respect to the opinions of mankind requires that they should declare the causes which impel them to the separation.

We hold these truths to be self-evident, that all men are created equal, that they are endowed by their Creator with certain unalienable Rights, that among these are Life, Liberty and the pursuit of Happiness. — That to secure these rights, Governments are instituted among Men, deriving their just powers from the consent of the governed, — That whenever any Form of Government becomes destructive of these ends, it is the Right of the People to alter or to abolish it, and to institute new Government, laying its foundation on such principles and organizing its powers in such form, as to them shall seem most likely to effect their Safety and Happiness. Prudence, indeed, will dictate that Governments long established should not be changed for light and transient causes; and accordingly all experience hath shewn, that mankind are more disposed to suffer, while evils are sufferable, than to right themselves by abolishing the forms to which they are accustomed. But when a long train of abuses and usurpations, pursuing invariably the same Object evinces a design to reduce them under absolute Despotism, it is their right, it is their duty, to throw off such Government, and to provide new Guards for their future security. — Such has been the patient sufferance of these Colonies; and such is now the necessity which constrains them to alter their former Systems of Government. The history of the present King of Great Britain is a history of repeated injuries and usurpations, all having in direct object the establishment of an absolute Tyranny over these States. To prove this, let Facts be submitted to a candid world.

He has refused his Assent to Laws, the most wholesome and necessary for the public good.

He has forbidden his Governors to pass Laws of immediate and pressing importance, unless suspended in their operation till his Assent should be obtained; and when so suspended, he has utterly neglected to attend to them.

He has refused to pass other Laws for the accommodation of large districts of people, unless those people would relinquish the right of Representation in the Legislature, a right inestimable to them and formidable to tyrants only.

He has called together legislative bodies at places unusual, uncomfortable, and distant from the depository of their public Records, for the sole purpose of fatiguing them into compliance with his measures.

He has dissolved Representative Houses repeatedly, for opposing with manly firmness his invasions on the rights of the people.

He has refused for a long time, after such dissolutions, to cause others to be elected; whereby the Legislative powers, incapable of Annihilation, have returned to the People at large for their exercise; the State remaining in the mean time exposed to all the dangers of invasion from without, and convulsions within.

He has endeavoured to prevent the population of these States; for that purpose obstructing the Laws for Naturalization of Foreigners; refusing to pass others to encourage their migrations hither, and raising the conditions of new Appropriations of Lands.

He has obstructed the Administration of Justice, by refusing his Assent to Laws for establishing judiciary powers.

He has made Judges dependent on his Will alone, for the tenure of their offices, and the amount and payment of their salaries.

He has erected a multitude of New Offices, and sent hither swarms of Officers to harrass our people, and eat out their substance.

He has kept among us, in times of peace, Standing Armies without the Consent of our legislatures.

He has affected to render the Military independent of and superior to the Civil power.

He has combined with others to subject us to a jurisdiction foreign to our constitution, and unacknowledged by our laws; giving his Assent to their Acts of pretended Legislation:

For Quartering large bodies of armed troops among us:

For protecting them, by a mock Trial, from punishment for any Murders which they should commit on the Inhabitants of these States:

For cutting off our Trade with all parts of the world:

For imposing Taxes on us without our Consent:

For depriving us in many cases, of the benefits of Trial by Jury:

For transporting us beyond Seas to be tried for pretended offences:

For abolishing the free System of English Laws in a neighbouring Province, establishing therein an Arbitrary government, and enlarging its Boundaries so as to render it at once an example and fit instrument for introducing the same absolute rule into these Colonies:

For taking away our Charters, abolishing our most valuable Laws, and altering fundamentally the Forms of our Governments:

For suspending our own Legislatures, and declaring themselves invested with power to legislate for us in all cases whatsoever.

He has abdicated Government here, by declaring us out of his Protection and waging War against us.

He has plundered our seas, ravaged our Coasts, burnt our towns, and destroyed the lives of our people.

He is at this time transporting large Armies of foreign Mercenaries to compleat the works of death, desolation and tyranny, already begun with circumstances of Cruelty & perfidy scarcely paralleled in the most barbarous ages, and totally unworthy the Head of a civilized nation.

He has constrained our fellow Citizens taken Captive on the high Seas to bear Arms against their country, to become the executioners of their friends and Brethren, or to fall themselves by their Hands.

He has excited domestic insurrections amongst us, and has endeavoured to bring on the inhabitants of our frontiers, the merciless Indian Savages, whose known rule of warfare, is an undistinguished destruction of all ages, sexes and conditions.

In every stage of these Oppressions We have Petitioned for Redress in the most humble terms: Our repeated Petitions have been answered only by repeated injury. A Prince whose character is thus marked by every act which may define a Tyrant, is unfit to be the ruler of a free people.

Nor have We been wanting in attentions to our Brittish brethren. We have warned them from time to time of attempts by their legislature to extend an unwarrantable jurisdiction over us. We have reminded them of the circumstances of our emigration and settlement here. We have appealed to their native justice and magnanimity, and we have conjured them by the ties of our common kindred to disavow these usurpations, which, would inevitably interrupt our connections and correspondence. They too have been deaf to the voice of justice and of consanguinity. We must, therefore, acquiesce in the necessity, which denounces our Separation, and hold them, as we hold the rest of mankind, Enemies in War, in Peace Friends.

We, therefore, the Representatives of the united States of America, in General Congress, Assembled, appealing to the Supreme Judge of the world for the rectitude of our intentions, do, in the Name, and by Authority of the good People of these Colonies, solemnly publish and declare, That these United Colonies are, and of Right ought to be Free and Independent States; that they are Absolved from all Allegiance to the British Crown, and that all political connection between them and the State of Great Britain, is and ought to be totally dissolved; and that as Free and Independent States, they have full Power to levy War, conclude Peace, contract Alliances, establish Commerce, and to do all other Acts and Things which Independent States may of right do. — And for the support of this Declaration, with a firm reliance on the protection of divine Providence, we mutually pledge to each other our Lives, our Fortunes and our sacred Honor.

John Hancock

Button Gwinnett
Lyman Hall
Geo Walton

Wm Hooper
Joseph Hewes
John Penn

Edward Rutledge
Thos Heyward Junr
Thomas Lynch Junr
Arthur Middleton

Samuel Chase
Wm Paca
Thos Stone
Charles Carroll of Carrollton
George Wythe
Richard Henry Lee
Th Jefferson
Benja Harrison
Thos Nelson jr
Francis Lightfoot Lee
Carter Braxton

Robt Morris
Benjamin Rush
Benja Franklin
John Morton
Geo Clymer
Jas Smith
Geo Taylor
James Wilson
Geo Ross
Caesar Rodney
Geo Read
Tho M'Kean

Wm Floyd
Phil Livingston
Frans Lewis
Lewis Morris
Richd Stockton
Jno Witherspoon
Fras Hopkinson
John Hart
Abra Clark

Josiah Bartlett
Wm Whipple
Saml Adams
John Adams
Robt Treat Paine
Elbridge Gerry
Step Hopkins
William Ellery
Roger Sherman
Saml Huntington
Wm Williams
Oliver Wolcott
Matthew Thornton

time, it was referred to as Independence Hall. From 1802 to 1820, the entire second floor of the building was used by the famous portrait painter Charles W. Peale as a museum. Between 1818 and 1895 it served as a municipal building, and from 1898 to the present day it has operated as an historic shrine.

The main part of the Georgian-style, red-brick structure is a two-level rectangular block, measuring 105 by 45 feet (32 by 14 m), and featuring a gabled shingle roof. Flanking the main part of the building are double-story, hipped-roofed, brick attachments known as the east and west wing buildings. Arcades made from the same material join the east and west wings to the main building. Offices for the province's administrative agencies were housed in the wings. The inability to ensure adequate fire-proofing of the original wings and arcades resulted in their demolition in 1812. These structures were replaced with large office wings designed by the architect Robert Mills. It was Mills who was also responsible for tearing down the committee room and library, adjacent to the Assembly Room, which had been added to the State House in the 1750s.

A brick tower rises from the center rear of the main building. Originally, the State House was supposed to be a rectangular structure without a tower. In 1750 the Assembly ordered that '... a suitable place thereon for hanging a bell ...' be constructed. Master builder Edmund Wolley, who had been responsible for overseeing the building of the State House, supervised the construction of the tower. Attached to the tower is a wooden steeple, 167 feet 8 inches high (7.9 m), which is topped with an octagonal belfry, small cupola and spire. The original wooden tower and steeple, completed in 1753, were not to remain in place long; rotting timber forced their removal in 1774. Thanks to the fine work of Philadelphia architect, William Strickland, they were restored to their original design and replaced in 1828. From here the State House bell or Liberty Bell, weighing 2,000 pounds (909 kg), was hung. Cast around the bell's crown are the words from Leviticus: 'Proclaim liberty throughout all the land unto all inhabitants thereof.' Upon the first public reading of the Declaration of Independence on July 8, 1776, the Liberty Bell rang in Independence Square, formerly the State House yard, outside

TOP LEFT    *Rising Sun Chair used by George Washington*
TOP RIGHT    *Portrait of Benjamin Franklin,* David Rent Etter, c 1854
ABOVE    *United States Constitution and quill pen*
OPPOSITE    *Liberty Bell*

Independence Hall. On July 8, 1835, when the bell was being tolled in honor of John Marshall, Chief Justice of the Supreme Court, it cracked. This was the last time it rang. The bell, an international symbol of freedom, is now on display in Liberty Bell Pavilion.

After the transfer of the federal capital from Philadelphia to Washington, the future of the Old State House became unclear, and in the years following the creation of the Union it was sadly neglected. In response to the rumor that the buildings on Independence Square might be demolished and the land sold for building lots, Independence Hall and the land where it stands were bought for $70,000 by the city. The deed of sale was formally executed in June 1818. When Marquis de Lafayette visited

Philadelphia in 1824, a function was held in his honor in the Assembly Room. In 1830 John Haviland commenced work on the much-needed restoration of the Declaration Chamber, and by 1854 the restoration was complete. In 1869 a statue of Washington, sculpted by J. A. Bailly and paid for out of funds raised by children from the city's public schools, was placed in front of the refurbished doorway. During the 1840s and 1850s, exhibitions and official receptions were held in the Assembly Room. The bodies of John Quincy Adams, Henry Clay and Abraham Lincoln are among those which lie in state in the room. Restoration work on the entire building continued intermittently well into the 20th century, and in 1942 the Independence Hall Association was formed.

The furniture displayed in Independence Hall's restored chamber is original and is that used from 1775 to 1781 by the Congress. Among the furnishings are the inkstand with quill box and shaker used to sign the Declaration of Independence and the Constitution, and the Rising Sun Chair used by George Washington when he presided over the Constitutional Convention. At the end of proceedings, Benjamin Franklin revealed his fascination with the sun carved on the back of Washington's chair: 'I have often and often in the course of the session and vicissitudes of my hopes and fears as to its issue, looked at that behind the president without being able to tell whether it was rising or setting. But now at length I have the happiness to know that it is a rising and not a setting sun.' Also housed in Independence Hall are uniforms, documents and relics of the revolutionary period, as well as a complete set of portraits, mainly by Charles Willson Peale, of the signers of the Declaration. The Assembly Room also features a statue of Washington by William Rush.

Independence Hall is one of several historically important buildings on Independence Square. Adjoining Independence Hall to the west is Congress Hall, formerly the County Courthouse, where the House and Senate met during the 1790s. Congress Hall, built after the Revolutionary War, is where Washington's second inauguration as President of the United States took place (his first inauguration was held in New York City on April 30, 1789), where his last message to Congress was delivered in 1796, and where the inauguration of the second President, John Adams, was held. Nearby, on the eastern side, is Old City Hall, the Supreme Court building, which was begun in 1789 and completed in 1791. The Supreme Court of the United States met on the second floor of this building from 1791 to 1800. While the interiors of these buildings have been altered, their external appearances have changed very little since the late 18th century.

Visitors to Independence National Historic Park should be aware that it is difficult to see all the sites in one day. Most park buildings are open seven days a week from 9 am to 5 pm, with extended hours in summer. Except for Independence Hall and the Liberty Bell Pavilion, all buildings are closed on Christmas Day and New Year's Day. Admission to Independence Hall itself is by tour only. Those wanting to know more about the park's many sites should make time to view the audiovisual exhibits, films, and interpretative displays found in the visitor center.

Cast around the bell's crown are the words from Leviticus:

*'Proclaim liberty throughout all the land*
*unto all inhabitants thereof.'*

*Further Information: Independence National Historical Park, 313 Walnut Street, Philadelphia, Pennsylvania 19106.*

# GRAND CANYON

## NATIONAL PARK

THE PRESERVATION OF THE GRAND CANYON of the Colorado
River expresses a modern idea of scenery and of conceptions
of the grandeur, beauty and power of nature. Its isolation, precipitous cliffs, awesome depths and dangerous rapids were once
regarded as ominous, severe and forbidding. Not anymore. In 1992,
4.3 million people came to see the Grand Canyon. Among the first
group of sites accepted for World Heritage listing in 1979, the Grand
Canyon preserves what is still one of the outstanding natural
wonders of the planet.

The first legislative attempts to set aside the Grand Canyon
as the United States' second national park after Yellowstone were
made in 1882. The bill failed to pass, as did others in 1883 and 1886.

John Muir visited the canyon in 1896 and described it as 'the
most tremendous expression of erosion and the most ornate and
complicated I ever saw.'

President Theodore Roosevelt followed Muir in 1903 and
was equally impressed. He urged the canyon's preservation, and
advised, 'Do nothing to mar its grandeur. Keep it for your children
and your children's children, and all who come after you, as the one
great sight which every American should see.'

In 1906 Roosevelt signed a bill that created Grand Canyon
Game Preserve, affording protection to game animals but not their
predators. Unsuccessful bills to create Grand Canyon National Park
were introduced in 1910 and 1911. Another bill was introduced in
1917. Finally, in 1919, thirty-seven years after the first attempt,
President Woodrow Wilson signed the bill creating Grand Canyon
National Park. Subsequent additions increased the park area to
1,218,375 acres (493,344 ha).

The park lies within the arid Colorado Plateau in the Four
Corners region of the United States, where the boundaries of
Arizona, New Mexico, Utah, and Colorado meet. An area of high
altitude, averaging more than 5,000 feet (1,500 m) above sea level,
the plateau is built up of extensive areas of nearly horizontal sedimentary rock through which deep and walled canyons have been
cut. The 1,450 mile (2,335 km) long Colorado River drains most of
the plateau.

At the southwestern part of the Colorado Plateau, the
Grand Canyon, at 277.4 miles (446.6 km), is the longest and deepest
of the many canyons through which the Colorado River flows.
Through the canyon the river drops an average of 7.9 feet per mile
(1.5 m per km). About 50 percent of the river descent occurs at
abrupt rapids.

Time, erosion and uplifting created the great canyon. It is fair
to say that without the Colorado River there would be no canyon,
but it is an inaccurate oversimplification to say simply, 'the Colorado
River did it.' It is now recognized that the origin and evolution of the
river itself is enormously complex, and resulted from the integration
of several smaller independent streams. The river has played an
important role in the canyon's formation as an erosive agent, but it
has been by no means the only agent. Rain, snow and ephemeral
streams have also played a role.

The river cuts only its channel. Widening of the canyon has
been, and is being, accomplished by other erosive forces. Frost cracks
the rocks. Plant roots wedge into the cracks, gradually prying them
wider. Rain, wind and the force of gravity work the loosened materials down to the river, where the debris helps to scour the river
channel and lower its bed.

The river's average depth is 50 feet (15 m) and varies in
width between 200 and 300 feet (60 and 90 m). At the narrowest
spot, canyon walls squeeze the river down to a width of 60 feet (18 m).

ABOVE   *North Rim*
OPPOSITE   *Colorado Plateau, the beginning of the Grand Canyon*

The canyon is over one mile (1.6 km) deep at several points along either rim. The width at the top varies from less than 1,000 feet (300 m) to 18 miles (29 km).

The bottom of the canyon is a desert, with an average precipitation of under 10 inches (250 mm). Most rain evaporates before it reaches the river. High summer temperatures are common. But deep within the canyon, springs and streams issue from tributary points, creating garden spots.

A highland climate prevails in the cool and moist areas along and behind the higher canyon rims. The average annual precipitation on the South Rim exceeds 15 inches (375 mm), much of it snow. The considerably higher North Rim is covered by snow until well into May. Snowfall there averages 12.5 feet (3.8 m) per year and rainfall averages 25 inches (635 mm).

Between the extremes of river and rim top, climates range from desert, temperate woodland, coniferous forest, to tundra. The variation allows a rich range of wildlife - mountain animals such as bighorn sheep are neighbors of such desert creatures as rattlesnakes. The canyon's great divide ensures that certain animals never meet - tassel-eared squirrels of the North Rim are a quite different subspecies from those of the South Rim.

Riparian animals include ringtail cats, spotted skunks, river otters, beaver, rock pocket mouse and long-tailed pocket mouse. Canyon wren and large black ravens are common. Colorado River squawfish, humpback sucker, and the bonytail chub are endemic.

Blackrush, Mormon tea, sego lily, mesquite, sand verbena, beaver tail cactus, narrow-leaf yucca, dollarpoint prickly pear, cataclaw, desert trumpet, desert thorn, Utah agave, desert prince's plume, pale evening primrose, white bursage, ocotilla, cholla and barrel cactus all grow in the canyon.

ABOVE   *Kaibab squirrel*
OPPOSITE   *Toroweap east*

The Colorado still flows through the Grand Canyon, but the living, wild river has been controlled. Owing to a dam upstream at Glen Canyon, the flow now hardly varies.

Pinyon pine & Utah juniper grow along and behind both the North and South Rims. Mule deer, desert cottontails, cliff chipmunks, gray foxes and wood rats live here. The rare white-tailed Kaibab squirrel is found only in the ponderosa forest of the North Rim. At altitudes above 8,200 feet (2,500 m), in areas of heavy snow fall with short growing seasons, are found Engelmann spruce, blue spruce, Douglas fir, white fir, aspen and mountain ash.

Originally 4,000 mule deer inhabited the North Rim, but the early policy of eliminating predators, including mountain lion, coyotes, and bobcats, resulted in an explosive population growth. By 1924 mule deer numbers rose to 100,000. Overgrazing caused the population to crash. Present numbers are around 10,000.

Deer, coyote, bobcat and mountain lion range freely from vegetation zone to vegetation zone. Most animals stay in the zones to which they are adapted. Reptiles are the most frequently seen animals of the inner canyon: small earless lizards, fast-moving leopard lizards, large plant-eating chuckwalla, collared lizards and the banded black and white Boyle's king snake. There is also a rare form of rattlesnake, the Grand Canyon rattler, whose pink color blends in with the background.

Mammals of the Lower Canyon include the antelope ground squirrel - which scurries from shrub to shrub with white tail held aloft like a flag - desert wood rat, pocket mice, kangaroo rat - which hops along on its hind feet and never needs a drink - little spotted skunk and bighorn sheep.

Reptiles are fewer in the upper zones. Mammals include the prairie dog, cottontail rabbit, grasshopper mouse, gray fox and various white-footed mice and wood rats. Further up are mantled ground squirrels, bushy-tailed wood rats, several varieties of pocket gophers, the porcupine and the Arizona skunk.

The park contains the largest breeding population of peregrine falcons in any land management area in the lower states.

Prior to the building of the dam in 1964, the flow of the river varied enormously: from less than 1,000 cubic feet (28 cubic m) per second to as much as 320,000 cubic feet (9,200 cubic m) per

RIGHT   *Grand Canyon Temples from desert-view tower, South Rim*
BELOW   *Prickly pear cactus, blossum and buds*

'Do nothing to mar its grandeur. Keep it for your children and your children's children, and all who come after you, as the one great sight which every American should see.'

President
Theodore Roosevelt,
1903

ABOVE *Elves Chasm*
RIGHT *Peregrine falcon*

second. When in flood the river carried hundreds of thousands of tons of scouring sediment a day. The Colorado still flows through the Grand Canyon, but the living, wild river has been controlled. Owing to the dam upstream at Glen Canyon, seasonal variations in flow are much diminished.

Large floods are needed to move the grosser detritus - the coarse gravel, rocks and boulders - brought down into the canyon by the tributaries. Without floods, detritus piles up at the mouth of the side canyons. This will result eventually in the formation of a series of impassable rapids trapping the river behind a series of boulder dams.

At the rim, increased visitation has caused traffic congestion and crowding at popular attractions. Tourist development includes lodgings, shops, parking lots, roads, and even a hospital.

Local coal-powered plants, aluminum smelters at Los Angeles, and copper smelters in Northern Mexico have adversely affected air quality, and a haze of pollution frequently hangs in the canyon.

Overhead, the South Rim experiences more air traffic than most major airports. Mid-air collisions are an ever present danger,

and the buzz of planes and whop-whop of helicopters is widespread. In recent years, flight-free air corridors have been set up over the park to deal with this problem.

The South Rim is more easily accessible and as a consequence is more heavily visited. The main gateways are Williams and Flagstaff, both less than two hours by car. Airlines serve the park, using an airport ten miles to the south, which is served by a shuttle bus from Grand Canyon Village, where there is an excellent Visitor Center. Accommodation is widely available. The North Rim is not often congested and is accessible via Jacob Lake, Arizona. Accommodation is available at the Grand Canyon Lodge and at a camp-ground near the ranger station. The Inner Canyon may be reached by foot and there are many primitive camp-grounds for hikers. Tour operators conduct journeys by mule or boat.

*Further Information: Superintendent, Grand Canyon National Park, Box 129, Grand Canyon, AZ 86023.*

ABOVE *Bobcat*
MAIN PICTURE *Red indian paintbrush, Toroweap Point*

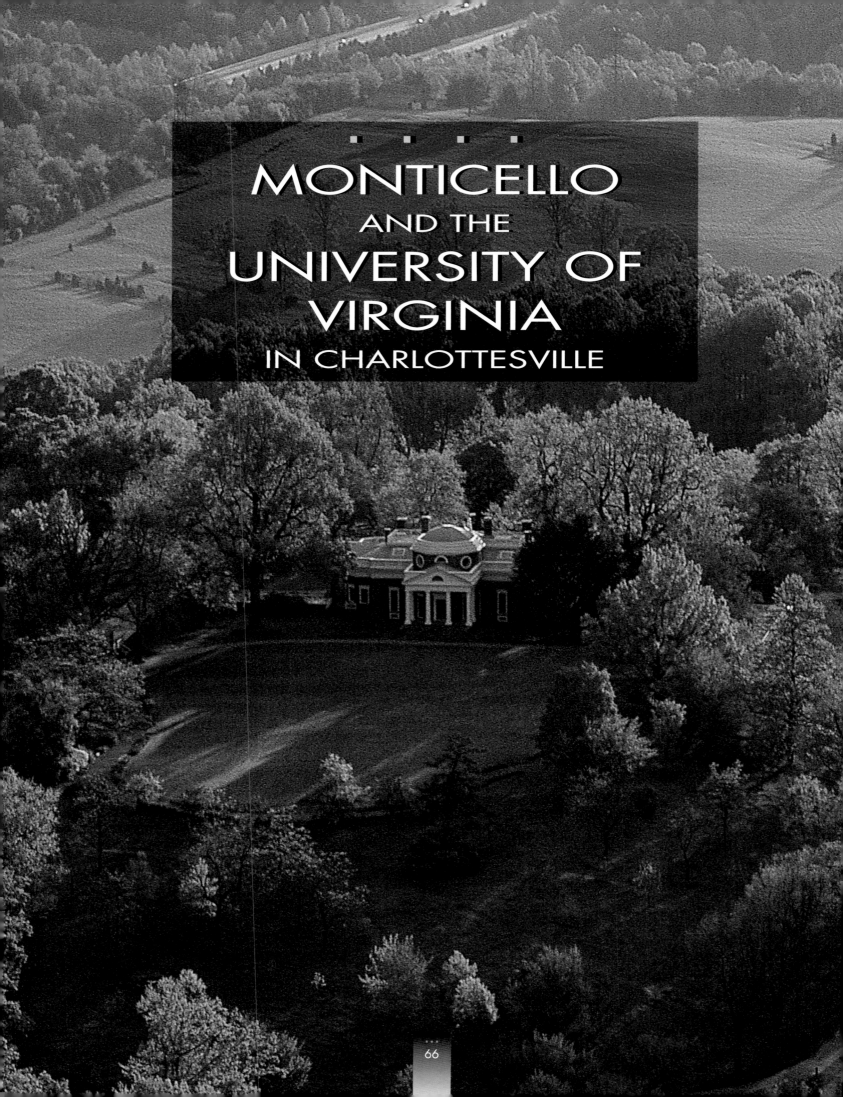

# MONTICELLO
## AND THE
# UNIVERSITY OF VIRGINIA
### IN CHARLOTTESVILLE

'I AM AS HAPPY NOWHERE ELSE, AND IN NO OTHER SOCIETY, and all my wishes end, where I hope my days will end, at Monticello', wrote Thomas Jefferson, the author of the Declaration of Independence and the third President of the United States, about his magnificent residence set in Albemarle County, central Virginia. Monticello, with its breathtaking views of the Blue Ridge Mountains and the surrounding countryside, was not only the former president's home for fifty six years, it was in the words of one of Jefferson's biographers, ' ... his body, the center of his personal universe.' The mansion, perched on a leveled mountain 867 feet (263 m) above sea level, is located two miles (3.2 km) southeast of the University of Virginia, Charlottesville, which Jefferson founded in 1819. From its exterior, the magnificent red brick house appears to be one story, but in fact consists of three levels and a cellar. Behind its large, columned entrance portico lie thirty three rooms. The house is around 45 feet (13 m) high and measures 110 by 88 feet (33 by 26.5 m). This national historical landmark, designed by its owner, a self-taught architect, is a unique mix of continental and colonial architecture. 'The quintessential example of the autobiographical house', is how the scholar William Howard Adams described Jefferson's grand dwelling. In 1987 Monticello became the only North American home to be World Heritage listed.

When his father died in 1757, Jefferson inherited the 1,000 acre (417 ha) property at the age of twenty one. Twelve years later, after studying philosophy, mathematics and the classics at the College

PREVIOUS PAGE   *Aerial view of Monticello*
TOP   *West front of Monticello*
ABOVE   *Monticello north terrace, cistern and Charlottesville view*
OPPOSITE   *Monticello's vegetable garden*

of William and Mary, and spending five years as a legal apprentice, the young bachelor commenced work on the architectural plans for his mansion. Without the benefits of formal study in architecture, Jefferson gained his inspiration from illustrated books and prints, as well as from his travels. By the time of his death, the so-called sage of Monticello owned the most important collection of books on architecture in the country. To him, the architecture of colonial Virginia was uninspiring and unsophisticated. Of the private dwellings in Williamsburg, Jefferson said, 'It is impossible to devise things more

ugly, uncomfortable, and, happily, more perishable...' The buildings of Williamsburg, he concluded, were proof that 'the genius of architecture seems to have shed its maledictions over the land.' It is not surprising then, that Monticello, in its original and revised form, bore no resemblance to the Georgian-style mansions prevalent in the former state capital.

The leveling of the mountaintop for Jefferson's new home had begun in 1768. Monticello, translated from old Italian as 'little mountain', was designed and remodelled over the next four decades into an adaptation of the neoclassical villa. In 1809, the year the house was completed and the year he left the presidency, Jefferson confessed to a visitor to the estate that ' ... architecture is my delight, and putting up and pulling down one of my favorite amusements.' To him, the remodeling of Monticello was his 'essay in architecture.' In the words of one scholar, 'All Jefferson's changes and additions were toward one end: to monumentalize the building.' He wanted to give the house 'a special presence.' That, he achieved.

The south pavilion, the first building erected on the site, served as Jefferson's bachelor quarters after fire destroyed his paternal home at Shadwell, Virginia, in February 1770. From this small, one-story brick building he supervised the construction of the central structure of the house. Known as the Honeymoon Cottage, the southern pavilion is where he brought his new bride, Martha Wayles Skelton, in January 1772. Work on the main house commenced in 1770 and was substantially completed by 1782, the year his wife died.

The structure seen by visitors to Charlottesville today is vastly different from the original Monticello. The first house was inspired by the architecture of the 16th century Venetian architect, Andrea Palladio. Although less grand than the present structure, the original house was, in the words of one visitor to Jefferson's residence, ' ... infinitely superior to all other houses in America in point of taste and convenience.' Built with red brick, the original Monticello featured a two-story central portico with massive columns where the Doric order supported the Ionic. This was flanked by one-and-a-half story wings.

In 1793, after having spent five years in France as United States Minister and Trade Commissioner, as well as three in Philadelphia as George Washington's Secretary of State, Jefferson returned to Virginia armed with fresh ideas on how to remodel and enlarge his beloved Monticello. While abroad he had become fascinated with the way the French had adapted the Roman style of architecture. In addition to studying many of the Old World buildings first-hand and purchasing works of art, furniture and other items to fill Monticello's interior, he held discussions with distinguished European architects. Jefferson planned to increase the size of his home dramatically and experiment with new architectural ideas. Over two decades, the entrance hall was replaced, the floor space doubled, the windows extended, the existing second floor demolished and another level added to the house. To save money and maximize space, Jefferson installed two unobtrusive stairways, each measuring only 24 inches (61 cm) in width.

The most dramatic modification was the addition of a large dome with a stepped octagonal base over the existing parlor, just behind the western portico. The dome was the first of its kind to be erected in an American home and was inspired by that of the Hôtel de Salm in Paris, a building with which Jefferson admitted he was 'violently smitten.' Beneath the dome is the dome room. The exact purpose of this room is unclear, though it is known that it was used as a bedroom and eventually became a storage room. On the same level are three small bedrooms, all featuring skylights. While the finished product has many Roman neoclassic features, the overall result is an Italian-style villa with Roman and French elements.

The first floor, which along with the basement is open to the public, is dominated by the large entrance hall, surrounded in part by a low balcony which connects the nursery and several small bed chambers found on the second floor. Referred to as 'Jefferson's museum', the entrance hall contains elk antlers brought back from the Lewis and Clark expedition which Jefferson had sent out to the northwest in 1803, as well as fossil bones, maps, paintings and busts. Also found in the entrance hall is the famous clock designed by Jefferson himself, which is operated by Revolutionary War cannon ball-like weights. The clock displays not only hours and minutes but days of the week. According to one of Jefferson's granddaughters, except for the drawing rooms in Washington, ' ... the hall with its gravel-colored border is the most beautiful room I ever was in.'

Behind the entrance hall, and separated from it by unique automatic glass doors, lies the parlor. The room's cherry and beech parquet floor, designed by Jefferson, was the first of its kind in America. Fifty seven works of art once adorned the walls of the parlor. The dining room, with its Wedgewood-blue walls and white trim, is located in the northern wing of the first floor. On either side of the mantle are dumbwaiters which slaves once used to hoist bottles of wines from the cellar below and to return them when empty. Food arrived via a revolving service door. Separated from the dining room by double sliding glass doors is a small, semi-octagonal tea room which Jefferson referred to as his 'most honorable suite', for it is filled with busts of several of his heroes, such as Benjamin Franklin, George Washington and the Marquis de Lafayette.

The master bedroom, library, study (or cabinet) and a glassed-in piazza are located in the private southern wing. Jefferson's bedroom is just off the entrance hall. Unlike all the other beds in the house which were set in recesses in the wall, Jefferson's bed was placed in an open alcove between his bedroom and study. It was in this bed that Jefferson died. This section of the house contains many examples of Jefferson's inventiveness: for instance, there is a revolving chair, as well as a revolving tabletop for letter writing and record keeping. Jefferson could enter the library through the study, which has a door to his bedroom. The large ceremonial chair in the library suite is the one he used when he served as vice-president, between 1797 and 1801. His architect's table, telescope, copying machine and magnifying glass are also found in these rooms. In 1815 a year after the library in the US Capitol building and other government buildings were burned down by the British, Jefferson sold his books, totaling over 6,000 volumes, to the nation. Soon after parting with them, Jefferson wrote to John Adams, 'I cannot live without books', and proceeded to assemble a new library, which eventually held over 2,000 volumes.

Unlike most Virginian estates, Monticello's service buildings were housed in a series of rooms at right angles to the central structure rather than as separate buildings. These auxiliary buildings were situated along passageways beneath long terraces, with tunnels connecting them to the cellars of the house. The kitchen, cook's room, two servants' rooms, dairy and smokehouse were located under the south terrace; situated at the end of this terrace is the Honeymoon Cottage. The stable, coach house, feed storage, icehouse and laundry were positioned under the north terrace. Rooms for wine, beer, cider and foodstuffs are found in the basement passages. By making the dependencies part of the main structure of the house, Jefferson ensured that the panoramic view would not be obstructed and that the outbuildings would be inconspicuous from the exterior.

Jefferson also had a passion for gardening which he spoke of in the following terms: 'No occupation is so delightful to me as the culture of the earth and no culture comparable to that of the garden.' Included in his landscape plan were ornamental and vegetable gardens, two orchards, a vineyard, beds of figs and other fruits, and a grove. Using Jefferson's original garden schemes as a guide, Monticello's gardens and orchards have been recreated.

Following Jefferson's death at the age of 83, on July 4, 1826, his only surviving child, Martha Jefferson Randolph, was forced to sell off much of Monticello's contents, including household furnishings, books, engravings, sculptures and historical portraits, as well as slaves,

stocks, grain and farm equipment. It is estimated that Jefferson's debt amounted to over $100,000. In November 1831 the house was sold for $4,762 to James T. Barclay, a druggist from Stanton, Virginia, who converted the property into a silkworm farm. After Barclay's venture failed, he sold the house in 1834 to a United States naval officer, Uriah Phillips Levy. Upon his death in 1862, Levy bequeathed Monticello to the nation, but over a twenty-year period Levy's heirs contested the will and, eventually, Jefferson Monroe Levy, a nephew, took ownership of the estate. Finally, in 1923, the newly formed Thomas Jefferson Memorial Foundation purchased the house and grounds for half a million dollars, and set about retrieving the original furniture and artwork. On July 4, 1926, the one hundredth anniversary of Jefferson's death, the estate was dedicated as a national shrine.

After the completion of the second Monticello, Jefferson, aged 74, began work on his last major architectural project, the University of Virginia. Between 1817 and 1826, in what he described as his 'last service' and 'the hobby of my old age', Jefferson designed and oversaw the construction of the nation's first public university. In 1976 the American Institute of Architects declared the 'academical village' the most significant architectural achievement of the past two centuries, and eleven years later, along with Monticello, it was added to the World Heritage List.

Rejecting the idea of housing a community of scholars in one large building, as had been the case at other places of learning, Jefferson arranged his so-called 'academical village' in a U-shape with pavilions positioned around a long terraced lawn, bordered by colonnades. A majestic rotunda, built between 1822 and 1826 and modeled on the Pantheon, served as a library. Sadly, Jefferson died before the 'temple of knowledge' was completed. On either side of the Rotunda lie two parallel rows of double-story pavilions; each of the ten pavilions is based on a different architectural order. In Jefferson's words, they were '...models of taste and good architecture, and of a variety of appearance, no two alike, so as to serve as speci-

ABOVE   *University of Virginia*
OPPOSITE (BACKGROUND)   *Looking down in the Dome Room of the Rotunda*

mens for architectural lectures.' A continuous loggia connects the ten buildings, providing protection from the elements.

Originally, professors resided on the upper floors and classes were held on the main floor. Today, senior faculty members still live in nine of the pavilions and classes are still held in two. Outstanding fourth-year students are selected to live in the one-story Lawn rooms located between the pavilions. Behind both rows of pavilions are additional student rooms. These are separated from the main pavilions by gardens enclosed by serpentine brick walls.

The epitaph engraved on his tombstone in the family graveyard at Monticello lists what Jefferson saw as his three greatest achievements: 'Author of the Declaration of Independence, of the Statute of Virginia for religious freedom, and Father of the University of Virginia.' There is no mention of the many public offices he held - Governor of Virginia, Secretary of State, Vice President and President.

Monticello is open from 9 am to 4.30 pm from November to February and 8 am to 5 pm from March to October. Except for Christmas Day, it is open daily. Tours of the house are conducted every five minutes and an admission fee is charged. Apart from visiting the house, visitors to Jefferson's mountaintop estate are able to stroll through the magnificent grounds, gardens, orchard and vineyard. Guided tours of the gardens and grounds and of the plantation community are available daily during Spring, Summer and Fall as part of general admission. Free guided tours of the University of Virginia's Rotunda and Lawn are provided all year round, except for three weeks over the Christmas/New Year period. Visitors are also welcome to explore the academic village on their own.

*Further Information: Thomas Jefferson Memorial Foundation, Inc., PO Box 217, Charlottesville, Virginia 22902.*

# EVERGLADES

## NATIONAL PARK

THE DECLARATION OF EVERGLADES NATIONAL PARK in 1934 was a landmark. Here, for the first time, the centerpiece of a park was an ecological setting rather than a scenic marvel. Almost all the first national parks in the United States were located high in mountain ranges. Lower-elevation forests, wetlands, grasslands and coastal areas were absent from the system. When President Harry Truman dedicated the Everglades National Park in 1947 he said, 'Here are no lofty peaks seeking the sky, no mighty glaciers or rushing streams ... Here is land, tranquil in its quiet beauty, serving not as the source of water but as the last receiver of it.' However, full recognition of the Everglades, which culminated in their inscription on the World Heritage List in 1979, came slowly.

At the turn of the century, the area was known as the home of many varieties of birds of striking beauty. Some, like the egrets, were prized for plumes on women's hats. To supply the plume trade, hunters shot large numbers of waterbirds. Many came near to extinction. The Audubon Society engaged a warden, Guy Bradley. His murder in 1905 gave impetus to both the bird conservation movement and to the preservation of the area.

Even at 1,400,533 acres (567,215 ha), the third largest national park in the country, Everglades National Park is actually only a corner of the whole Everglades. They begin at Lake Okeechobee, a 480,000 acre (190,000 ha) natural reservoir one-third of the way up Florida's peninsula.

As the summer rainy season, which drops 50 to 60 inches (1,270 to 1,520 mm) of water, saturates the land above it, Lake

PREVIOUS PAGE   *Whitewater Bay*
TOP   *Atlantic bottlenose dolphin*
ABOVE   *American alligator*
OPPOSITE   *Sawgrass plain*

Okeechobee rises, overflows shallow banks and floods the already saturated grassy swamplands below it with more water than can be absorbed.

The Everglades become an enormous freshwater river, moving south slowly over the 100 miles (160 km) to the bottom of the peninsula, to the coastal mangrove fringe, the sandy storm dunes and the brackish estuaries of Florida Bay and the Gulf of Mexico. By midsummer the flow is more than 50 miles (80 km) wide, inundating some 3,500 square miles (9,000 sq km) of sawgrass and other vegetation with up to one foot (0.3 m) of gently moving water.

The sawgrass that covers up to 70 % of the Everglades is technically a water sedge. It has three sharp edges set with fine, serrated teeth of silica that cut like glass. The plant grows, flowers, and seeds in the rainy season, then dies back each winter as water levels drop. Its ten foot-long (3 m) blades fall and decompose, adding seasonally to the thick interwoven mat of roots and leaf litter that make up the wetland floor.

Perched here and there on higher ground are small islands, called hammocks, where slightly deeper soil and drier footing support small but dense stands of bald cypress, palmetto, mahogany, strangler fig and coppery-barked gumbo-limbo and other plants.

Few landscapes on Earth have a more intricate interplay of physical and biological elements than the Everglades.

The plain is old sea floor exposed only a few thousand years ago by the last retreat of the sea during an Ice Age buildup. The land that emerged came out flat and tilts barely enough - two to three inches per mile (3.2 to 4.8 cm per km) - to keep water flowing across it. This flow integrates the whole of peninsular Florida into one vast ecological entity.

Although the Everglades are fundamentally watery, their most distinctive characteristic is drought. There is little rain in southern Florida from November to April, and the dying off is so widespread that the possibility of life ever reviving with the May to October wet season appears remote.

LEFT   *Coastal prarie*
BELOW   *Everglades kite*

ABOVE  *Endangered Florida panther*
TOP RIGHT  *Raccoon*
RIGHT  *Armadillo*
OPPOSITE  *Southern bald eagle*

Some of the more wide-ranging animals - birds, mammals, and flying insects - escape death by leaving. Others go into a torpid state called aestivation: they wall themselves off in chambers or capsules that stay damp under the crust of sun-baked muck or marl.

Some creatures find refuge in scattered ponds, holes and depressions that retain water even after the River of Grass has dried up its bed. Alligators gnash and slosh out pools - known as 'gator holes' - in the muck or marl, where most of the aquatic creatures of the region find asylum.

When the rainy season arrives in late spring, the inhabitants of gator holes, crayfish burrows and holes and cracks in the bedrock repopulate the newly flooded plain. Bacteria, protozoa and tiny crustaceans come out of their drought-resistant eggs or cysts. New green algae begin their production of sugar to provide the food base for the reviving community. As these smaller forms of life regain their abundance, the flying aquatic insects return.

Little fish appear, at first in small posses and then in bigger schools. Snails, glass shrimp, crayfish, turtles, garfish, mud eels and catfish emerge from their various shelters. Aquatic plants sprout and grow. Bull frogs and tree frogs sing, mate and lay eggs that quickly produce tadpoles. Half a dozen kinds of turtles climb out on to the few high places and leave their eggs to hatch wherever the marl or peat rises above the lap of the River of Grass.

Even the bass and bream come back - the first to die when the water levels fell in winter. Alligators re-establish their territorial patterns, bellow, build new nests and breed. Waterbirds disperse throughout the reviving landscape. This pattern has continued uninterrupted since the Ice Ages.

For all their ecological vagaries, the Everglades provide a refuge for many animals that are declining outside southern Florida. Most of the endangered species are birds. The Everglades also serve as a refuge for the manatee, or sea cow, the American crocodile and the Florida panther.

These days droughts and floods are more stressful. There is both a growing water famine and a water surplus. Since 1948 massive dikes and drainage canals, constructed around the park to divert water for the benefit of large-scale agriculture and real estate, have severely disturbed the natural balance of the environment.

First, water levels began falling. Then the dry seasons became longer and more pronounced, and catastrophic drought and fires occurred more frequently. Fauna thinned out in the River of Grass, and salt water rose in freshwater wells.

Some remedial action has been taken. The establishment of Big Cypress National Preserve in 1974 helped safeguard the natural flow of fresh water. In 1979 Congress voted to add 108,000 acres (44,000 ha) to the national park to further improve the water supply. The Florida Panther National Wildlife Refuge, covering almost 25,000 acres (10,125 ha), was established in the same year to help restore a species whose numbers had fallen to dangerously low levels.

North of Lake Okeechobee, the Corps of Engineers, which once converted the lake's 98 mile (158 km) Kissimmee River tributary into a wide, deep channel, is now working to return the river to its original meandering bed.

Nevertheless, threats remain. As more and more fresh water is pumped from the ground to supply the municipal and recreational needs of southern Florida, it is replaced by nutrient-rich waters from

surrounding agricultural lands. These, in turn, have spawned an explosive growth of plants that were never part of the Everglades ecosystem. Exotic animals and plants such as casuarina, melaleuca, cajeput and Brazilian pepper are driving out or inhibiting many native species. Birds that had recovered from near destruction at the hands of plume hunters are once again in decline.

The inscription of Everglades National Park on the World Heritage List was made in recognition of what is probably the largest area of sawgrass marshes in the world, coupled with an extent of mangrove vegetation that is surpassed in only a few parts of the globe outside the Australasian region. Its complex of habitats, high number of endemic plants and small but important collection of endangered animals, add further weight to its inclusion on this list of places of outstanding universal significance. Yet now this magnificent and vitally important ecosystem is seriously endangered.

In 1995 the system of canals and dikes that keep southern Florida's cities and farms dry, channeled the floodwaters of two years of unusually heavy rains on to the greatly depleted Everglades. The result was catastrophe. The water drowned normally dry islands, killing trees and vegetation and destroying habitat for wildlife. Ecologists fear that with only half the Everglades left and the ecosystem already reeling from years of abuse, the land may never recover. In 1993 the park was placed on the List of World Heritage in Danger. The Federal Government has now begun a seventeen year, $2 billion ecosystem restoration project to improve water inflow and quality to the park.

Access to Everglades National Park is via Key West, to Homestead. There is a Visitor Center on the approach to the park on Florida Highway 27. Boat tours are available from Everglades City, as are canoe tours. Look for accommodation in Key Largo, Homestead, Florida City or Islamorada. Camp sites are located at Long Pine Keys and Flamingo. Primitive camping is permitted in the park by first obtaining a permit from a ranger station or park headquarters in Homestead.

*Further Information: Superintendent, Everglades National Park, Box 279, Homestead, FL 33030.*

TOP AND BELOW LEFT    *Manatees*
BACKGROUND    *Palmetto leaf*
BELOW    *Brown pelican*

When President Harry Truman dedicated the Everglades National Park in 1947 he said, 'Here are no lofty peaks seeking the sky, no mighty glaciers or rushing streams ... Here is land, tranquil in its quiet beauty, serving not as the source of water but as the last receiver of it.'

LEFT   *Tri-colored heron*
ABOVE   *Great blue heron*
RIGHT   *White ibis*

# CAHOKIA MOUNDS
## STATE HISTORIC SITE

PREVIOUS PAGE   *Artists impression of Cahokia Mounds village*
TOP   *Aerial view of Monks Mound*
ABOVE   *Artists impression of inhabitants below Monks Mound*

NEAR THE TOWN OF COLLINSVILLE IN SOUTHERN ILLINOIS, just 8 miles (5 km) across the Mississippi River east of St. Louis, Missouri, is Cahokia Mounds State Historic Site. It was inscribed on the World Heritage List in December 1982, due to its significance as a major center of prehistoric American Indian culture.

Cahokia Mounds was the largest prehistoric settlement north of Mexico. Its exact size at any one time is unknown, but at its peak, between AD 1100 and 1200, it may have had a population of 10-20,000 people. It included at least 120 mounds spread over more than 5 square miles (13 sq km). Permanent occupation of the site began around AD 700, during the Late Woodland period. A significant increase in population accompanied the Emergent Mississippian period (AD 800-1000), as corn agriculture expanded the food base and social, political, religious and economic organization became more complex. During the Mississippian period (AD 1000-1450) Cahokia literally 'exploded', becoming the regional capital; the northernmost city of the time. By the 13th century Cahokia had begun to decline and by the 15th century it had been abandoned.

There is no record of what the people called themselves or their city, but archaeologists use the term 'Mississippian' for them, as that was the cultural tradition of which they were part. The name 'Cahokia' was given to the site during the 1800s to commemorate a later group of Illini Indians who had moved into this area in the 17th century, although they had not built the mounds.

Most of the mounds were not for burials, but rectangular platforms for important buildings such as temples and residences of the leaders. The greatest of these is Monks Mound, rising in four terraces to a height of 100 feet (30 m), and covering more than 14 acres (34 ha) at its base. It is the largest wholly earthen prehistoric mound in the Western Hemisphere. Today visitors can climb the 144 steps to the top for a wonderful panoramic view of the site and the wide Mississippi flood plain known as the American Bottom.

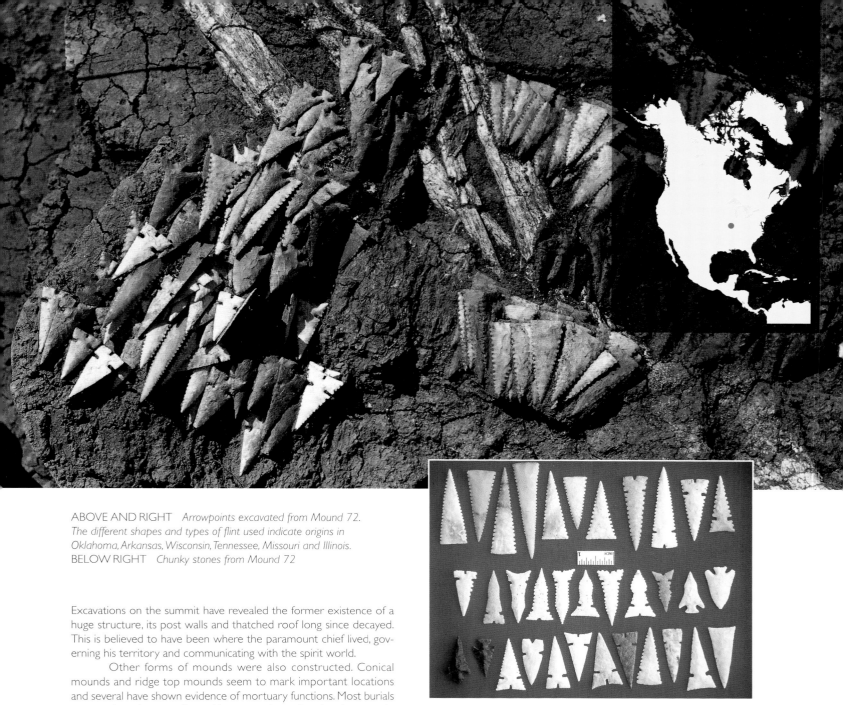

ABOVE AND RIGHT    *Arrowpoints excavated from Mound 72.*
*The different shapes and types of flint used indicate origins in*
*Oklahoma, Arkansas, Wisconsin, Tennessee, Missouri and Illinois.*
BELOW RIGHT    *Chunky stones from Mound 72*

Excavations on the summit have revealed the former existence of a huge structure, its post walls and thatched roof long since decayed. This is believed to have been where the paramount chief lived, governing his territory and communicating with the spirit world.

Other forms of mounds were also constructed. Conical mounds and ridge top mounds seem to mark important locations and several have shown evidence of mortuary functions. Most burials seem to have been performed in cemeteries rather than in mounds, but it is thought that these two mound forms are sometimes associated with burials of special significance. Almost all mounds that have been examined show evidence of several stages of construction, perhaps representing cycles of renewal or dedications to successions of leaders.

One small ridge top mound, known as Mound 72, was partially excavated and nearly 280 burials were revealed, many in mass graves. The primary burial may have been an early leader of Cahokia, buried on a platform of some 20,000 marine shell beads, with several people buried around him. Tribute offerings included many chunky game stones, a large pile of southern Appalachian mica, a roll of Lake Superior copper, strings of marine shell beads, and over 800 perfect arrow-points made from chert (flint) originating throughout the Midwest. This tribute attested to the importance of this man and the wide extent of Mississippian trade. Mass graves of young women are indicative of human sacrifice. Four men were lying with arms interlocked, but their heads and hands had been removed; some people had been carried there on litters, others were tossed into pits; still others had been reburied from other locations. These differential burial treatments are important in providing clues to the intricate social status systems which prevailed.

Among the many accomplishments of the Mississippians at Cahokia was the construction of a sun calendar, known today as Woodhenge. This remarkable construction consists of a circle of large red cedar posts, with a central observation post. From the central position, the rising sun aligns with certain posts on the circle's perimeter that mark important dates, such as the equinoxes and solstices. Excavations have revealed that Woodhenge was constructed at least five times, each circle with a different diameter and number of perimeter posts. The reasons for the changes are not clear, and it is possible that the Woodhenges had uses other than astronomical - perhaps as aligning devices for community planning and mound placement. Researchers believe there were other Woodhenge locations around Cahokia.

Visitors today can view the third circle, which has been reconstructed at the original location. It is 410 feet (124 m) in diameter and has forty eight perimeter posts and a large central observation post. Public observations of the equinox and solstice sunrises are held throughout the year.

The presence of conflict and warfare in this ancient society is indicated by four constructions of the log Stockade wall, nearly two miles (3 km) long around the central precinct of the city. At regular intervals along the wall, bastions projected outward, where warriors could launch arrows against attackers. The wall also served to separate the classes within their own society. It is believed that the ruling elite lived within the walled district. Most of the commoners

TOP   *Woodhenge reconstruction*
ABOVE   *Woodhenge, Spring equinox, Monks Mound in background*
OPPOSITE TOP   *Artists' and archaeologists' reconstruction of fishing*
OPPOSITE BELOW   *Artists impression of market life*

would live outside, but there also were several elite districts beyond the limits of the Stockade. It is likely that most of the general population would have been allowed inside for public gatherings in the Grand Plaza for festivals, ceremonies, markets, games and other special occasions. They would also have been permitted inside to assist in defending the city when it was under attack.

The Mississippians were an agricultural people, growing corn, squash, pumpkin, sunflower, and several seed-bearing plants. They also hunted deer, waterfowl and smaller animals, and caught huge amounts of fish from the nearby rivers, lakes, sloughs and marshes. Their diets would no doubt have been rounded out with the addition of many wild fruits, nuts, seeds and roots.

The houses were primarily one-family dwellings, small and rectangular, with wall posts set in trenches and covered with mats or a plaster of clay. The roofs were covered with bundles of prairie grass. Some buildings were used for storage, for meeting places or public facilities. Small circular dome-shaped structures were used as sweatlodges for purification rituals.

The decline of Cahokia was probably not due to any one cause, but a combination of factors. Depletion of resources in the region may have contributed, as would increased competition with others for the remaining resources. Climatic changes may have affected crop production and surpluses. Loss of economic and political controls over the region is also believed to have contributed. Whatever the causes, by the 1400s Cahokia had been abandoned, and we do not know who are the direct descendants of this once extraordinary community, as the population apparently scattered gradually in many directions.

Visitors can relive the story of this unique site, told in the magnificent Interpretative Center. This building houses many innova-

ABOVE   *Artists impression of aerial view, c AD 1100*
OPPOSITE TOP   *Birdman Tablet recovered from Monks Mound, front and reverse view*
OPPOSITE CENTRE RIGHT   *Bird-like pottery*
OPPOSITE BELOW LEFT   *Pottery*
OPPOSITE BELOW RIGHT   *Pottery pipe figurine of man*

tive exhibits, created to tell the story of the Cahokia site and the people who lived here. An award winning orientation show introduces the visitor to the site and provides a stimulus to learn more from the exhibits of artifacts, dioramas, models and graphics. The focal point of the exhibit gallery is a full-scale recreation of one of Cahokia's neighborhoods, complete with houses, a sweatlodge, a granary and more than a dozen mannequins (cast from living Native Americans) representing citizens engaged in a variety of daily activities. Administered by the Illinois Historic Preservation Agency, the Center, is open every day, except for several holidays, from 9 am to 5 pm, and the grounds are open from 8 am to dusk.

Throughout the year there are many programs, activities and special events, including Native American craft demonstrations, education programs, Kids Day, a Native Harvest Festival, a winter lecture series, solstice and equinox observances, and performances of Indian dance. The biggest event of the year is Heritage America, held during the last weekend in September, with Native Americans from across the country gathering at Cahokia Mounds to perform traditional dancing, songs, music, storytelling and crafts.

*Further Information: Cahokia Mounds State Historic Site, P.O. Box 681, Collinsville, IL 62234.*

# PUEBLO DE TAOS

ON A VALLEY FLOOR IN NORTHERN NEW MEXICO, at the foot of the sacred mountain Taos, lies North America's largest, best-preserved, and possibly oldest pueblo - Taos Pueblo or, more formally, San Gerónimo de Taos. In 1992 Taos Pueblo ('pueblo' is the Spanish word for town or village) was inscribed on the World Heritage List. This remote pueblo, surrounded by a fertile plateau, is sheltered by the Sangre de Cristo mountain range, of which Taos Mountain is a part. The most northern of the Rio Grande pueblos, Taos Pueblo is located about 70 miles (112 km) north of the state capital, Santa Fé. One of nineteen Native American pueblos still in existence, it is administered by the Taos tribe and governed by a mayor and a council.

It is believed that the first people to visit the Taos area were the Paleo-Indians, passing through more than 9,000 years ago, probably on a buffalo hunting mission. Taos Pueblo has been continually inhabited by Taos-Tiwa Indians for at least 600, and possibly 1,000, years. Its culture is largely derived from the traditions of the prehistoric Anasazi Indian tribes.

The Spanish first learned of Pueblo of Taos (pronounced 'touse', as in house) in the 16th century. In 1539 the missionary Fray Marcos de Niza led a small fact-finding expedition into New Mexico and confirmed earlier reports that there were areas of immense wealth in the Pueblo Indian country. The following year Captain Hernando de Alvarado, who was with the first Spanish expedition of the Francisco Vasquez de Coronado, failed to find the fabled cities or the untold wealth, but came upon the pueblo dwellings, including Taos.

Taos Pueblo is organized around two flat-roofed adobe buildings. As archaeologist John Bodine has noted, these sun-dried brick structures ' ... have become the most important visual symbol of Taos culture.' The Taos River, which divides the two irregular structures, flows through the large central plaza. The north and south side community houses are five and four stories respectively. With no internal stairways, the only access to the upper levels is by ladders. In the event of an attack, the ladders were pulled to the roofs. The traditional apartment buildings consist of two rooms, with one room used for food preparation and eating and the other reserved for sleeping. The lower rooms serve mainly as storage areas. Of the approximately 1,500 people who live in Taos Pueblo today, about 150 reside in the original apartments.

To preserve the distinctive style of architecture, any building modifications are bound by strict rules, and traditional materials and methods must be used in any repair work. Furthermore, restoration work is carried out by members of the preservation project, all of whom are members of the Taos tribe. Several obvious changes in the structures have occurred over the past century. For instance, doors and windows, which were once kept to a minimum for defensive reasons, have been cut into the adobe walls and interior fireplaces have been added. In the old pueblo, modern facilities like electricity or running water are not permitted. In the view of John Bodine, this is ' ... symptomatic of the kind of resistance the Taos have mounted against wholesale acceptance of Anglo and Spanish-American values and attitudes.' Close to the houses are ovens for baking. An eroding adobe wall, constructed originally for defensive purposes, surrounds the north and south sides of the pueblo. While the wall no longer serves as a physical barrier, it is still of cultural and psychological importance, and the area within the wall is sanctified. Beyond the wall, and well out of view of the old pueblo, other styles of architecture are evident. Six underground kivas are found at Taos Pueblo. Apart from being used as meeting places for the male members of the tribe, young men enter the kivas to receive instruction on ancient ceremonies and traditions. Only on certain ceremonial occasions are women permitted to enter the kivas.

The most important event of the year in Taos Pueblo is held on September 29, the eve of the fiesta of San Gerónimo, the patron saint. Visitors are able to witness the Sundown Dance, which is performed in the central plaza. Prior to the festivities, the terraced houses are replastered and hundreds of candles are positioned on the rooftops. Apart from the annual procession of the Virgin on Christmas Eve, this is the only time visitors are allowed into the old pueblo. After mass on Christmas Day, the traditional race between the two pueblos is held. D.H. Lawrence, one of the many members of the creative world who visited the pueblo, believed that the Taosans ran the race ' ... in an effort to gather into their souls more and more of the creative fire, the creative energy that shall carry their tribe through the coming year ... in the unending race of humanity along the track of trackless creation.'

A permanent Spanish settlement was founded in New Mexico in 1598, sixty years after the first expedition. The Spanish brought with them, among other things, horses, cattle and sheep, and introduced various food crops, such as wheat and fruit. Within two decades of settlement Taos was established as a trading center. Yet while the Indians and the conquerors farmed the area and created an irrigation system, their relationship was far from harmonious. It was not long before any respect the Pueblo Indians had for the new settlers turned to resentment, and attacks against colonial rule became a frequent occurrence. There were several reasons for the Indians' hostility, one of which was the Spanish determination to convert the Indians to the Christian way of life. Indians caught practicing their own religion faced severe punishment and sometimes even death. The new economic system introduced by the Spanish, the encomiendas, also caused widespread dissatisfaction. This system allowed some Spaniards to force taxes upon inhabitants of the pueblo. Additionally, the Pueblo Indians faced exploitation at the hands of Spanish landowners. To make matters worse a drought, which lasted from 1667 to 1672, resulted in crop failures and starvation. The Spanish were blamed for the major climatic changes that had occurred since European settlement.

Bitterness towards the Spanish settlers culminated in the Pueblo Indian revolt of 1680 in which the colonial government was overthrown and seventy Spaniards killed. The leader of the revolt, Popé, planned his attack from inside a kiva at Taos Pueblo. The general revolt took place on August 10, 1680, and resulted in the deaths of many colonists and missionaries, and the destruction of all signs of Spanish religious worship and other reminders of the European settlement. During the revolt the first church was destroyed by fire. Those Spaniards who survived the revolt headed south, and for the following twelve years the Pueblo Indians were the sole rulers of their land.

Colonial rule returned in 1692 when Don Diego de Vargas seized New Mexico for the King of Spain. In doing so he met surprisingly little resistance from the Pueblo Indians. Within four months, he had gained the support of twenty three pueblos from ten Indian nations. As de Vargas later explained, he did this ' ... without wasting a single ounce of powder, unsheathing a sword, or without costing the Royal Treasury a single maravedí.' However the hostile attacks against the colonists continued; by 1694 only four of the pueblos had kept their earlier promises of loyalty. On June 4, 1696, five Franciscan missionaries, along with several Spaniards, were murdered. The inhabitants of Taos and other pueblos fled to the mountains, abandoning their dwellings. Eventually, after six months of hostilities, the Indian leaders at Taos submitted peacefully to de Vargas. The rebellion marked the Pueblo Indians' last serious attempt to expel the Spanish from New Mexico.

In the 18th century, the frequency and severity of attacks by Comanche, Navajo, and Apache Indians brought the Pueblo Indians into an alliance with the Spanish. With peace restored, the town prospered as a market center, with visitors traveling from afar to partake in the trading: the French traded furs and guns, the Mexicans silver, and the Navajo blankets as well as pottery. One of the negative effects of the trading was that the French sold firearms to the Comanche who then used the weapons to attack many Taos

properties. The Comanche attacks in the early 1760s, together with the spread of disease, particularly smallpox, resulted in a rapid decline in the population of the Taos area. Over the hundred years to the end of the 18th century, the Pueblo population was halved.

Mexico assumed control of New Mexico in 1821, but lost the territory to the United States twenty five years later when Brigadier-General Stephen Kearney captured Santa Fé with little opposition and formed a civil government. On September 9, 1850, the United States Congress established the territory of New Mexico. Initially, at least, it seemed the Pueblo Indians were pleased to be rid of the Spanish and Mexican rule and would accept the United States; but as one military advisor pointed out, in portentous terms, 'A people conquered but yesterday, could have no friendly feeling for their conquerors, who have taken possession of their country - changed its laws and appointed new officers, principally foreigners.' The bitter resentment eventually expressed itself in the form of a general revolt, with the Indians joining the Mexican resistance to American rule. A plot to overthrow the Americans was concocted in Taos. In mid-January 1847, a group of Indians and Mexicans attacked the village of Taos. The first United States territorial governor of New Mexico, George Bent, was scalped and left to die, and five other United States officials were also killed. Bent's home, containing original furnishings, still stands and is open to visitors. In early February, with the rebels entrenched within the pueblo, United States troops attacked. Before surrendering, the Indians lost one hundred and fifty men, while seven Americans were killed and another forty five wounded. Fifteen rebels were put to death. The remains of the church where the final assault took place still stand.

D. H. Lawrence, who lived in the Taos area for about eighteen months between 1922 and 1925, was spellbound by the landscape. He reflected: 'I think that New Mexico was the greatest experience from the outside world that I have ever had. It certainly changed me forever ... the moment I saw the brilliant, proud morning shine high up over the deserts of Santa Fé, something stood still in my soul, and I started to attend. There was a certain magnificence in the high-up day, a certain eagle-like royalty...In the magnificent fierce morning of New Mexico one sprang awake, a new part of the soul woke up suddenly, and the old world gave way to new.' The breath-taking beauty of the Taos region has continued to attract artists and inspire writers.

Taos Pueblo is open to the public during daylight hours. Visitors are not permitted to enter kivas and graveyards, nor are they allowed to enter homes unless invited. While outsiders are welcome to view the traditional feast day ceremonies held at the pueblo, they are asked to be respectful. Cameras are not permitted into Taos Pueblo during feast days.

*Further Information: Taos Pueblo, PO Box 1846, Taos, New Mexico, 87571.*

# CHACO CULTURE
## NATIONAL HISTORICAL PARK

PREVIOUS PAGE  *Chaco Canyon*
ABOVE  *Ancestral Puebloan ruins*

I N THE NORTHWEST CORNER OF NEW MEXICO, at the center of the San Juan Basin, lies Chaco Canyon, which from roughly AD 900 to 1500 was the heart of Chacoan culture. The Chacoans were a unique group of Anasazi (Navajo for 'ancient enemies') Indians - now often known as Ancestral Puebloans - who oversaw an extensive system of satellite communities. Chaco Canyon served as an important trading and religious center. Comprising close to 34 square miles (54 sq km), the complex contains eighteen major ruins and about 2,800 sites, of which more than 1,800 are associated with Chaco culture. While the ten mile long Chaco Canyon is the main area, the park itself covers 33,149 acres (13,800 ha), and includes three smaller separate areas: Kin Bineola, Kin Ya'a, and Pueblo Pintado. Chaco Culture National Historical Park is the largest archaeological site in the United States. The so-called Chaco phenomenon permeated well into present-day Arizona, Utah and Colorado.

Like the Ancestral Puebloans who settled at Mesa Verde to the north, the Chacoans left behind massive and impressive ruins. Fortunately the excellent building techniques employed by the Chacoans, together with the dry climate and remote location, have aided in the preservation of the spectacular ruins. Chaco Canyon is characterized by impressive multi-storied and multi-roomed adobe apartment houses, earthen mounds, enormous kivas (partially subterranean chambers used for religious ceremonies) capable of holding more than 500 people, sophisticated and effective irrigation works, and an elaborate and well-engineered road system, which extended across the San Juan Basin linking the large towns with satellite villages. The area is filled with remnants of Chaco culture, which reached its zenith between about AD 1020 and 1110. By the start of the 13th century, Chacoans had deserted the canyon.

In addition to small habitation sites and isolated great kivas such as Casa Rinconada and Kin Nahasbas, are the remains of nine multi-storied buildings known as the Great Houses of Chaco:

Peñasco Blanco, Pueblo Alto, Kin Kletso, Hungo Pavi, Pueblo del Arroyo, Chetro Ketl, Una Vida, Wijiji and Pueblo Bonito. It is estimated that to build a single small room in one of the Great Houses, about 99,000 pounds (45,000 kg) of sandstone, hand-cut from the surrounding cliffs, was required. The walls were up to six feet (1.8 m) thick and forty feet (12 m) high. Fifty million pieces of sandstone would have been used in the construction of Chetro Ketl alone. About 200,000 wooden beams were needed to build the roof of one Great House. Each of these structures features a variety of doors - full-length rectangular, T-shaped, and small corner doors, which were less common. Inside many of the rooms were wall niches, windows and fireplaces. With no machines or draft-animals to assist them, the Chacoans transported massive ponderosa pines from forests located miles from the canyon. The wood was used for beams, ceilings and floors, as well as for heating and cooking.

The largest single Anasazi building, and the most impressive of the nine Great Houses, is Pueblo Bonito - Spanish for 'beautiful village'. Covering three acres (1.25 ha) of ground, this pre-Columbian village is situated near the base of a sandstone cliff, on the north side of the canyon. Along its rear wall it rose five stories. Entrance to the pueblo was by ladder. Built over four construction periods between AD 900 and 1115, the huge semi-circular or D-shaped structure features 800 rooms, two well-defined plazas and thirty seven kivas, making it the largest single ruin in the national park system. The pueblo's east and west wings were added after AD 1075. More than one million stones were used in its construction. The storage rooms were located at the back side, with the living quarters facing the plaza, housing perhaps as many as 1,200 people. After the pueblo was abandoned, many of the upper walls collapsed. Furthermore, twenty three ground floor rooms of this prehistoric apartment complex were damaged in 1941 when a massive piece of the cliff, known as Threatening Rock, crashed into the back wall of the pueblo. Prior to the building of the Spanish Flats in New York in 1882, this pueblo was the world's largest apartment house.

The Chacoans used rubble core masonry, which involved laying sandstone walls and filling the gaps with masses of adobe and stone. The beautiful masonry work led archaeologist Brian Fagan to describe Pueblo Bonito as ' ... a Sistine Chapel of Native American architecture ... [and] ... an astounding testimony to the skill of Native American architects.' Pueblo Bonito is an amazing architectural achievement considering no wheels, metals, or domesticated draft-animals were used in its construction. Centuries after the Chacoans abandoned the area, the masonry walls (some five stories) still stand.

It is difficult to estimate what the total population of Pueblo Bonito, and indeed of the other large ruins, would have been, because not all the rooms served as living quarters. Additionally, new rooms were built and old rooms were used for storage. Though, as Francis Jennings has pointed out, those storage rooms could have been dwellings during peak population and converted after a decline. Estimates of the total number of people in Chaco Canyon range from 1,000 to 6,000 people. Other magnificent ruins are found along the canyon. Located southeast of Pueblo Bonito is Chetro Ketl, which contains 500 rooms and more than twelve kivas. It was constructed in fifteen stages from about AD 1010 to 1105.

The Great Houses as well as the remote outliers were connected by a network of perfectly straight roads. The roads were built between AD 1079 and 1140 and range from 25 to 45 feet (7.5 to 13.6 m) in width. More than 400 miles (640 km) of roads have been mapped, of which 300 miles (480 km) are outside the park. This is an extraordinary achievement given the absence of surveying equipment. The roads at the base of the canyon were joined with those on the mesa-top by hand-cut stairways. It has been suggested that apart from transporting Chacoans, as well as goods and building materials to and from the canyon, the roads served another purpose: they created a social and economic network between those living in the canyon and those residing in the outliers. William Ferguson and

Arthur Rohn view the road system as ' ... undoubtedly the greatest single achievement of prehistoric man in the Southwest ... the crowning achievement of the Chaco Culture.'

A multitude of artifacts has been unearthed, including black and white Chaco pottery, large amounts of turquoise jewelry, and painted objects crafted from stone, bone and wood, copper bells, macaw feathers, drilled beads and tools. Much of the material needed to make these pieces came from well outside the region. For example, the turquoise used to make jewelry was from the Santa Fé region 100 miles (166 km) to the east.

Exactly when the Chacoans abandoned the area is impossible to determine, though it is known that by AD 1300 there were no Chacoans in the Canyon. It is thought that some people from Mesa Verde, another World Heritage Site, were temporary residences in Chaco Canyon. The barren and isolated canyon was inhabited by the Navajo in the 18th century. The deforestation of the land, which led to soil erosion and loss of soil fertility, is one reason put forward to explain the end of the Chaco civilization. More likely, it was over three decades of drought that forced the Chacoans to settle in small communities with better water supplies.

The site was discovered in 1849 by a United States Army topographical engineer, Lieutenant James H. Simpson, who along with a small team spent two days mapping and drawing some of the dwellings. Simpson later published his journal, providing the oldest eyewitness account of the prehistoric sites at Chaco Canyon. He wrote of ' ... the grandeur of their design and the superiority of their workmanship.' As useful as Simpson's journal has been, it does however contain some erroneous assumptions, such as his claim that the ruins were built by the Aztecs and not the Ancestral Puebloans.

The first major excavation of the communal dwellings in Chaco Canyon took place in 1896, and was led by Richard Wetherill, who had earlier discovered the cliff dwellings at Mesa Verde in

Colorado. Wetherill's involvement in what was called the Hyde Exploration Expedition was financed by two brothers from New York, Fred and Talbot Hyde. Over a four-year period, the expedition excavated 190 of Pueblo Bonito's 800 rooms. The Hydes donated hundreds of artifacts from the excavation to the American Museum. Seven National Geographic expeditions excavated the site between 1921 and 1927, removing 100,000 tons of rubble. They were led by Neil M. Judd, the curator of American Archaeology at the Smithsonian Institution, who stabilized the ruin. In 1971 the National Park Service and the University of New Mexico commenced a fifteen-year research project of the site.

In 1907 President Theodore Roosevelt signed legislation that established Chaco Canyon National Monument, to preserve the ancient pueblo ruins. In December 1980, legislation passed by Congress designated it a national historical park and extended its boundaries. Over 13,000 acres (5,400 ha) were added to the park, and the canyon and outlying sites were renamed Chaco Culture National Historical Park. Seven years later, in 1987, it was placed on the World Heritage List.

The park is open to visitors all year, except for Thanksgiving, Christmas and New Year's Day. The Visitor Center is 60 miles (96 km) from Thoreau along New Mexico Highway 57. A simple campground is maintained.

*Further Information: Chaco Culture National Historical Park, SR #4, Box 6500, Bloomfield, New Mexico 87413.*

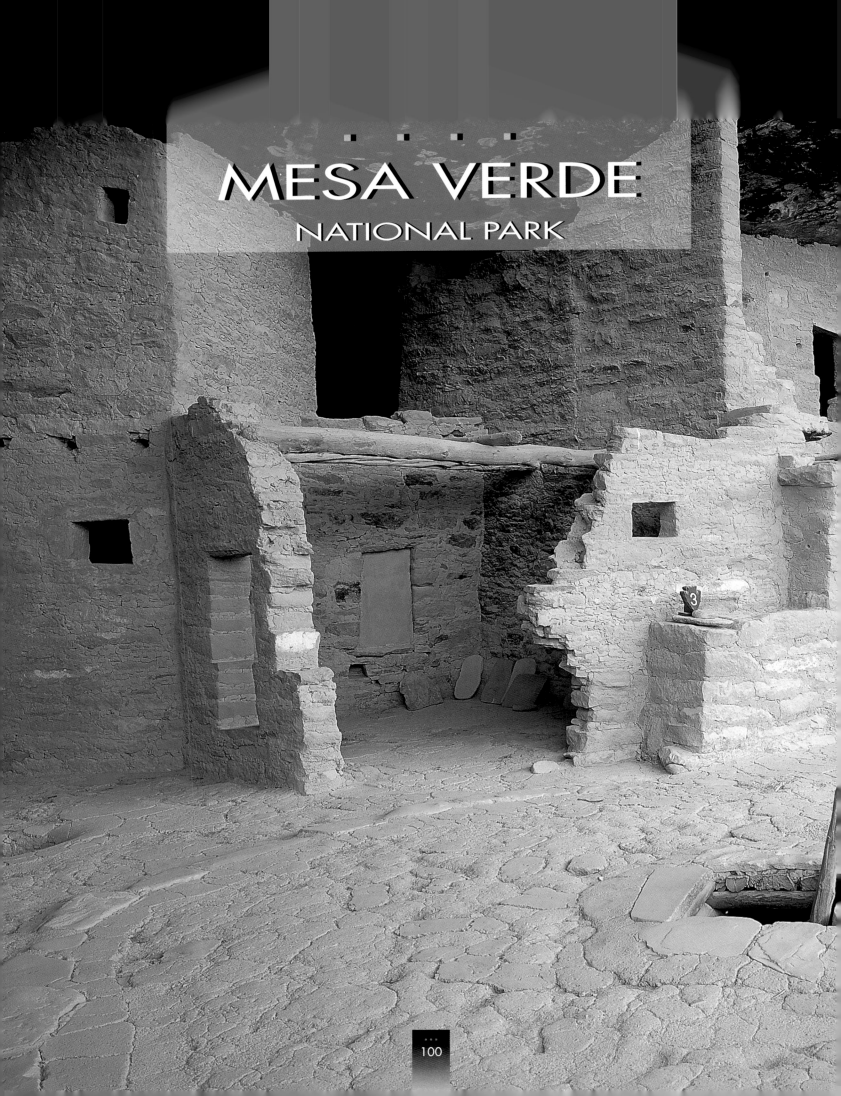

# MESA VERDE

## NATIONAL PARK

N THE WORDS OF ARCHAEOLOGIST BRIAN FAGAN, 'There is a paradisal quality about Mesa Verde. It is one of those quiet places where time seems to stand still, where the air is clear, and you feel very close to the people who once lived here.' Today, over half a million people annually visit what are widely viewed as the finest prehistoric Indian cliff dwellings in the United States. Mesa Verde occupies just over 50,000 acres (20,833 ha) of the southwest corner of Colorado. The tableland rises up to 1,739 feet (527 m) above the surrounding plains. Covered with pinyon-juniper woodland and measuring 20 miles (32 km) long and 18 miles (29 km) wide, the mesa is littered with nearly 4,000 ancient sites. The area, cut by a score of enormous, deep canyons, houses a multitude of sandstone alcoves. Within many of these large niches are massive cliff dwellings. While cliff dwellings are found in the other three states that make up the so-called Four Corners (Utah, Arizona and New Mexico), Colorado's are arguably the most spectacular, extensive and well preserved. Six hundred cliff dwellings have been identified in Mesa Verde National Park alone.

These cliff dwellings were built by the ancestors of the modern Pueblo Indians. It is not known what they called themselves, but they have become known to archaeologists as the 'Anasazi' - a rather inappropriate name as it is a Navajo word, rather than a Pueblo one, and it translates as 'ancient enemies'. These ancestral Puebloan people occupied the area from about AD 600 to 1300, an occupation that has been divided into four periods of cultural development: Basket Maker III (AD 450 to 750); Pueblo I (AD 750 to 900); Pueblo II (AD 900 to 1100); and Pueblo III (AD 1100 to 1300). It is believed that they came upon Mesa Verde by accident while hunting. Initially they lived in pit houses, which were built into the ground and covered with logs and adobe plaster. These first occupants were masters in weaving baskets for food and making sandals and other items from straw, vines and yucca. Animal skins, plant fibers and turkey feathers were used to make simple clothing. Over time the Indians moved from their pit houses to above-ground structures

PREVIOUS PAGE   *Spruce tree house*
RIGHT   *Spruce tree house in winter*

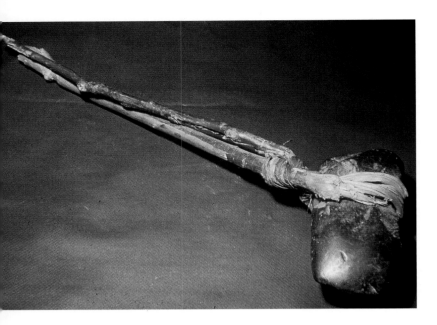

ABOVE *Shafted axe*

known as 'pueblos' (a Spanish word for town or village). Hundreds of villages were scattered throughout the Mesa Verde region, particularly on the high flat lands. By AD 1200 something had prompted them to move into the canyons -perhaps it was the desire for defensive locations or the need for protection against inclement weather.

The Ancestral Puebloans lived together in two to four story structures that were constructed of stone, mud and poles. Access to rooms was through small rectangular openings or T-shaped doorways. Windows were not a common feature and those that did exist were very small. Each cliff dwelling had circular, underground rooms, measuring around 12 feet (3.6 m) across, known as 'kivas'. These rooms were used as a community space and for ceremonial purposes. Entrance to the kiva was through a small square hole in the roof. The inhabitants of Mesa Verde spent their time farming, making pottery and digging ditches to irrigate their crops of maize, beans and squash.

For decades scholars have tried to ascertain why these people left their vast cliff dwellings and where they went. Serious archaeological exploration has offered some answers to these puzzles. It seems protracted drought probably forced them to relocate. With widespread crop failure, the people would have died of starvation had they not abandoned the area. Lacking any means of transport, they had little choice but to leave most of their possessions behind. For centuries the items they left behind remained untouched. These people never returned to Mesa Verde. Many moved southward to the Rio Grande valleys and the Little Colorado River valley where they constructed smaller pueblos. These areas are still occupied by their descendants, the modern Pueblo Indians.

No written records of the Ancestral Puebloan civilization exists. Still archaeologists have been able to reconstruct their culture from the plethora of items they left behind. In addition to unearthing objects made of wood, plant fibre, pottery and stone, bones of people and mummies have also been found. The archaeological evidence even includes the fingerprints of those who laid the stones in the mud mortar for the building of their homes.

The age of trees in the Mesa Verde has been determined by using tree-ring dating, a process which involves counting a tree's layers of wood to reveal its age. This method also provides information on weather patterns, as the layers of wood are smaller during dry spells and larger during wet years. Thanks to the work of Dr A E Douglass of the University of Arizona, who devised a tree-ring calendar,

scholars are now able to determine when a tree was logged for building purposes. This tree-ring calendar has revealed that these people inhabited the cliff dwellings for approximately eighty years.

When Colorado became part of the United States in 1848, Mesa Verde had yet to be discovered; the site had remained untouched for six centuries. Spanish explorers had ventured into the region as early as 1765 but were unaware of the many 'silent cities' located nearby. While not able to claim credit for the discovery of the ancient dwellings, the Spanish were responsible for giving Mesa Verde - translated as 'green table' - its name.

Under the supervision of F.V. Hayden, the United States government, having purchased the land from the Ute Indians, sent an expedition to the area in the 1870s. In 1874, William H. Jackson, a photographer with the team, located and photographed what he had named Two Story House in the canyon of the Mancos River. The following year, a second dwelling was discovered and named by a member of another government survey. The many holes in its lower wall led to it being called Sixteen Window House.

In 1888 two ranchers, Richard Wetherill and his brother-in-law Charles Mason, from the nearby Mancos River valley, discovered Cliff Palace. While they were searching the area for stray cattle, the pair stumbled upon the site that was built under the shelter of an overhanging cliff in the womb of a single alcove. The recess itself measures 325 feet (98 m) across the front, and has eight levels containing more than 200 rooms.

The homes were built of regular blocks of stone. After cutting the stones into blocks using crude stone axes, the blocks were placed in a mud mortar to hold them in place. The small, square-shaped rooms, built on top of one another, each housed one family. A flat slab of rock, pressed tightly against the opening, served as a door. Those rooms that did not serve as living quarters were used to store corn. From a distance, this 'strange and indescribable' structure, wrote the young Swedish archaeologist Gustav Nordenskiöld, resembled 'an enchanted castle'. To reach their homes the Anasazi traveled up precipitous trails. This was the way logs and other material needed for construction purposes were transported to the cave. Access to the mesa farmland high above was also by steep trails.

Spruce Tree House, discovered by Richard Wetherill, is the third largest of the cliff dwellings and has 114 rooms and 8 kivas. On a return trip to Spruce Tree House, the two men discovered by accident a four-story structure with a tall square tower, and named it Square Tower House. With its 85 feet (26 m) high tower, Square Tower House is the tallest structure in the national park. Covered in debris from fallen walls and collapsed roofs, the dwellings discovered by Wetherill and Mason looked far different from the sites visitors view today. Fortunately many of the cliff houses are still in excellent condition.

In 1891 after hiring three laborers together with one of the Wetherill brothers as his guide, Gustav Nordenskiöld spent four months excavating the cliff dwellings. Upon returning to Europe, he published the first scientific study of the sites, 'The Cliff Dwellers of the Mesa Verde'. In it he wrote, 'The Mesa Verde ruins are so magnificent that they surpass anything of the kind known in the United States.' Few would disagree with Nordenskiöld's assessment. He donated the artifacts he unearthed to the Finland National Museum in Helsinki. Meanwhile Richard Wetherill went on to explore 180 sites and sold various artifacts from the cliff dwellings. Later he turned his attention to what is now another World Heritage site, Chaco Canyon in New Mexico.

After nearly two decades of destructive commercial excavation and theft of artifacts, Mesa Verde National Park was created in 1906 to preserve the cliff dwellings. Sadly for some of the dwellings, it was too late. Long House for example, once the second largest of the cliff dwellings, had been carelessly excavated. In the same year, the Federal Antiquities Act was passed, which put an end to the pillaging of artifacts from Mesa Verde.

*From a distance this 'strange and indescribable' structure, wrote the young Swedish archaeologist Gustav Nordenskiöld, resembled 'an enchanted castle'.*

In 1908 Cliff Palace was excavated by Dr Jesse Walter Fewkes. Between 1915 and 1916, Fewkes uncovered two more large ruins: the Sun Temple, thought to be used as a place of worship; and Far View House. In the 1930s Cliff Palace, Spruce Tree House, Balcony House and Far View Ruin were repaired and 'stabilized'. Between 1958 and 1962, the National Geographic Society and the National Parks Service carried out a massive project; around the same time, the University of Colorado commenced a two-decade project of surveying and excavating. In 1977 representatives from various institutions and agencies completed a detailed archaeological study of the national park. Mesa Verde became a World Heritage Site in September 1978.

Airlines operate services to Durango, where car hire is available. A modern camp-site operates only five miles from the park entrance. Visitors are able to go on naturalist-conducted walks and tours, or explore the national park by car. Apart from the magnificent cliff dwellings, the area contains pit houses and pueblos, enabling visitors to trace the development of the Ancestral Puebloan culture. A visit to the excellent museum and library is a must. Sun Temple, Cliff Palace and Balcony House can be visited year round, as can the hundreds of Basket Maker pit houses on Ruins Road. It is the archaeological sites that most visitors come to see but there is much more to view at Mesa Verde National Park: 160 different kinds of birds, including some endangered species, live in the park, as well as many different types of animals, such as mule deer, black bear, fox, coyote, bobcat, badger, porcupine, prairie dog and chipmunk.

*Further Information: Superintendent, Mesa Verde National Park, Colorado, 81330.*

# OLYMPIC
## NATIONAL PARK

THE GREATEST CONIFEROUS FOREST ON EARTH, once extending from Alaska to California, reached its climax growth on Washington state's Olympic Peninsula, in the northwestern corner of the United States. A tiny remnant of that vast domain has been preserved within Olympic National Park. The park was inscribed on the World Heritage listing because its undisturbed mountains, luxuriant rain forests and rugged, wave-battered coastline preserve an area of great physical and biological diversity.

The story of that forest's preservation is the story of the conflict between those who believed that the world had to be passed on 'to future generations undiminished in richness and beauty' (John Muir) and those who believed that each generation has an opportunity and a right to get as much out of nature as it possibly can with little thought to the future.

The Olympic Mountains, which dominate the peninsula, were first explored by Europeans in the 1890s. The newcomers were so impressed with what they discovered that they recommended the area be made a national park.

In 1897, out of one of the most heavily forested regions in the country and including the Olympic Mountains, President Cleveland created the 2,188,800 acre (886,464 ha) Olympic Forest Reserve. Timber interests opposed the reserve and succeeded in getting timber lands removed. Further withdrawals followed.

In 1909 the federal government created Mt. Olympus National Monument, partly to preserve the largest remaining herd of Roosevelt elk. Half the reserve was withdrawn from protection during World War I. Conservationists continued to press for preservation and in 1938, over strenuous opposition, the federal government established the 648,000 acre (262,440 ha) Olympic National Park. Further additions were made, including a separate coastal strip, so that when the park was designated a World Heritage Site in 1981 it comprised 897,232 acres (363,379 ha).

The Olympic Mountains were created by the collision of drifting continental plates which uplifted a 59 mile diameter (95 km) dome containing contorted beds of shale, slate, and sandstone. As the dome rose it began to capture moisture from the Pacific Ocean. Eleven major rivers and many glaciers (sixty of which remain) carved the dome into an area of deep canyons and jagged peaks.

Mt. Olympus, the highest mountain at just under 8,000 feet (2,440 m), is a massive cluster of rock peaks that poke upward through a sprawling cloak of ice that covers more than 7,600 acres (3,100 ha). Some 200 inches (5,000 mm) of precipitation a year, mostly snow, falls on Mt. Olympus. The mountains' western slopes and valleys are also deluged and receive a staggering 12 feet (3.6 m) of precipitation a year.

PREVIOUS PAGE  *Hoh Valley rain forest*
BELOW  *Baby mountain lion*
RIGHT  *Hurricane Ridge*

*The Olympic Mountains were created by the collision of drifting continental plates ... Eleven major rivers and many glaciers (sixty of which remain) carved the dome into an area of deep canyons and jagged peaks.*

From glaciers and snowfields on the higher peaks in the center of the mountains, a multitude of tributary brooks and creeks tumbles down, sometimes plunging over cliffs in ribbonlike cascades. The rivers spiral outward from the interior, tending to curve counterclockwise as they flow through the mountains.

In the first few miles the rivers descend sharply to the bottoms of deep, narrow canyons. Farther downstream the valleys broaden to form deep troughs. These are usually V-shaped, but valleys like the Hoh and Queets are more spacious, displaying the U-shaped level floor and truncated lateral spurs characteristic of glaciated country.

On the relatively wide bottomlands the rivers meander and spill out into channels. As they cross the lowlands the rivers straighten and, amid obstructions of boulders and drift logs, flow rapidly toward the sea.

The unique North American rain forest of giant Douglas fir, Sitka spruce and western red cedar flourishes here. Many of the trees are hundreds of years old and are up to 12 to 13 feet (3.6 to 4 m) in diameter.

With their trunks set close and their branches interlocking, the firs lift rough, wind-torn crowns. Trunks resembling fluted columns are frequently free of limbs for 100 to 150 feet (30 to 45 m). The massive bell-bottomed spruces sometimes grow as tall as the firs.

The conifers overshadow smaller deciduous trees, although the big-leaf maples and black cottonwoods often reach large proportions. Still another understory of shrubs and low-growing trees grows below. Most prominent is the vine maple, with crooked and sprawling limb-like trunks.

ABOVE *Mountain goat*
OPPOSITE *Mist flowing over forest*

The rain forest has a strange, muted appearance, owing to thick growths of mosses, liverworts, ferns and lichens. These adorn the trees and cover the ground. In some of the valleys the forest aisles are cloaked with yellow-green and brownish lichen. Giant fallen trees - the 'nurse logs' for new forest growth - are upholstered with mosses and oxalis. Tree trunks are cushioned with moss; almost every branch is draped with long, pendent festoons. Tropical-looking ferns grow in profusion - on the ground, on fallen trees and on tree limbs.

More than 150 varieties of mosses thrive in the Olympic rain forest dampness. Colors are varied: green, gray, golden yellow, emerald, and brown. Some kinds are feathery, forming plume-like sprays. Others resemble ferns.

The densest forest grows on the lowlands - the bottom-lands, benches and low ridges between the mountains and the seas. Dark stands sweep up the mountainsides, the trees gradually diminishing in density and height with increasing altitude.

Pacific silver fir and western hemlock, together with western white pine, Douglas fir and western red cedar, grow on the mountain slopes. The crowns of the Pacific silver fir create a canopy so dense that even in summer the light reaching the forest floor is soft and indirect. The air is cool, fragrant and moist. The evergreen covering is so thick that it intersects the first winter snows, which often melt on warm succeeding days, never having reached the ground.

At the timberline, trees give way to a land of low-growing plants. Here, flowers bloom with a sudden rush at the height of the brief summer season when snow, which covers the meadows for eight or nine months of the year, melts. Hundreds of different kinds of blossom, exhibiting every color and hue, flood the mountainsides with vivid color. Meadows are also richly carpeted with grasses and ferns.

An estimated 3,000 to 5,000 Roosevelt elk, the largest mammal on the peninsula and second largest member of the deer family in America next to the moose, live on the peninsula. Formerly present along the entire coastal region from northern California to southern British Columbia, the park is one of its last strongholds.

The Olympic wolf, a local subspecies and once numerous, is believed to be extinct, a victim of ruthless persecution before the park was established.

Endemic fauna include three species: Olympic marmot, Beardslee trout, and Crescenti trout. Cougar, coyote, mule deer, fisher, and snowshoe hare thrive in forest and mountains.

The Pacific coast of North America is a major flyway for migratory birds. Millions of marine birds settle in the coastal regions of the park. Other species, including the peregrine falcon and the spotted owl, live inland - along the rivers, on logged-off lowlands, in the dense mountain forests or on the high meadowlands.

Most of the peninsula's old growth forest, described by Spanish seafarers as 'an infinity of trees,' has been cut, especially on the accessible lowlands. The logged-off land is now covered with farms and second growth forest, or else lies barren. Huge blackened stumps are all that remain of the former forest. The devastated land vividly illustrates the power of humans to alter the surface of the earth.

The core of the Olympic Mountains is still largely undisturbed mountain and forest. Nevertheless, illegal timber felling has occurred within the park. Outside, old growth forests continue to be felled. A 1988 survey found that in the park's buffer zone less than half of the old growth trees claimed to be present by the Forest Service remain - only 106,000 acres (42,930 ha) of the 211,000 acres (87,885 ha) claimed. Herbicides in timber-producing areas threaten water quality. Introduced mountain goats erode and over-graze high-elevation plant communities.

Over 2.5 million people visit the park annually. Visitors find that spur roads lead to many major attractions, including the Hoh rain forest, Kalaloch and Rialto beaches, and the magnificent views of the Hurricane Ridges. Scattered around the park are enclaves of resorts, camp-grounds and interpretive centers. The backcountry can be reached through 600 miles (960 km) of trails. Visitor Centers are located at Hoh and at the southern edge of Port Angeles.

*Further Information: Superintendent, Olympic National Park, 600 E. Park Avenue, Port Angeles, WA 98362.*

Outside, old growth forests continue to be felled. A 1988 survey found that in the park's buffer zone less than half of the old growth trees claimed to be present by the Forest Service remain.

113

The park was inscribed on the World Heritage listing because its undisturbed mountains, luxuriant rain forests, and rugged, wave-battered coastline preserve an area of great physical and biological diversity.

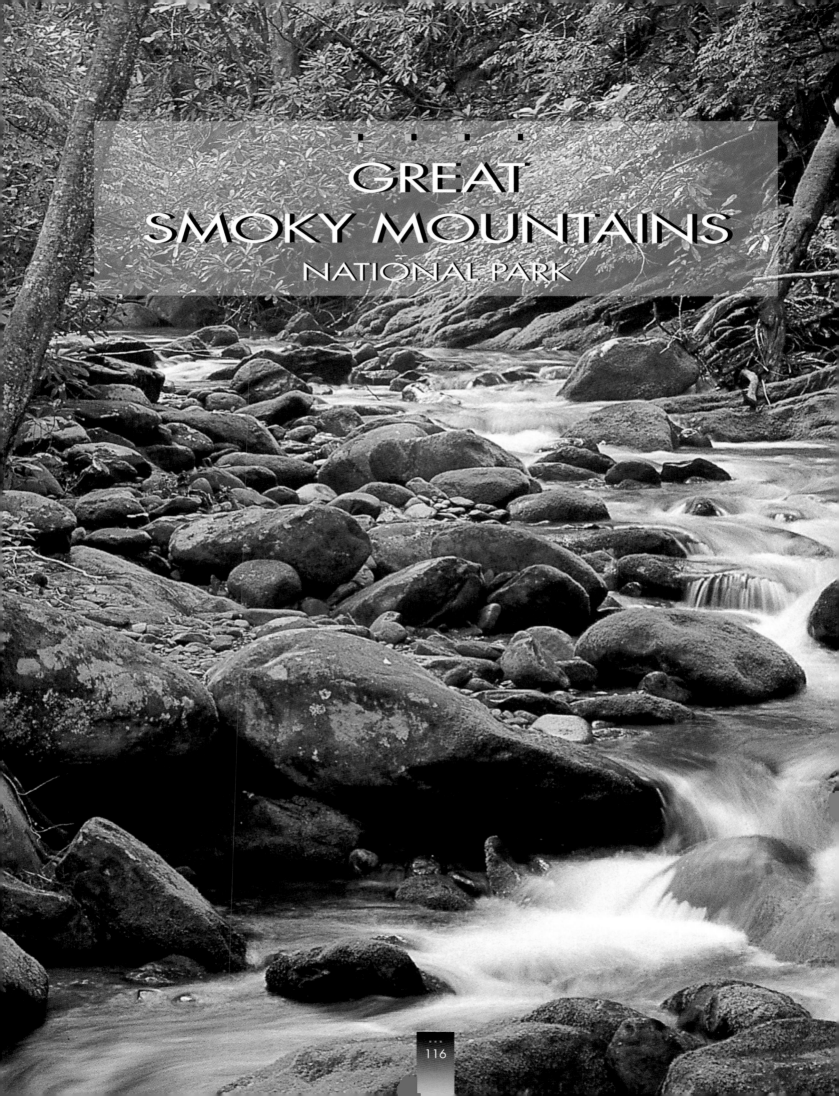

# GREAT
# SMOKY MOUNTAINS
## NATIONAL PARK

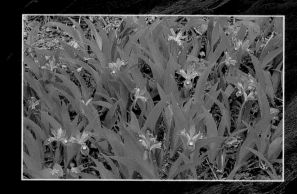

ABOVE *Racoon*
INSET RIGHT *Mountain laurel*
INSET BELOW *Dwarf iris*

BEGINNING IN CANADA'S GASPE PENINSULA as a limestone finger only 1.5 miles (2.5 km) wide, the Appalachian mountain system that dominates eastern North America slants about 3,100 miles (5,000 km) southwest across New England and the Atlantic and border states to culminate in the grandeur and complexity of the Great Smoky Mountains. The density of forest cover and the exuberance of plant life and its attendant transpiration help account for the misty character from which the Great Smoky Mountains are named.

The Smokies, the misty forest-laden mountains which constitute the Great Smoky Mountains National Park, mark the dividing line between Tennessee and North Carolina. They are high - their thirty six mile (58 km) crest maintaining an altitude greater than 5,000 feet (1,500 m) above sea level. They are also ancient, containing rocks estimated to be 500 - 600 million years old. Because the Smokies encompass most of the eastern major forest types, in addition to containing large stands of rare eastern virgin forest, the park was designated an International Biosphere Reserve in 1976 and inscribed on the World Heritage List in 1983.

The first proposal to make the area a national park, made in 1899, was renewed in 1923 by Mr and Mrs Willis P Davis of Knoxville, Tennessee. But establishing a 500,000 acre (208,000 ha) national park in the southern Appalachians, or anywhere in the East, demanded a different approach from the West.

ABOVE  *Columbine*
RIGHT  *Small purple-fringed orchids*

The eighteen national parks in existence in the 1920s had been created from lands already owned by the federal government. The Smokies lands were in private ownership in more than 6,600 tracts. Eighteen timber and pulpwood companies owned 85% of the land and were logging the last large stands of old growth southern conifers and hardwoods. Farms comprised 1,200 tracts, while more than 5,000 were lots and summer homes.

By the late 1920s logging and settlement had turned dense wilderness into a ravaged landscape and had at least partially cleared more than 75% of the land in the Great Smoky Mountains.

Nevertheless, about 25% of the area remained uncut and unsettled - this alone constituting the East's most extensive old growth forest landscape.

The federal government would not purchase land for national parks so the Davis family launched a movement to raise funds for land purchase through private subscription. Every local grazing, irrigation, power, timber, mining and resort interest opposed agitation on behalf of a park.

With great perseverance, the park movement endured and the money was raised. When the final lot was purchased, the land was donated in total to the federal government. It was declared a national park in 1926.

A federal committee, which surveyed the entire mountain region for the best location for a national park, reported: 'The Great Smoky Mountains easily stand first because of the height of the mountains, depth of valleys, ruggedness of the area and the unexampled variety of trees, shrubs and plants.'

Indeed, diversity is the defining feature of the Great Smoky Mountains. Warm, humid summers and relatively mild winters coupled with high rainfall, averaging 90 inches (2,285 mm) in some places, nourish vigorous plant growth. The region contains about 1,300 native species of vascular plants, including 130 trees - more than in all of Europe. There are 60 types of ferns, 800 briophytes (mosses and hepatics) and lichens, and well over 2,000 macro fungi, especially conspicuous because abundant moisture encourages them to fruit several times a year.

There are 50 mammal species and 200 bird species. The park's 1,898 miles (3,057 km) of streams, many thickly bordered by laurel and rhododendron, support 70 fish species, or more than in the fresh waters of any other national park on the continent. There are about 80 species of reptiles and amphibians, and more species diversity in salamanders (around 30 species in 12 genera) than in any other part of the world.

The Smokies' great diversity of life partly arises from the fact that during the last Ice Age the southern end of the Appalachian ridge remained free of the great coverings of ice and snow that lay on the northern half of the chain. This enabled the plants already living in the region, augmented by many northern refugees, to go on evolving with relatively little interruption.

Unlike the lowlands, the range of elevation of the mountains made it possible for species to adjust their living conditions by moving higher and lower as the climate warmed and cooled. Today the Smokies are the true meeting-ground of northern and southern types of forests.

ABOVE   *Mountain dusky salamander*
BELOW   *Little Pigeon River*

Areas that were farmed or logged have been recovering for varying periods of time and present a range of successional states. Deciduous broad-leaved and evergreen coniferous forests predominate, but treeless grass and heath balds, open wet meadows, cliff communities and many other types of natural communities also occur. Vegetation changes continuously with elevation, slope, aspect, geology, topographic position and disturbance regime.

Ecologists estimate that 6.5 feet (2 m) in elevation is the rough climatic and ecological equivalent to one mile (1.6 km) in latitude. The Smokies' 6,000 feet (1,800 m) of elevation contain almost as many varieties of habitat as all of the land from Atlanta to Montreal, from the oak and pine forests of northern Georgia, the oak-hickory forests of central Virginia, the northern hardwoods of Massachusetts, and into the spruce-fir forests of Maine and Canada.

Like the plants, many of the animals in the Smokies have strong biological preferences for specific altitudes and habitats. A few move seasonally between these habitats instead of migrating north or south each spring and fall. Some birds migrate vertically; from the valleys to the mountaintops in summer and back down in winter - equivalent to a journey from Georgia to New England.

Beaver, once common, are beginning to reappear in several valleys. River otter and red wolves have been reintroduced. Fisher and wapiti once occurred in the Smokies and may be reintroduced. Bison have been considered for reintroduction, but would be problematic due to concerns for visitor safety.

In autumn, oaks, hickories, beeches and other trees shed their fruits. Many animals, especially bear - of which there are some 400 to 600 in the park - deer, gray squirrel, chipmunk, turkey and ruffed grouse, are dependent on this mast, as it is called, for their autumn and winter survival. Chestnuts once supplied winter food as well, but a fungal blight from east Asia virtually eliminated the chestnut trees earlier this century, adding to the importance of acorns.

Although the park suffers from traditional problems such as poaching, and trampling due to heavy visitor use, these usually affect contained sites, rather than whole ecosystems. More problematic are

BELOW  *Whitetail buck*

TOP   *Gray squirrel*
ABOVE   *Gray fox*
LEFT   *Sugar maples*

the threats from introduced species such as wild boar, introduced in the early 1940s, and now thought to number around 2,000. In feeding, these animals move together and root up the ground and stream beds with devastating thoroughness. They damage ground cover, inhibit tree reproduction and increase erosion. German brown trout is another major pest, as it threatens to wipe out the populations of native trout. Introduced plants number around twenty five species and constitute perhaps the most serious threat of all. In conjunction with introduced insects and diseases, this front of 'biological pollution' has decimated extensive areas of the park and extinguished several species.

Air pollution is another major concern. Higher peaks intercept acid rain, while gaseous ozone appears at high levels from time to time. The effects of these changes is uncertain and remains a contentious issue.

As recovery from past logging and settlement continues well into the next century, issues such as fire control and loss of buffer zone habitat will become even more vital than they are today. The National Park Service policy of total suppression of fire is already threatening some habitats where frequent low intensity fires are required for survival. These problems epitomize the difficulties of maintaining natural ecosystems in parks, in a country where human influence is ubiquitous.

The Smokies lie about one hour's drive from Asheville, North Carolina, or from Knoxville, Tennessee. They are within a day's driving time of almost all the large cities of the East and Midwest.

As a consequence, the park receives about 8.8 million visitors each year and is the most visited national park in the country. To minimize visitor impact, the park service encourages use of camp-grounds, trailer parks, hotels and other facilities outside the park. Inside the park there are three visitor centers, ten camp-grounds (three primitive), and eighteen shelters along the Appalachian Trail and other backcountry trails, ten picnic areas, numerous backcountry camp-grounds, and 900 miles (1,450 km) of trails.

*Further Information: Superintendent, Great Smoky Mountains National Park, Gatlinburg, TN 37738.*

BELOW   *Black bear cub*

The density of forest cover and the exuberance of plant life and its attendant transpiration help account for the misty character from which the Great Smoky Mountains are named.

# REDWOOD
## NATIONAL AND STATE PARKS

BEFORE TWENTY-FIVE MILLION YEARS AGO, redwood trees grew widely across the Northern Hemisphere. Changes in climate have, in relatively recent times, confined the coast redwood (Sequoia sempervirens) - the earth's tallest living tree - to the moist and warm climate of southwestern Oregon and northern California. The World Heritage Committee inscribed Redwood National and State Parks on its World Heritage List in 1980 in recognition of these surviving remnants of coastal redwoods.

In their natural range coastal redwoods cover about 2,000,000 acres (810,000 ha) in a strip 5 to 35 miles (8 to 56 km) wide and along 450 miles (725 km) of the Pacific Coast, from the Chetco River in Oregon to the Santa Lucia Mountains of Monterey County, California. In the northern part of the range, an annual average of 60 to 100 inches (1,530 to 2,540 mm) of rain soaks the coastal land, providing ample moisture for the lush forest. In the drier south, the redwoods are confined to shaded valley bottoms.

In 1964 a National Park Service survey revealed that only 15% of the original forest remained. Of this amount, only 2.5%, or approximately 50,000 acres (20,250 ha) was protected in state parks. At the then annual rate of redwood logging, it was estimated that virtually all old growth redwoods not protected in parks would be gone within twenty or thirty years.

The first successful redwood preservation effort came in 1902, with the establishment of Big Basin Redwoods State Park in the southern redwood belt near Santa Cruz. The establishment of Muir Woods, just north of San Francisco, in honor of John Muir, followed in 1908.

In 1918 the Save the Redwoods League was formed. In half a century, with matching funds provided by the state of California, the league placed large acreage of old growth redwood forest in the Californian state park system. Three of these parks - Jedediah Smith

ABOVE  *Rainbow trout*
INSET  *Striped skunk*
OPPOSITE  *Stands of Redwood*

Redwoods, Del Norte Coast Redwoods, and Prairie Creek Redwoods - form the core of what, in 1968, became Redwood National Park. In 1978 Congress expanded the park by an additional 48,000 acres (19,440 ha), bringing the total size to 110,246 acres (45,936 ha), including 4,246 acres (1,770 ha) of submerged lands. In April of 1994, the National Parks Service and California Department of Parks and Recreation signed a memorandum of understanding to provide for co-operative management of this area, and to designate it as Redwood National and State Parks.

Not all the park is old growth. Only about 39,000 acres (15,800 ha) contain trees aged 400 years or older. Nevertheless, Redwood National and State Parks, which occupies a narrow corridor along 33 miles (53 km) of California's rugged north coast, preserves 42% of all the remaining old growth coastal redwood stands.

The redwood is the earth's tallest living tree, commonly growing more than 200 feet (60 m) high, occasionally more than 300 feet (90 m), and sometimes more than 350 feet (106 m). The tallest tree stands 367.8 feet (112.1 m). Trunks are 15 to 20 feet (4.5 to 6 m) in diameter, with exceptional specimens up to 25 feet (7.6 m).

Redwoods are also old. As a species they are remnants of the age of dinosaurs; as individual trees, some have been growing a thousand years or more. The average age of old growth giants is 500 to 700 years. The oldest known tree, felled long ago, was more than 2,200 years old.

The park's elevation ranges from sea level to 3,100 feet (944 m). Three major watersheds drain its rain-soaked forests. The northernmost river, the Smith, rises high in the Siskiyou Mountains and is the last major undammed river in California. Its turquoise blue waters flow through steep canyons and narrow redwood-lined valleys.

The middle river, the larger Klamath, begins in Oregon and meanders through flatter country. Redwood Creek drains the lower southern third of the park. On its alluvial (stream-side) terrace thrive two of the three tallest measured trees on Earth.

Upstream logging continues. All remnant old growth stands outside the park will be cut during the next decade. Second growth harvest has begun on lands outside the park.

Alluvial terraces and low-elevation slopes within a few miles of the ocean provide ideal growing conditions for redwoods. Here they develop the greatest volume of living matter per acre on Earth.

Protected from drying or toppling winds, valley redwoods - close to water and moisture-laden fog - may grow 2 to 3 feet (up to one meter) in a year. On hill slopes exposed to sun and drying winds, redwoods may grow only an inch (25 mm) or so per year. Generally a seedling takes about 200 years to reach canopy size - a fraction of its life expectancy.

Because of their tolerance to shade, resistance to fire and disease, their height and their ability to sprout from burls, coast redwoods dominate where they grow in a self-perpetuating 'climax' forest that has been stable for millennia.

In the forest shadow grow Douglas fir, western hemlock and Sitka spruce. Abundant winter rain produces a thick understory: rhododendrons 40 feet (12 m) tall, red-barked madrone, alder, maple, azalea, California laurel and bay. Tan oak acorns germinate and grow in forest duff, formed from decaying leaf litter, twigs, and other organic matter.

Duff is an unfavorable sprouting medium to most other trees. However, shrubs, herbs, ferns and skunk cabbage that grow in the soft, muted light cover the forest floor tangled by fallen logs and limbs. Wild flowers - redwood violets, showy trilliums and Douglas iris - grow in the springtime woods.

The forest litter supports a number of invertebrates: banana slugs, crane flies, millipedes and fifteen of western North America's twenty-two species of salamanders.

Because of a limited variety of food, bird life is relatively scarce in the forests. Several species that prefer mature redwood groves thrive: winter wren, Stellar's jay, ravens and marbled murrelets, which, although ocean-going birds, nest, along with the spotted owl, in old growth trees.

Grassy knolls and prairie vegetation supersede the forest as slope and dryness increase. The prairies on the eastern ridges and slopes above Redwood Creek are islands of grasslands and wild flowers; the realm of hawks, kestrels, and great horned owls that feed on meadow mice, gophers, brush rabbits, and squirrels. Mountain lions, bobcats, foxes, coyotes, gopher, snakes and other wildlife hunt and live on the prairies.

ABOVE *Bobcat*

ABOVE   *Roosevelt elk*
LEFT    *One of the ancient trees at Jedediah Smith Redwoods*
RIGHT   *Coast redwood (Sequoia sempervirens)*

The park's largest land mammal, Roosevelt elk, uses the forest mainly for cover and shade, but favors the open prairies and previously logged-over lands for food.

Nearly one hundred black bears live in and around the park, mainly in the Redwood Creek area, where new growth of plants following logging provides an abundance of food.

A coastal shrub borders the seaward side of the forest. Fragrant flowers of blue-blossom and large-leafed vines of wild cucumber, or manroot, trail over coyote bush. Sparsely vegetated sand dunes give way to surf and life in the shallow offshore sea. Shorebirds - black oyster catchers, black turnstones and several species of gulls - probe the sand beaches and tide pools for worms, crustaceans, shellfish and other bits of food.

About half of the more than 200 species of birds in Redwood are associated with the seashore and ocean. Offshore rocks provide a nesting area for common murres, puffins and three species of cormorants.

Endangered birds present in the park include the marbled murrelet, northern spotted owl and American peregrine falcon. Transient endangered birds include the brown pelican, bald eagle and western snowy plover.

Harbor seals appear in the surf, and large groups bask in 'haulouts' (sheltered coves). California and Stellar's sea lion also haul out in several places. Pods of gray whales pass close to the coast on their spring migration to arctic feeding areas and on their fall migration to their breeding and calving grounds in Baja California.

When the national park was established in 1968, critical problems remained. Upstream logging had greatly altered Redwood Creek, laid thousands of acres of forest bare, eroded the land and filled the creek with debris and great quantities of sediment. The stream bed and water table rose, and floodwaters undercut the stream banks.

The 1978 expansion did not solve the problems. The additional area comprised mostly cut-over lands - with 200 miles (320 km) of logging roads, 3,000 miles (4,800 km) of skid trails and thousands upon thousands of burned stumps. A major rehabilitation effort began: seeding logging roads, reshaping contours to cope with gullies and landslides, and reforestation.

Upstream logging continues. All remnant old growth stands outside the park will be cut during the next decade. Second growth harvest has begun on lands outside the park. Proposed offshore oil and gas developments, coupled with other proposed mining and subdivisions, also threaten the park's integrity.

Park Information Offices are located in Orick and Crescent City. Visitors may purchase tickets for a shuttle service to Tall Trees Grove on Redwood Creek from Orick Center on the west side of Highway 101, near the mouth of Redwood Creek. Park headquarters are located at the Newton B. Drury Center at Crescent City, 24 miles (38 km) south of the Oregon border. Campgrounds in Prairie Creek State Park are usually full in summer - a better time to visit being from Labor Day to early November.

*Further Information: Redwood National and State Parks, Drawer N, 1111 Second Street, Crescent City, CA 95531.*

*The redwood is the earth's tallest living tree, commonly growing more than 200 feet (60 meters) high, occasionally more than 300 feet (90 meters), and sometimes more than 350 feet (106 meters)*

# HAWAII VOLCANOES
## NATIONAL PARK

HAWAII VOLCANOES NATIONAL PARK is the youngest part of the United States. Here the earth is being made - born and born again in earthquakes, sudden eruptions of fume and steam, hissing fumaroles, smoldering fire pits, pungent sulphur banks and flows of lava.

Two hundred and thirty thousand acres (93,000 ha) of the youngest part of the island of Hawaii constitute the park. Hawaii Island, part of the Hawaiian Islands chain, is a coalescence of five separate mountains, all of volcanic origin. The entire island is composed of lava - constantly forming as layer after layer of the earth's magma (molten rock) extrudes from volcanic vents and solidifies as it flows to the sea.

Hawaii Volcanoes National Park encompasses two of the mountains of Hawaii. It spreads from the shore up over the low, dome-shaped tops of two of the most active volcanoes on earth: Mauna Loa - 13,680 feet (4,169 m) and Kilauea - 4,090 feet (1,246 m). In 1987, this park was inscribed on the World Heritage List in recognition of these two volcanoes. Constantly changing, they generate extensive lava flows and other landscape upheavals, including fire pits, rifts and earthquakes.

Like an iceberg, the bulk of Mauna Loa lies beneath the sea, hidden by 18,000 feet (5,455 m) of ocean. Measured from floor to summit, it stands as the greatest volcanic mass on Earth - a 30,000 feet high (9,090 m) giant.

The crust of the earth consists of several huge plates, which drift slowly over a deeper, more flexible mantle. Much of the world's volcanism occurs at the zones of weakness where two or more plates collide. The Hawaiian Islands are an exception, as they lie on the middle of the Pacific plate. Mauna Loa and Kilauea lie above a 'hot spot' - the route that magma travels in its periodic surfacing.

This hot spot has produced the Hawaiian Islands, and although it has remained relatively stationary throughout geologic time, the ocean floor has not. As volcanoes emerged and grew, the Pacific plate continued its slide to the northwest at 3 to 5 inches (75 to 125 mm) each year. Slowly, each mountain was rafted from its place of birth, eventually forming a chain, arching northwest over 1,500 miles (2,400 km) across the northern Pacific.

Mauna Loa and Kilauea began on the ocean floor 2 or 3 million years ago and emerged above the sea only 500,000 years ago. Since written records began in Hawaii two centuries ago, the lavas of Mauna Loa have covered some 160,000 acres (64,800 ha) and those of Kilauea some 38,000 acres (15,400 ha).

The avenues that magma travels are not simple, nor is its rise steady. Magma may accumulate in a huge reservoir, or magma chamber, a mile or two beneath the summit of a volcano. As pressure builds, even stone gives way under the tremendous force. The volcano inflates - often as much as several feet over a period of months or years - swelling like an inflating balloon. When a critical limit of expansion is reached, magma wedges into countless fractures and begins to rise.

Magma outbreaks often begin at the summits, where lava bursts into the air as a line of spectacular lava fountains, a 'curtain of fire', rising from newly opened fissures. With temperatures often exceeding 2,000°F (1,093°C), the lava begins to flow. Such enormous temperatures mean that the molten rock remains highly fluid and it will advance until it is ultimately slowed by the sea or halted as eruptions end.

Around the turn of the century, interest grew in studying Hawaii's volcanoes in a systematic fashion. Early visitors were enthusiastic. 'Here was room for the imagination to work,' exclaimed Mark Twain.

Agitation to secure the area as a public park began in 1906. The world famous Volcano Observatory, now of the US Geological

PREVIOUS PAGE  *Eruption and steam from rainfall, Kilauea volcano*
RIGHT  *Mauna Loa*

Survey at Kilauea, was established in 1911. In 1916 President Woodrow Wilson signed the nation's twelfth national park into existence.

Initially the park consisted of only the immediate summits of Mauna Loa and Kilauea on the island of Hawaii, and Haleakala on the island of Maui. Again and again the park was enlarged as other features were recognized for their value: the dry mountain forests of Mauna Loa, the Ka'u Desert, the rain forest of Ola'a and the Kalapana country.

The Hawaiian Islands are the most isolated islands on earth; the continents, with their rich assemblages of life, are at least 2,400 miles (3,864 km) away. Yet, when the islands of Hawaii rose from the sea, they were not long without life. The air was adrift with insects, spiders and the seeds and spores of plants that fell on the land even before the rocks had cooled to survival level.

Like a vast net across 1,500 miles (2,400 km) of ocean, the older portion of the Hawaiian chain received the passing forms of life and accumulated a reservoir of species. These speeded the colonization of the 'Big Island' as it grew from the sea.

In isolation, and with time, island evolution diverged from that on the continents and produced many species unique to the new land. Among the native flowering plants, 98% are found only in Hawaii, while 65% of ferns are unique. From 150 ancestral insect species, some 7,000 present-day species evolved. Twenty-two species of honeycreeper evolved.

Life is governed by the volcanoes. Volcanic activity formed the topography that influenced the climate. Geology and climate made the soils. As vegetative growth and decay changed the soil, plant communities reformed.

Recovery often depends on rainfall, elevation and on the texture of the lava. Smooth textured lava, known as 'Pa-hoe-hoe', has a web of fine cracks over its surface in which seeds readily take root. The rough-textured lava, known as 'A-A', has far fewer footholds for germination, and plant succession is much slower.

There are few days without rain on the windward slopes of Mauna Loa and Kilauea. This is rain forest country, a mass of green from soil to treetop. Great ferns rise 20 feet (6 m) or more and huge fronds may rise yet another 20 feet (6 m), fanning out and leafing together in a second canopy of green that allows little light to filter through. Epiphytes grow in rich profusion. A single large ohi'a may support a ton or more of mosses, ferns and flowering plants.

LEFT  *Hapuu forest, Ohia*
ABOVE  *View of Mauna Loa from Kilauea Crater*

ABOVE   *Another 'curtain of fire' erupts*
LEFT   *Helecho plant growing from lava*

Low, dense clouds rise up the forested northwestern slope of Kilauea, then rapidly dissipate to nothing as they pass over Kilauea Caldera. The northeastern caldera rim is often drenched in showers while the southwestern rim sits under cloudless skies. Between these two extremes lies the dry open forest so widespread on Kilauea, where a mixture of scattered 'ohi'a, pukiawe, 'a'ali'i, 'ohelo and 'uki thrives.

Annual rainfall drops off quickly along this path. At park headquarters the rain forest receives more than 100 inches (2,540 mm) of rain a year. At Halemaumau, 2 miles (3 km) away, rainfall is half that. Another 3 miles (5 km) southwestward and rainfall is 20 to 30 inches (500 to 760 mm) or less.

This is the heart of the Ka'u Desert, a vast tract of lava and ash, where life is marginal. The few plants grow in the shade of cracks that ameliorate the heating and drying effects of wind and sun. The stresses that plants and animals must contend with are compounded by the Volcanic fumes which release sulphur dioxide, chlorine and other gases to the atmosphere.

Because the park contains many flows of different ages in different climates, it is one of the best places in the world to study vegetative recovery and change. Yet indigenous life on Hawaii is under threat. In the last century and a half more birds have become extinct on this one island than in all of North America.

Introduced pigs, cats, mongoose, dogs and birds threaten the remaining endemic life. Approximately 600 non-native plant species occur in the park and at least 40 of these invade and diminish native ecosystems; 30% of the indigenous park flora are endangered or rare.

There is only one native land mammal in the park, the Hawaiian hoary bat. Most endemic birds are rare or endangered. They include Hawaiian goose, Hawaiian hawk, dark-rumped petrel, and short-eared owl.

Advance and burial is the repeated story of life on Mauna Loa and Kilauea. Lava flows destroy all previous vegetation. Cracks in the flow are filled by ferns and flowering plants common to the adjacent area. At the same time, a heavier plant covering, filling in between the cracks, develops. Animals and insects are attracted to the plants, until finally an ecological community little different from surrounding areas establishes itself.

No doubt it is the sheer size and ferocity of these two slumbering giants which draws the numerous visitors to the park each year. But perhaps this ceaseless cycle of regeneration, the constant rebuilding after destruction, also plays a part in attracting curious

TOP  *Wahaula Heiau*
ABOVE  *Honey creeper*
RIGHT  *Nene*

visitors. Fortunately, despite their immense power of destruction and creation, Mauna Loa and Kilauea are both relatively gentle giants, rarely threatening human life, even while venting their molten fury.

Mauna Loa was first climbed by Europeans in 1794; and as a result of descriptions written in 1823, Kilauea had by 1840 become an important tourist attraction. The first Volcano House was constructed in 1866 and successive structures were built over the years to serve volcano-watching visitors. One of the early constructions is now used as the Volcano Art Center, while a later construction is the park's only hotel. Present day facilities include the Volcano House and two camp-grounds. Hiking and fishing are two of the major activities. Direct flights to the Big Island depart from Honolulu, Kona and the mainland. Guided tours are available on the island, as are hire cars.

*Further Information: Superintendent, Hawaii Volcanoes National Park, HI 96718*

ABOVE   *Kilauea Volcano*
RIGHT   *Kalapana coast*
OPPOSITE   *Lava flow on Big Island*

'Shortly the crater came into view. I have seen Vesuvius since, but it is a mere toy, a child's volcano, soup-kettle, compared to this ... Here was a yawning pit upon whose floor the armies of Russia could camp, and have room to spare.'

Mark Twain

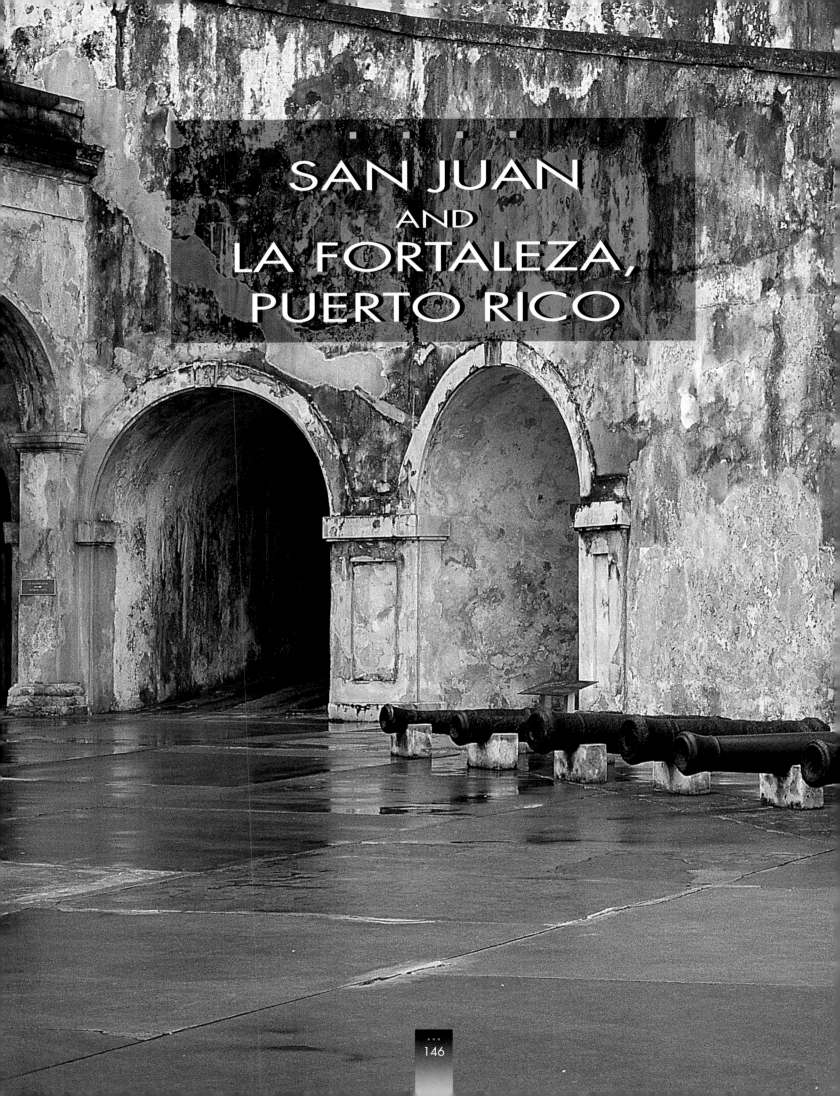

# SAN JUAN
## AND
# LA FORTALEZA,
# PUERTO RICO

S ITUATED BETWEEN THE CARIBBEAN SEA AND THE ATLANTIC OCEAN, Puerto Rico, and more particularly its capital San Juan, is home to some of the Western Hemisphere's greatest military architecture. The city's forts, the largest of their kind in the Americas, are found within the old area of metropolitan San Juan. In 1983 the San Juan National Historic Site, together with the city's first fort, La Fortaleza, were added to the World Heritage List.

Discovered by Christopher Columbus on November 19, 1493, on his second voyage to the Americas, and colonized by Juan Ponce de León in 1508, Puerto Rico became one of Spain's important military sites in the New World. At the time of Columbus' arrival, the native inhabitants of the island, the Taínos Indians, called it Boriquén, meaning 'the land of the valiant lord'. Columbus changed the name of the island to San Juan Baustista de Puerto Rico. Upon his arrival on August 12, 1508, Ponce de León, who had been appointed the first governor, named the harbor Puerto Rico, meaning fine or rich port, and established the first settlement at Caparra, two miles (3.2 km) south of the harbor. Disease and inaccessibility to water forced the early colonists to relocate the capital across the bay. In 1519 the seat of government was moved to San Juan, a three-and-a-half mile (5 km) islet at the entrance of San Juan Bay. Two years later, the capital city was renamed San Juan and the island took the name of the former capital, Puerto Rico.

During the 16th, 17th and 18th centuries, the English, French and Dutch tried repeatedly to invade San Juan. Initial aggression from European powers in the Caribbean in the late 15th century came in response to Spain and Portugal signing the Treaty of Tordesillas in 1494 which, in effect, divided the New World between the two nations. In May of the previous year, Pope Alexander VI had issued a bull preventing all ' ... persons, regardless of rank, estate, degree, order or condition ...' from entering those lands, discovered and yet to be discovered, without a special license issued by the Catholic Kings. In the words of one scholar, by the middle of the 16th century, ' ... the vast area of the New World, from Florida through Mexico down through Central and South America and encompassing the whole Caribbean area, was part of the new Spanish Empire.' In response, the French and British challenged Spain's monopoly on trade in the West Indies. Given its strategic importance, it was not surprising that Puerto Rico became a main target. Between 1595 and 1625 the island was attacked three times.

PREVIOUS PAGE   San Cristobal Fortress
ABOVE   Main plaza of San Cristobal Fortress
RIGHT   El Morro Castle

By 1530 despite orders issued eight years earlier to defend it, the island still lacked any effective means of protection. In 1530 San Juan's colonial council sent a missive to Emperor Charles V stating, 'Let the port be fortified, or the island will be deserted.' There were two main factors responsible for the exodus of Spaniards from Puerto Rico in the 1530s: first, the island's gold deposits had been exhausted; and second, the disappearance of the Indians, the major source of labor, meant that there was a critical shortage of workers. If the situation was not remedied, concluded Puerto Rico's governor, Francisco Manuel de Lando, Spain would lose the colony. Eventually the governor passed an order promising severe punishment upon those who tried to leave. The labor problem was solved by the importation of black slaves. With its small population and its limited economic value, the real importance of Puerto Rico lay in its strategic location.

Finally, in response to the threat from other European powers, the Spanish injected vast sums into the building of dozens of fortresses to defend its territory. The fortification of San Juan was later to become even more important after the great Spanish Armada was destroyed by Sir Francis Drake in 1588. In 1532 the construction of the colony's first true fort began. Completed in 1540, and situated in the interior of San Juan Bay, the medieval-style fort, known as La Fortaleza, was, however, poorly positioned from a military point of view. In the 1640s, and again in 1847, El Palacio de Santa Catalina, as it is formally known, underwent major reconstruction. Today, apart from being a major tourist attraction, it serves as the governor's official residence; as it has done since the middle of the 17th century. Even before La Fortaleza was completed, the construction of a new fort, El Morro (meaning 'the headland'), at the entrance of San Juan Bay, had begun. The Italian architect Bautista Antonelli drew the plans for the final form of the fort. In a letter to the Council of the Indies, Governor Diego Menéndez de Valdés explained that El Morro ' ... standeth in a good situation, and in a convenient place on a high mount which doeth lye upon the entering in of the harbor.' He predicted that when finished El Morro would be ' ... the strongest that his majestie hath in all the Indies'.

After nearly seventy years, El Morro, known formally as El Castillo de Felipe, was finished; 700,000 tons (636,000 tonnes) of masonry had been used in its construction, and its walls, made of sandstone, lime brick and crushed rock, stood 140 feet (42 m) above sea level. In the words of one scholar, El Morro and the several other imposing forts in San Juan, were ' ... unquestionably jewels of military architecture' in the Spanish colony. Today El Morro is preserved by the National Park Service, and visitors are able to tour through the site.

Further improvements to the island's defenses were made between 1580 and 1595. In an attempt to strengthen the defense of its colony, Spain introduced an annual subsidy in 1586, known as the 'situado mexicano'. The royal treasury of Mexico City funded the scheme. Thanks to the annual subsidy and the strong leadership of Governor de Valdés, more forts were constructed in the latter part of the 16th century: El Boquerón was built in the eastern part of San Juan, and San Elena built between El Morro and La Fortaleza.

The first test of El Morro's strength came in 1595 with an English attempt to seize the island. Queen Elizabeth sent Sir Francis Drake and John Hawkins to Puerto Rico, which at the time was being defended by 750 Puerto Rican and Spanish soldiers, along with 800 Spanish seamen. Their mission was to capture a treasure from the damaged flagship of a Spanish fleet which was believed to have been deposited in La Fortaleza. Accompanying Drake and Hawkins, and arriving in Puerto Rico on November 22, 1595, was a fleet of six royal ships and twenty one other vessels, carrying 4,500 men. Despite outnumbering the Spanish, the English plan to seize the island 'with all speed' failed. Hawkins, in fact, died in the process. But the English were not so easily defeated. Three years later, Sir George Clifford, third Earl of Cumberland, launched another attack on the island.

Between the two attacks, the Spanish continued to strengthen the defense of Puerto Rico: the size of the garrison was increased substantially and improvements were made to the forts. Yet by the time the English attacked in 1598, the island's human shield had been weakened considerably for an epidemic had wiped out many soldiers, slaves and citizens. Furthermore, unlike Drake, Clifford decided against sailing directly into San Juan Bay. Instead, he landed his troops on the east coast of the island, thus enabling him to stage an assault on the interior and eventually capture San Juan. However, Cumberland's occupation lasted only a few months. Realizing it was impossible for his weakened troops to fight against the 3,000 Spanish troops rumored to be heading his way, Cumberland evacuated the island. Before leaving, the English wreaked havoc, destroying sugar plantations, houses and crops. In the aftermath of the occupation, further improvements were made to the defense of Puerto Rico.

In the early 17th century, the Dutch emerged as the new adversary. In 1625 war broke out between the Netherlands and Spain. On September 25, 1625, seventeen Dutch ships with one thousand men on board, under the command of Balduino Enrico, sailed into the harbor, and landed over the following two days. Despite being in an unwinnable position, the Governor of Puerto Rico, Juan de Haro, refused to surrender and retreated to El Morro. Enrico retaliated by burning the city, destroying the civil archives, Bishop Bernado de Balbuena's house and library, dozens of wooden homes and part of La Fortaleza. Still the governor refused to succumb and instead turned 150 soldiers on the invaders. The Dutch finally left the island in early November. As the former Governor Diego Menéndez de Valdés had predicted in 1560, El Morro proved to be the strongest fort in the Indies.

As had been the case following the English attack, further improvements were made to the defense of Puerto Rico. In 1631 the construction of another fort, even larger than El Morro, commenced. The main purpose of this fort, San Cristóbal, was to guard the city's land approaches. Additionally, between 1630 and 1650, San Juan was encased in a great wall, which was in some places 15 feet (4.5 m) high; the walled area covered 62 acres (26 ha). It was not until 1897 that the land side of the wall was deemed useless and demolished. Of the four original gates, San Juan is the only one remaining.

In 1796 Spain declared war on England, and in the following year General Sir Ralph Abercromby arrived at San Juan with a large fleet of six vessels and 600 cannon. Faced with fierce fighting from the Spanish troops and local militia, the English failed in their attempt to break the defenses. It was largely due to the recommendations propounded by Field Marshal Alejandro O'Reilly, who had arrived on the island in 1765 to inspect its military conditions, that Puerto Rico's system of defense was stronger than ever. During the Spanish-American war in 1898, Puerto Rico fell to the United States, and its capital was occupied by foreign troops. One of the shells fired from a vessel under the command of Admiral Sampson blasted through an eighteen-foot wall at El Morro and exploded in an interior chamber. On December 10, 1898, by the Treaty of Paris, the island was ceded to the United States, thus making San Juan the oldest capital city under the United States flag.

*Further Information: San Juan National Historic Site, Box 712, San Juan, Puerto Rico, 00902.*

RIGHT *Ramp leading to the Santa Barbara Battery, El Morro Castle*

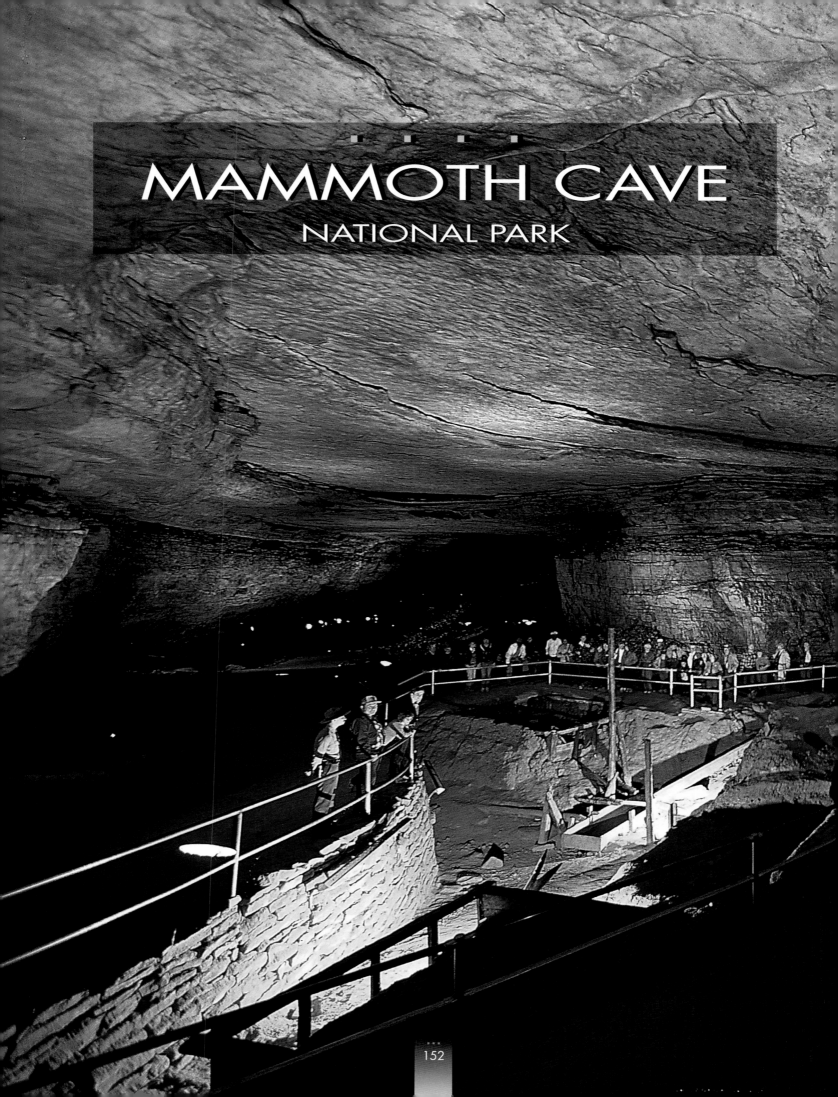

# MAMMOTH CAVE

## NATIONAL PARK

Down in south-central Kentucky, water and time has created the longest cave system in the world. Mammoth Cave National Park, internationally recognized as both a World Heritage Site and an International Biosphere Reserve, boasts passageways filled with spectacular rock formations and domes that extend for more than 350 miles (560 km).

Prehistoric Indians used the cave for shelter, and chipped gypsum and mirabilite off the walls. The first European settler entered the cave around 1797. By the early 1800s the cave was privately owned, and during the War of 1812 it was mined for nitrate, used in the manufacture of gunpowder. As many as seventy African slaves worked the operation, providing a substantial portion of the gunpowder needed to fight the war.

Successful promotion by a series of private owners resulted in the cave becoming an internationally renowned tourist attraction by the middle of the 19th century. In 1849, the last of the private owners, Dr John Croghan of Louisville, Kentucky died, and willed that Mammoth Cave be retained as a natural preserve until the last of his seven nieces and nephews died. It was then to be sold at public auction. The Mammoth Cave Estate maintained the cave enterprise for seventy-seven years.

In 1924 when the cave was about to be disposed of in accordance with the bequest, a group of concerned citizens who wished to see Mammoth Cave become a national park formed the Mammoth Cave National Park Association. They raised money to purchase land in the area and operated the cave until the National Park Service assumed control in 1941, declaring it a national park. Five years later, in 1946, the cave and the minimum number of required acres above it (50,000 acres - 20,830 ha) were formally dedicated as a national park.

The natural creation of the longest cave in the world began about 350 million years ago when a shallow sea covered most of today's southeastern United States, including Kentucky. The warm waters teemed with tiny organisms whose shells were made from calcium carbonate precipitated from sea water. As these creatures died, their shells accumulated on the sea floor.

The buildup continued until some 500 feet (150 m) of limestone formed under the sea that covered the Kentucky area. Subsequently a large river that emptied into the shallow sea covered the limestone with several hundred feet of sand that later turned to sandstone.

PREVIOUS PAGE   'Wright's Rotunda', an enormous room 142 feet (43 m) long and nearly as wide.
RIGHT   'Frozen Niagra', stalagtite formation
BELOW   Illustration of the Mammoth Cave system

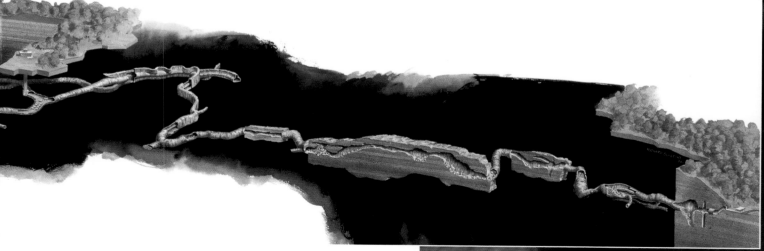

About 280 million years ago the sea level began to drop and the land rose. Cracks formed across layers of limestone and sandstone. The resultant porosity provided ideal cave-making conditions.

Rainwater combined with carbon dioxide in the soil to form a weak acid. This acidic water seeped down through the millions of tiny cracks and crevices and dissolved a network of micro-caverns along the cracks.

As the land rose, the water table dropped, and the water in the micro-caverns drained through the limestone toward the lowest point, which, by twenty-five million years ago, was the Green River. Along the way, the draining water converged into a few underground channels. With continued seepage, more limestone dissolved, and the channels enlarged, becoming the cave's major passageways.

The Green River cut deeper, the water table dropped farther, new underground drains formed at levels lower than the older ones and the older channels emptied. Mammoth Cave contains at least three, and possibly five, levels of major passages. Seepage, dissolution and drainage continue, and new cave passageways are forming at water-base level.

As well as eroding, the water also deposits dissolved limestone in travertine formations - shapes created by dripping water - such as stalagmites, stalactites, columns, drapery and flowstone. To these cave decorations - known as 'speleothems' - impurities added colors: reds from plant compounds, oranges and yellows from iron oxides, and black from manganese.

Chambers and passageways bear such names as 'Grand Central Station' and 'Wright's Rotunda'. The rotunda is an enormous room 142 feet (43 m) long and nearly as wide. The ceiling arches 40 feet (12 m) above the floor and is 140 feet (42 m) underground.

Deposits of orange-white gypsum cling to the walls of mile-long (1.6 km ) 'Cleaveland Avenue' an enormous elliptical tube formed more than 700,000 years ago. These deposits form only in very dry cave passages. When gypsum-laden water passes through limestone and reaches dry cave walls, the water quickly evaporates, leaving gypsum crystals, white to gold flower-like structures that seem to ooze and curl from the wall, ceiling or floor.

Visits to the cave are by tours, which range from easy half-mile ambles to rugged four-to-six-hour expeditions involving belly crawling. On guided tours visitors experience a traditional lights-out ceremony: guides flip the light switch, then in complete blackness light a grease lantern similar to those used by the guides of the 1800s.

About 130 species of animals have been found in Mammoth Cave, but their populations are small. In the absence of green plants, they depend on material carried into the cave by water, or in the faeces of animal visitors that feed outside the cave.

Animals that live inside but feed outside include raccoons, bats, pack rats, and cave crickets. Using smell, chemical trails and touch, they can find their way in and out of the cave in the dark.

Permanent cave-dwellers have evolved to maximize their ability to detect scarce food and reduce their expenditure of energy.

PREVIOUS PAGE *Green river*
ABOVE *Echo river, tour boat*
ABOVE RIGHT *Blind cave fish*
RIGHT *Blind cave shrimp*
BELOW RIGHT *Cave cricket*

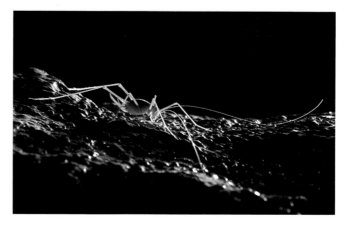

They live in an environment that is constantly dark, with an unvarying temperature of 54°F (12°C) and an average relative humidity of 87%. In response, most have lost functional eyes, coloration and the ability to cope with variable temperature and moisture conditions. The most renowned of these are the eyeless fish and the Kentucky cave shrimp.

Terrestrial cave-dwellers include beetles, spiders, millipedes, mites, springtails and bristletails. Aquatic cave dwellers include fish, crayfish, shrimp, isopods, amphipods and flatworms.

Without change of day length as a cue to time of year, crayfish and fish depend on internal clocks that ready them to mate and lay eggs whenever subtle changes in water chemistry signal an inflooding of organic matter.

Cave-dwellers are extremely vulnerable to toxins. Few or no pollutants originate in the park, but much of the water in the big stream passages comes from outside the park - from sinking streams, and sinkholes on the sinkhole plain, recharged by an annual precipitation of 44 inches (1,120 mm). Water from Park City, Cave City, an

TOP    *Forest above the cave system*
ABOVE    *Stalagtite formations*
RIGHT    *Cathedral Dome's impressive vertical shaft*
OPPOSITE    *Drapery Room ceiling*

interstate highway and railroad corridors flows to the Green River by way of the cave.

Industrial and domestic sewage in the Green River back-floods and enters downstream parts of Mammoth Cave. Most pollution however, originates upstream from the sinkhole plain, from fertilizer and pesticide runoff and through the dumping of wastes into sinkholes. Pollution has also come from a wrecked chemical tanker on the interstate highway and leakage from a gas station.

Electric lighting has led to the growth of mosses, fungi and algae in the cave. This growth may eventually spoil the natural beauty of the formations.

Bats no longer frequent the public areas of Mammoth Cave because the presence of people disturbs them. Elsewhere they continue to thrive. In winter thousands of social bats hibernate in dense patches in the coldest and windiest spots near cave entrances not open to the public. The bats need this cold air to slow their metabolism enough for their fat to last through the winter.

Most of the park above the cave is successional forest. As recently as 1941, when the park opened, farms were common; their outbuildings, fields, fence rows and pastures dotted the landscape. Red cedars now grow among oaks.

Luxuriant surface vegetation includes eighty-four tree species, ferns and flowers. Big Woods, the preserve above the cave, is one of the largest and best remaining examples of the ancient oak-hickory forest of North America that once covered Kentucky. In the wooded hills and valleys live white-tailed deer, woodchucks, cotton-tails and squirrels.

In 1981 UNESCO designated Mammoth Cave National Park a World Heritage Site in recognition of its stature as the longest cave system in the world. In addition, Mammoth Cave reveals the clearest and most complete record of geomorphic and climatic changes in the past ten to twenty million years of any readily accessible conti-nental feature. Mammoth Cave also has one of the most diverse cave ecosystems in the world, with the greatest variety of sulfate minerals of any cave. The park and a portion of the sinkhole plain - 100,000 acres (40,500 ha) in all - became an International Biosphere Reserve in 1990.

Access to the park is generally via either Nashville or Louisville, both around 90 miles (144 km) away. Cave City, Park City and Horse Cave are smaller towns nearby where accommodation is available. Cave tours are conducted every day of the year except Christmas Day. Special tours are available for the disabled.

*Further Information: Superintendent, Mammoth Cave National Park, Mammoth Cave, Kentucky 42259.*

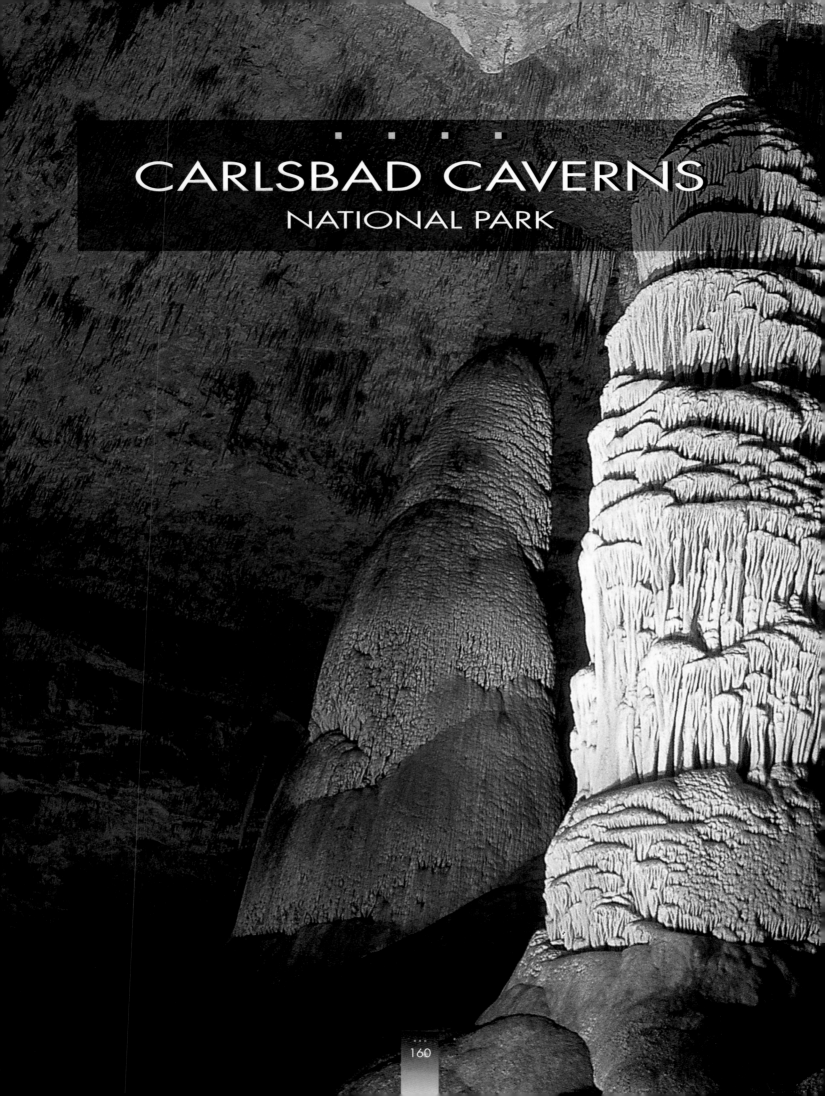

# CARLSBAD CAVERNS
## NATIONAL PARK

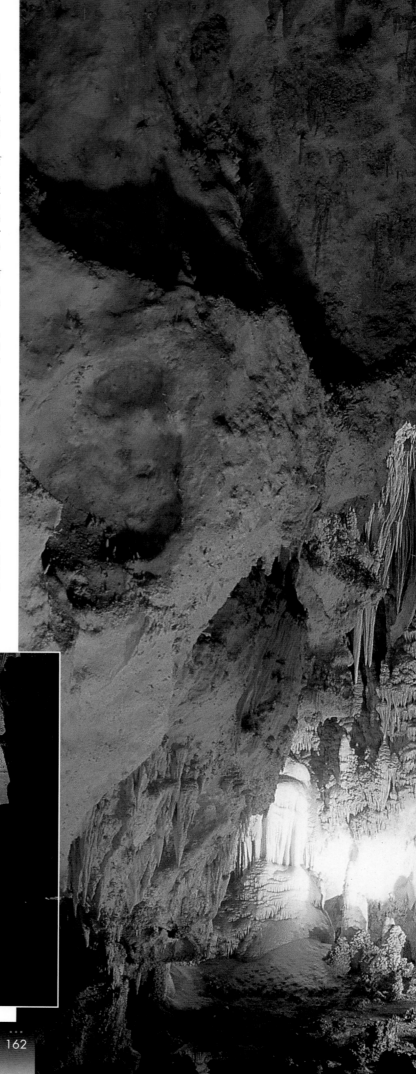

EAR THE FOOTHILLS OF THE GUADALUPE MOUNTAINS in southern New Mexico, a few miles north of the Texas border, desert-like flatlands sweep away to remote mountains. Below this arid, bare landscape lies a vast maze of caves: caves that boast the largest chambers of any such system in North America. These are the Carlsbad Caverns.

Pictographs and artifacts found in the natural entrance of Carlsbad Cavern, the largest of the park's eighty four caves, demonstrate an early Indian knowledge of these caves, thought to date back to BC 6,000. The park boasts several outstanding pictograph sites, including the profusely decorated Painted Grotto site (on the National Register of Historic Places). The art found in Slaughter Canyon Cave is thought to represent the oldest examples of deep cave art in North America.

In the 1880s ranchers and settlers in New Mexico knew of Carlsbad Cavern as the Bat Cave. At first they left the cave to the bats. A local boy, lowered into the cave at the end of a rope by his father in 1883, became the first known European to enter the cave.

Later, the deposits of bat guano drew commercial attention, and mining began. The guano filled one long tunnel near the entrance: it reached a depth of 100 feet (30 m) and sloped away hundreds of yards over the cave floor.

Between 1903 and 1923, miners working with hand tools removed an estimated 100,000 tons (91,000 tonnes) of guano. One of the workers began exploring. His stories of the magnificent cave led others to join on his trips. Eventually geologists from the United States Geological Survey explored Carlsbad Cavern and recommended Federal protection.

In 1923 President Calvin Coolidge proclaimed Carlsbad Cave and 719 acres (291 ha) around it a National Monument. Carlsbad quickly became famous. Visitors flocked to the attraction to be lowered by windlass in a miner's bucket almost 200 feet (80 m) to the cavern floor.

The cave did not remain a national monument for long. In 1930 a bill to make Carlsbad Cavern and additional surrounding acreage a National Park passed Congress without opposition and was approved by President Herbert Hoover. Since then, many more

PREVIOUS PAGE   The Hall of Giants

caves have been discovered and further additions have been made to the park, which now occupies 46,766 acres (18,926 ha) and includes eighty-four separate caves. In 1978 approximately two-thirds of Carlsbad Caverns National Park was designated as wilderness.

Visitor development has been limited to the largest and most easily accessible cave, the mighty Carlsbad Cavern, with 30 miles (48 km) of passages, which reach 1,037 feet (316 m) below ground level.

Consisting of a network of great tunnels and chambers, Carlsbad Cavern fits perfectly the popular image of a cave: massive, well-decorated rooms that interconnect in a vast, three-dimensional labyrinth, like a huge warren. The cave contains the famous Big Room, the largest underground space in North America, with a ceiling reaching 255 feet (77 m) above a floor which is big enough to fit twelve football fields.

Carlsbad Cavern has two natural entrances. Two man-made elevator shafts also enter the cave, each 754 feet (229 m) deep, providing visitor access to the Big Room area. Additionally there are two abandoned 170 feet (52 m) deep bat guano mining shafts which once entered the east end of the Bat Cave section. These have now been sealed to restore natural conditions in the bat roost where the young are born each summer.

Recently, geologists have changed their minds about how these caves, at the south eastern end of a 350 mile (560 km) long fossil limestone reef, were formed. The old theory held that falling rain and snow absorbed carbon dioxide from decaying vegetation in the soil, forming weak carbonic acid. The acidic rainwater, seeping down through the joints and fissures of the earth, would slowly dissolve the rock, hollowing out the caves.

The new theory proposes that the limestone was dissolved by sulfuric acid that formed when hydrogen sulfide gas from underlying oil and gas deposits seeped upward and combined with ground and surface water. Reactions between sulfuric acid and limestone produced gypsum and other sulfate products, evident in most caves of the Guadalupe Mountains. The caves of Carlsbad are highly decorated with stalactites, stalagmites and other speleothems which formed in a variety of ways.

Carlsbad Cavern is the largest cave, but recent exploration of the Lechuguilla Cave reveals it to be one of the most pristine, extensive and decorated caves in the world. Lechuguilla Cave and its unmistakable 90 ft (27 m) deep entrance pit have been known since 1914. In the early 1980s, cavers noticed that the wind blew through cracks and rubble at the bottom of the pit, indicating there was more to the cave. Moreover, the quantity of air movement, which changed with barometric pressure, frequently shifted directions, sometimes blowing in, sometimes out, indicating the existence of a large cave.

Subsequent exploration, commencing in 1984, disclosed that cave. With a depth of 1,567 feet (478 m), Lechuguilla is the deepest known limestone cave in the United States; with more than 89 miles (144 km) of passages, it is the third longest in the United States and the fifth longest in the world. Lechuguilla is currently closed to the public to preserve the cave's extraordinary decorations and scientific features, which include rare microbes presently being studied for potential medical applications.

White gypsum flowers are common in Lechuguilla. Although Carlsbad Cavern has great quantities of multicolored calcite dripstone, which forms stalactites and stalagmites, Lechuguilla displays a great variety of all types of formations. Lechuguilla's 325 feet by 100 feet (100 m by 30 m) Glacier Bay area features large blocks of gypsum resembling icebergs sheered off a glacier, sitting below a massive, white bed of gypsum.

Rare hydromagnesite balloons grow from the ceiling of the 200 feet (61 m) long Windy City passage. These white, inch-sized bubbles are found in only four other caves in the world.

Beyond Lake Labarge, clusters of gypsum flowers curl outward from the walls with delicate twists and turns. In the Chandelier Ballroom, sparkling crystalline gypsum grows down from the ceiling like tree roots. These gnarled white lengths of up to 20 feet (6 m) are the largest in the world.

Recent biological research in Lechuguilla Cave has uncovered unusual micro-organisms in pools and hydroaerosols in the cave air. The bacteria may derive metabolic energy from sulfur, manganese, and iron.

Carlsbad Caverns also harbor migratory bat species, in particular the Mexican free-tailed bat, now numbering some one million, down from five million plus reported in the 1920s. Many still live in the Bat Cave during the summer. At nightfall, they leave the cave in huge swarms, during an exodus that can last up to an hour.

The land they fly over is semi-arid and ranges from desert to coniferous forest. It is a land of alkali flat and soda lake, of cactus and mesquite. The climate is one of seasonal extremes, with an average rainfall of 14 inches (350 mm) and a mean annual temperature of 62°F (17.3°C).

Some eight hundred plant species grow within the park, ranging from drought-resistant shrubs such as creosote bush and prickly pear; to walnut, hackberry, oak and soapberry trees in the canyons. Coniferous forest with pine and juniper grows at higher elevations. Four threatened plants grow in the park: shining coral root, sneed pincushion cactus, Lee pincushion cactus, and Lloyd's hedgehog cactus.

Besides the Mexican free-tailed bat, there are over sixty mammals in the park, including mule deer, gray fox, coyote, bobcat, and occasionally puma. The park's 331 recorded bird species include golden eagle, bald eagle, cave swallow, loggerhead shrike, scaled quail, roadrunner and great horned owl.

The limestone reef that underlies the park dates back some 280 million years and is rich in fossils. They include bryozoans, pelecypods, gastropods, echinoderms, brachiopods, fusulinds, sponges, trilobites and algae.

Little permanent damage to the caves occurred as a result of guano mining. However tourism, as well as bringing many benefits, has caused considerable damage. Speleothems near trails have been dulled from touching and some have been broken. Organic litter has caused some increase in bacterial growth and pollution. Lighting encourages the growth of algae, moss, fungi and even vascular plants in some places.

Bat populations have declined from years of DDT use - still found in residual quantities in surrounding agricultural land, and still in use in Mexico where the bats winter. Mexican attempts to eradicate vampire bats also endanger the insect-eating free-tailed bats.

Oil and gas exploration along the park's boundaries, and the accompanying transmission and storage areas, threaten the land's integrity, as do livestock grazing, invasion by exotic fauna, and the hunting of puma.

Carlsbad Caverns National Park was accepted for World Heritage listing in 1995 because it contains some of the most outstanding caves in the world. This exceptionally high concentration of caves represents a natural ensemble of spectacular beauty. The sheer size of the chambers, which are far larger than those in most other cave systems; along with the caves' unusual origin and the abundance and diversity of their decorative rock formations also marked them for listing as a group of outstanding universal significance.

Carlsbad Caverns National Park is a popular tourist destination, and visitor numbers continue to grow each year. In 1994, 617,087 visitors descended into Carlsbad Cavern. The town of Carlsbad, New Mexico, easily reached by air or by bus, is only 20 miles (32 km) from the park entrance, along US Highway 285. Car rentals and accommodation are available in the town.

*Further Information: Carlsbad Caverns National Park, 3225 National Parks Highway, Carlsbad, NM 88220.*

# CANADA
# AND THE
# UNITED STATES
# OF AMERICA

# KLUANE, WRANGELL - ST ELIAS, GLACIER BAY
## AND
# TATSHENSHINI - ALSEK
## PARKS

I N 1910 WHEN AMERICAN CONSERVATIONISTS BEGAN PUSHING FOR the creation of Glacier Bay National Park in southern Alaska, some politicians thought the idea preposterous. 'It seems to be protected by nature without our setting it aside', explained one senator. 'It is practically inaccessible.'

Remoteness, however, proved no protection. Seventy years later, in a comprehensive survey of the national park system, Glacier Bay was listed as the most beleaguered of all US parks, with fifty-six identified threats to its integrity.

Although many of the threats remain, Glacier Bay, together with Alaska's Wrangell-St. Elias Park and Canada's Tatshenshini-Alsek and Kluane Parks, now forms part of the largest internationally protected area in the world.

Reaction to the creation of Glacier Bay National Monument in 1925 was hostile. Editorialists believed that protecting a glacier was absurd: ' ... a monstrous crime against development and advancement.' Mining interests succeeded in having the protected area reduced by over half to 1,164,800 acres (471,744 ha).

Similar protests preceded and greeted the creation of the other parks that now form part of this vast, jointly listed World Heritage site of 38,744 square miles (100,345 sq km): 12,199 square miles (31,595 sq km) in Canadian territory and 26,545 square miles (68,750 sq km) in US territory. This joint listing qualifies for World Heritage status because of the breadth of the display of active natural processes: tectonic, volcanic, glacial, fluvial, aeolian, mass wasting, soil formation, plant succession and animal migration; the combination of spectacular marine, coastal, wild river and high mountain scenery; and for the diversity and abundance of habitat for wildlife and fisheries.

Kluane, in the southeast corner of Canada's Yukon Territory, was first declared a reserve in 1942. Game sanctuary status, added in 1943, prevented hunting but left mining interests free to operate,

OPENING PAGE    *Autumn Pond, Mt Sanford*
PREVIOUS PAGE    *Aerial view of Glacier Bay National Park*
RIGHT    *Kluane Glacier*
BELOW    *Arctic wolf*

unrestricted by any measures to protect the land. Mining interests continued to oppose a park, but in the 1960s conservation groups made a concerted effort to push park plans to completion. In 1972 the Canadian government declared the majority of the game sanctuary as National Park Reserve.

Wrangell-St Elias, in the southeast corner of Alaska across the border from Kluane is, at 13.2 million acres (5.5 million ha), the biggest US park. A large copper mine operated in the area between 1911 and 1938. Mining interests expected more mines in the future, but US President Carter proclaimed the area a national monument in 1978.

In 1979 Kluane and Wrangell-St Elias were added to the World Heritage List, the first joint international nomination inscribed on the list. The 3.3 million acre (1.4 million ha) Glacier Bay National Park, immediately south, joined the listing in 1992.

Between Glacier Bay and Kluane-Wrangell-St Elias, in the extreme northwestern corner of British Columbia, lie the wide valleys of the Tatshenshini and Alsek Rivers. The discovery of a large copper deposit at the head of Tats Creek (Windy Craggy), in the heart of this area, spurred conservation efforts.

Development of a mine at the site would have created the hemisphere's largest open-pit copper and gold mine. Water pollution and disruption of the migration of plants and animals in the entire region would have been among the serious consequences. The establishment of the 2.3 million acre (almost one million ha) Tatshenshini-Alsek region as a wilderness park in 1993 and its nomination for joint World Heritage listing with the surrounding parks extinguished the Windy Craggy mineral claims.

TOP   *Peregrine falcon*
BELOW   *Pika, collecting food for winter*
RIGHT   *Willow Lake and Wrangell Mountains*

ABOVE *Golden eagle*

The landscape covered by the joint listing is one of motion, disruption and creation. The St Elias Mountains, the highest range in North America, dominate the region. Hundreds of peaks exceed 10,000 feet (3,000 m) above sea level, while Canada's tallest mountain, Mount Logan, at 19,525 feet (5,951 m), is one of the world's most extensive massifs.

Most of the mountains moved into place over the last fifty million years - very recently in geological terms. They are still moving: both upwards, in defiance of the erosive powers of water, ice and wind, which constantly wear them away; and laterally, along faults - deep fractures in the earth's crust between blocks of rock - that shift periodically in relation to one another. This newly emergent land is vulnerable. Vehicle tracks, for example, last for decades.

Glaciers hang off the St Elias Mountains by the thousands. They have advanced and retreated several times in the last 3,000 years - the most recent advance started 450 years ago - and most of them are still advancing. From the icefield that straddles the divide between the Pacific Ocean and the Yukon River flow many of the world's largest non-polar valley glaciers: Hubbard Glacier, 70 miles (112 km); Walsh Glacier, 60 miles (97 km); Kaskawulsh, Logan, and Lowell Glaciers, 45 miles (72 km). Malaspina Glacier, in Wrangell-St Elias, is larger than Rhode Island.

In Glacier Bay, walls of ice 150 feet (45 m) high flow directly into the ocean. In their wake, coastal glaciers leave not only icebergs but, more permanently, inlets, fjords and bays.

These huge mountains and vast glaciers make their own weather, at times causing the fiercest imaginable wind and snow storms.

The St Elias Mountains present a massive barrier between the Pacific Ocean and the continental interior. The effects are striking. The range effectively divides the region into two moisture belts: the

ABOVE *Lynx*
RIGHT *Muskrat*

marine slopes along which water-laden Pacific air is cooled and deposited, and the semi-arid rain shadow zone of the leeward continental slopes. Some areas receive less than 4 inches (100 mm) of rain per year, while others receive about 80 inches (2,000 mm). On higher peaks, snowfalls over 60 feet (18 m) are common.

Temperatures vary according to altitude. Average monthly temperatures on the ice fields are below 32°F (0°C). The southern portion of the region, close to the sea, has an average summer temperature of 54°F (12°C) and of 27°F (-3°C) in winter.

Despite the harshness, a spectrum of microclimates occupies the continuum between the extremes. Moreover, conditions near large glaciers are not hostile to life. On the contrary.

Ecosystems on the lee side of big glaciers are subject annually to pulses of highly fertile rock dust and water liberated by the glaciers. Productive plant communities grow in the sunny climate and support a diverse assemblage of animals. In turn, the large grazers support a diverse group of carnivores, such as brown bears, wolves and mountain lions.

In Glacier Bay, golden-crowned sparrows chirp in willow bushes only a few yards from the ever rumbling glaciers with their coat of rock debris and mud. Grizzlies feed on soapberries that grow abundantly in the glacial out-wash. Grasses cling to the soil collected in hollows in the ice. Dwarf willow and mountain avens root securely in the lateral moraine at the glacier's edge. Beyond the moraine, in the meadows of subalpine vegetation, moose browse on willow leaves, sedges, fireweeds and valerian.

On Klutlan Glacier a few feet of volcanic ash supports forests of white spruce and poplar, alder thickets, and wide flats covered by willows and dwarf birch. Moose winter here, and caribou cross the area.

Extensive forest cover across the valley bottoms and the lower mountain slopes is often interrupted by meadows, lakes, fens and river systems.

Permafrost restricts much of the region's interior vegetation to grasses, sedges and low, scrubby trees and shrubs. However permafrost also creates ideal habitats for water-breeding insects, and for the waterfowl and wading birds that migrate here by the millions each spring to nest - by preventing rainwater and surface melt from soaking into the ground. Food is so plentiful that birds converge from every one of the world's continents: golden plovers from Asia and the South Pacific, wheatears from Africa, loons from northern Europe, China and Japan, Arctic terns from South America and Antarctica, and godwits from Australia.

The region contains the world's largest protected population of grizzly bear. The last major bands of Dall sheep live in the mountains; large numbers of moose inhabit the subalpine region; caribou occupy northern tundra uplands. The region is also home to mountain goats and wolverines.

This jointly listed World Heritage area preserves a sizeable part of the earth's remarkable wilderness, as yet scarcely touched by the ruinous economic rationalizations that have stripped away so much of the landscape in so many other parts of the globe.

RIGHT   *Wolverine*
BELOW   *Grizzly bear fishing*

TOP    *Bald eagle*
ABOVE    *Dall sheep*

TOP   *Rain forest, Bartlett Cove, Glacier Bay NP*
CENTER   *Bank vole*
ABOVE   *Bunchberry, Glacier Bay NP*
RIGHT   *Abbot Ridge Trail, Glacier Bay NP*

TOP    *Bagley Icefield*
ABOVE    *Hoary marmots fighting*
RIGHT    *Cowell Glacier, Kluane NP*
NEXT PAGE    *Tidewater glacier, Johns Hopkins Inlet*

# GLACIER-WATERTON
## INTERNATIONAL PEACE PARK

THE FORTY-NINTH PARALLEL separates the United States and Canada. Political boundaries, however, do not determine ecology and have no influence on geology or climate. Nature's wholeness in this region is preserved across political divides at Glacier-Waterton International Peace Park, a joint World Heritage listing of Canada's Waterton Lakes National Park and the United States' Glacier National Park.

Nearly 90% of the 1,098,269 acre (457,612 ha) Peace Park lies in the United States, in the northwest corner of Montana. Just over 126,000 acres (50,500 ha) of it crosses the border into southwest Alberta.

The park, united by the Rocky Mountains, has many geologic features. About 1.5 billion years ago the ocean invaded what is today the mountain region. Sediments, eroded from neighboring highland areas, filled this sea for over a half billion years. Tens of thousands of feet of sediment accumulated.

Buried and compressed deposits of sand, silt and carbonate mud formed sandstone, siltstone, shale, limestone and dolomite. Under heat and pressure, minerals in the sediments were metamorphosed and converted to quartzite, siltite, argillite and recrystallized limestone and dolomite - the colorful rocks of western Montana and Alberta.

Later, much later, the Rocky Mountains began to rise, exposing the sedimentary rock to erosion. Water, wind and gravity lowered the surface of this high plateau and rounded the mountains. Thousands of feet of eroded rock and soil accumulated in valleys.

With the coming of the Ice Age, high alpine snowfields gave rise to massive rivers of ice that flowed down existing stream valleys. At least four major glacial advances and retreats, as well as numerous minor ones, slowly sculpted the knife-edge ridges, jagged peaks, basins and U-shaped valleys of Glacier-Waterton.

PREVIOUS PAGE  *Upper Waterton and townsite*
TOP  *Upper Waterton Lake*
ABOVE  *Mule deer, doe and fawn*
RIGHT  *Cameron Falls*

The fifty or so glaciers found in Glacier National Park today are of recent origin. They cling to north and northeast facing slopes, where steep head-walls shade them from the melting rays of afternoon sunlight.

The Continental Divide follows the Lewis Range through the center of Glacier National Park into Canada, where it forms the western boundary of Waterton Lakes National Park. Water from rainfall and snowmelt on the Divide flows into the watersheds of three major drainages - to the Pacific and Atlantic Oceans and to Hudson Bay in the Arctic.

The more than one thousand species of plants that inhabit Glacier-Waterton migrated in from south, east, west and the Arctic; and include species common in the northern Rocky Mountains as

'If we cannot live in
harmony with other forms
of life, if we cannot control
our hostility toward the
earth and its creatures,
how shall we learn to
control our hostility toward
each other?'

Wallace Stegner

well as those from other areas. Plants from the Great Plains of the United States and the Great Canadian plains reach the western edge of their ranges in Glacier-Waterton. The park preserves rare fescue grassland - used by elk, coyotes and pocket gophers - as well as wild flowers such as lupine and shrubby cinquefoil.

Other plants, common in the Cascade and Coast Mountains of western Washington and British Columbia, reach the eastern edge of their distributions in the park. Several arctic-alpine species reach their southernmost extensions in the park.

The Continental Divide splits Glacier National Park into two climatic regions. To the west, Pacific fronts bring heavy precipitation of up to 100 inches (2,500 mm) and moderate temperatures. Some of this precipitation spills over into Waterton, particularly in the Cameron Lake region, where annual precipitation reaches 42 inches (1,072 mm). Along the lower eastern edges, including most of Waterton Lakes National Park, the drying chinook winds create a wide variety of climatic conditions within a relatively small area; a major contributing factor to the wide diversity of plant and animal life found in the region.

Nearly two-thirds of the park is forested with nineteen species of trees. The highest diversity occurs on the western, moist side of the Continental Divide.

Cedar-hemlock forests occur in the southwestern area of the park. Their dense canopy allows little light to reach the forest floor. Only shade-tolerant plants, including western yew, queen's cup beadlily and devil's club, grow there. Lush cushions of mosses and liverworts carpet the ground.

A transitional forest of lodgepole pine and Douglas fir covers the mountains and lower mountain slopes. Most valleys floors are covered with either prairie or aspen park land.

Above 4,000 feet (1,200 m), Engelmann spruce and subalpine fir forests blanket both sides of the Continental Divide and extend to the tree-line, where scrub forest of subalpine fir prevails. Huckleberries, gooseberries, thimbleberries, elderberries and serviceberries grow in the understory.

Above 6,000 feet (1,800 m) the forest gives way to widely spaced islands of dwarfed trees and lush meadows. With snowfall averaging up to 25 feet (7.6 m) per year and snow lingering into July, the growing season lasts a mere six weeks. Nevertheless, vivid alpine meadows spread over the high country.

The arctic-alpine zone occurs above 7,000 feet (2,100 m). This vast, treeless expanse covers nearly one quarter of the park. Several plant communities form a mosaic of vegetation, from wet alpine bogs to meadows. Heathers, avens and willows are among the few woody species present. Mature dwarfed willows, scarcely 6 inches (150 mm) high, form thick mats. Dense growth enables plants to conserve moisture and heat, in addition to trapping soil and seeds.

Slopes of loose rock, or talus, and year-round snowfields, cap the high country. Rocky and desolate mountain summits over 8,000 feet (2,400 m) support several hardy species. Alpine plants include sky pilot, stonecrop, alpine buttercup, Jone's columbine and woolly daisy.

Snowfields also support plant life. Some algae can survive in snow and ice, sometimes becoming so dense that they color the snow.

Ranging throughout the entire park, grizzly bear, bighorn sheep, mountain goat, mule, deer, moose and elk that are found in Glacier National Park are some of the last populations surviving in the lower United States.

Coyotes, mountain lions and wolves are the largest predators of the grasslands. Mountain lions prey on deer but will eat what is available, including elk, mountain goats, beaver and small mammals.

Resident wolf-packs have returned to Glacier National Park from Waterton Lakes and other adjoining areas in Canada. They have raised many litters of pups since the mid-1980s.

The park's more than 650 lakes and ponds support aquatic plants and ducks, geese, beaver, muskrat and mink, as well as native and introduced fish species. Many of the introduced fish compete with native species; some prey on them, while others interbreed with them.

Many of the birds in Glacier-Waterton's forests are only part-time residents, taking advantage of summer insects and fall berries. Flycatchers, waxwings and swifts catch flying insects on the wing; woodpeckers, nuthatches and creepers glean insects from tree trunks and branches.

In 1891 the US Congress authorized the establishment of the Lewis and Clark Forest Reserve over much of present Glacier National Park. Four years later the Canadian government created the Kootenai Lakes Forest Park on the other side of the border.

In 1910, US President William Taft signed legislation creating Glacier National Park. Efforts by Montana and Alberta Rotary International Clubs resulted in the establishment in 1932 of Glacier-Waterton International Peace Park, to commemorate friendship and goodwill between the two countries and to recognize that the natural character of the region was not severed by a political boundary.

Once part of an enormous wilderness of forested slopes, wide prairies and abundant wildlife, Glacier-Waterton is now a wilderness island amid a sea of development; a remnant of a pre-industrialized landscape.

Nearby mineral exploration and logging has produced air and water pollution and habitat loss, particularly of concern in buffer

OPPOSITE   *Upper Waterton Lake*
TOP   *Bison Paddock*
ABOVE   *Cameron Lake*

zones adjoining the park. Livestock trespass has proved problematic, as has the introduction of exotic plant species such as spotted knapweed, which is threatening indigenous species. Owing to years of suppression of wild fires, the natural fire cycle is out of balance.

Glacier and Waterton Lakes National Parks contain a stratigraphic record which, it is thought, may span more than 1,250 million years of sedimentary and tectonic evolution. Jointly inscribed on the World Heritage List in 1995 as Glacier and Waterton Lakes International Peace Park, this place offers many opportunities for solitude, wilderness experience and quiet contemplation of nature. Such aesthetics as peace and solitude are indivisible from the natural beauty and international character of this landscape. Its designation as a World Heritage site ensures its continued global importance as part of a functioning ecosystem.

# CANADA

# CANADIAN ROCKY MOUNTAIN
## PARKS

THE WORLD HERITAGE SITE known as the Canadian Rocky Mountain Parks, with a total area of 5,517,600 acres (2,299,000 ha), began as a public sanitation reserve of 6,400 acres (2,592 ha) around the hot mineral springs of Banff Station, Alberta, in 1885.

The springs, bubbling from the slopes of Sulphur Mountain, were the only convenient place for railroad workers and others in the area to have a hot bath. Two years later Banff Hot Springs Reserve was enlarged to 166,400 acres (67,392 ha) and officially became Canada's first national park. It was enlarged again in 1930 to 1,654,000 acres (669,500 ha).

Meanwhile, in 1886, the federal government declared a reserve of 6,400 acres (2,592 ha) in the vicinity of Mt Stephen in British Columbia. In 1901 the reserve was enlarged to 551,000 acres (223,000 ha) and named Yoho Park Reserve. Later boundary changes, including the removal of logging areas, reduced Yoho National Park to its current size of 324,480 acres (131,414 ha).

Jasper, the third reserve in the area, and now the largest and most northerly of Canada's four Rocky Mountain Parks, was first created as a forest park in 1907. The aim was to preserve the forests of the Rocky Mountains and to protect the rivers and streams that originated in the mountains and crossed the province of Alberta. Jasper became a 2,685,925 acre (1,087,800 ha) national park in 1930.

Construction of a road from Banff to Windermere provided the catalyst for the creation of the fourth mountain park, Kootenay. The government of British Columbia began the road in 1911. When costs escalated, the federal government completed the highway in exchange for the creation of Kootenay National Park, enclosing an area 5 miles (8 km) on either side of the road. Kootenay National Park was proclaimed in 1920. The park subsequently covered an area of 340,000 acres (137,788 ha).

After Banff became Canada's first national park, visitor activities centered around the mineral hot springs. Access to the park was by train, foot or horse. Motor cars were at first prohibited, for the protection of the wildlife and to maintain serenity. Cars had to be

OPENING PAGE   *Opabin Moor, Yoho NP*
PREVIOUS PAGE   *The Ramparts, Jasper NP*
RIGHT   *Lake O'Hara from Yukeness Lodge, Yoho NP*
BELOW   *Canadian lynx*

ABOVE   *Moraine Lake, Banff NP*
LEFT   *Trilobite fossil, Yoho NP*
RIGHT   *Bow River, Banff NP*
NEXT PAGE   *Bighorn sheep in a display of aggression*

becoming the Canadian Rocky Mountain Parks World Heritage site. Three adjoining British Columbian provincial parks - Mount Robson, Mount Assiniboine, and Hamber - were added in 1990.

The Canadian Rocky Mountains straddle the Continental Divide. They are young, having been pushed up some seventy million years ago, trend northwest-southeast, and form a series of parallel ranges including the Western Ranges, the Main Ranges, the Front Ranges, and the Foothills. Each of these ranges, along with their characteristic vegetation and wildlife, are represented in the four mountain parks.

All the ranges are composed of squeezed and uplifted sediments. During the formation of the sediments, changes in climate, in water depth, and in size and availability of the sediment particles, resulted in various rock types.

The Western Ranges, included in Yoho and Kootenay National Parks, are composed of soft shales and limestone beds. Shales are often rich in fossils. The Burgess Shale, one of the most significant fossil finds in the world, lies in Yoho National Park and extends south into Kootenay. The shale contains the 530 million year-old fossilized remains of more than 150 species from 120 genera. Most of these species, from soft-bodied creatures buried in an ancient sea, are found nowhere else in the world.

'checked' at the police barracks in Banff, and the motorists 'dismounted'. There were few roads suitable for motor cars anyway, but tremendous agitation for improvement and new road construction overrode the ban after 1916.

Ten thousand people visited Banff in 1900; 160,000 in 1930; 1,000,000 in 1960. In 1962 the Trans-Canada Highway opened and gave millions more people access to the mountains. Visitation soared. In 1966, 2,000,000 people visited Banff. Over 4,000,000 came in 1993.

The four contiguous national parks of Banff, Yoho, Jasper and Kootenay were added to UNESCO's World Heritage List in 1985; subsuming the former Burgess Shale Palaeontological site, and

The Main Ranges, underlain by quartzite and bordered by faults, were forced up as great rigid blocks. They contain the highest mountains in the four ranges. The Continental Divide runs along these peaks and plateaus, which rise more than 6,500 feet (2,000 m) above sea level. The Divide forms the western boundary of Banff and Jasper park.

The Main Ranges have been, and are being, sculpted by ice. Huge glaciers shaped great domes of limestone and gouged out hanging valleys, carving cirques and the present-day peaks. Permanent snow fields and icecaps in the higher peaks still send tongues of glacier ice down into the valleys.

As they ooze down, the glaciers grind rock to powder, which is carried away in rushing streams. The debris, known as 'rock flour', enters the lakes and gives them a cloudy appearance. In Banff's Lake Louise, the glacial silt, suspended in the water, reflects the blue-green spectrum, giving the lake a brilliant emerald hue.

Meltwater also seeps through rock and into cracks in the earth's crust. Here it is heated, pressurized and percolated back to the surface, to form the mineral hot springs that drew the first tourists to Banff a century ago.

The Columbia Icefield, at 92,592 acres (37,500 ha) the largest icefield in the North American sub-arctic interior, spans the Continental Divide and the boundary between Banff and Jasper. Its melt-waters serve as the headwaters of three rivers - North Saskatchewan, Athabasca and Columbia - that eventually flow into three different oceans - the Atlantic, Arctic and Pacific.

East of the Main Ranges lie the Front Ranges, built of lime-stone and shale and often showing a tilted, tooth-like appearance. The Foothills, the eastern-most extension of the Rocky Mountains, are rounded, rolling hills bordering the Front Ranges and the grass-lands of Alberta.

This varied landscape is reflected in a matching diversity of plant life. In the valleys, dense forests of aspen, pine, fir and spruce rim the lakes' edges. Higher up, meadows and gnarled sub-alpine trees give way to barren, wind-scoured heights. In spring, yellow glacier lilies push through melting snows. In summer, wild strawberries and blueberries are found in the sub-alpine meadows, which are pro-fusely decorated with Indian paintbrush and heather, amongst many other species.

BELOW   *Stream carrying glacial silt, Kootenay NP*
RIGHT   *Athabasca Glacier, Sunwapta River, Jasper NP*
INSET RIGHT   *Angel Glacier, Jasper NP*

TOP    *Black bear, cinnamon phase*
ABOVE    *Red squirrel*
RIGHT    *Wolves*
TOP INSET    *Waxwing*

Animal life is just as varied. There are 225 species of birds, from hummingbirds to eagles, and 53 species of mammal. The contiguity of the seven mountain parks assists, but does not guarantee, the protection of a relatively large, undisturbed tract of wilderness that supports this diversity.

Grizzly and black bear, mountain goats, bighorn sheep, mule deer and white-tailed deer, elk, moose and wolves thrive in this vast territory. These animals require large habitats. Each grizzly in Alberta, for example, needs somewhere between 46,000 and 300,000 acres (18,000 to 120,000 ha).

Humans too take up territory. They are also powerful; strong enough to suffocate the planet with carbon dioxide, and certainly strong enough to overwhelm the Rocky Mountain Parks with roads, parking lots, resorts and amusement parlors.

The Lower Athabasca Valley makes up only 10% of Jasper National Park but supports 90% of the park's wildlife in winter, including elk, sheep and deer. This area is also most favored for development and includes Jasper townsite, as well as highway, railway, airport, utility corridors, camp-grounds and other facilities.

Each new development causes loss of more wildlife habitat. Sewage is polluting the Kicking Horse River, which cuts through Yoho National Park.

Poaching and hunting along the World Heritage site's boundaries, coupled with incompatible development on adjacent lands, further threatens wildlife. Toxic spills along highways and the railway pollute land and water. Exotic weeds threaten native plants. Logging of old growth forests outside the parks is reducing habitat. Logging roads enable poachers to prey on park wildlife.

The nomination of this site for inclusion on the World Heritage List broke new ground. Previous sites on the list focused on a single major ecosystem - the Canadian Rocky Mountain Parks represent many ecosystems. The Canadian Rockies made the list because of the unique properties of the Burgess Shale, the glacial landforms of the Columbia Icefield, the karst formations of the Maligne Valley, the exceptional beauty of the landscape and for the protection the parks afford to wildlife habitats.

BELOW   *Black bear*
RIGHT   *Elk bulls, Jasper NP*
NEXT PAGE   *Maligne Lake, Jasper NP*

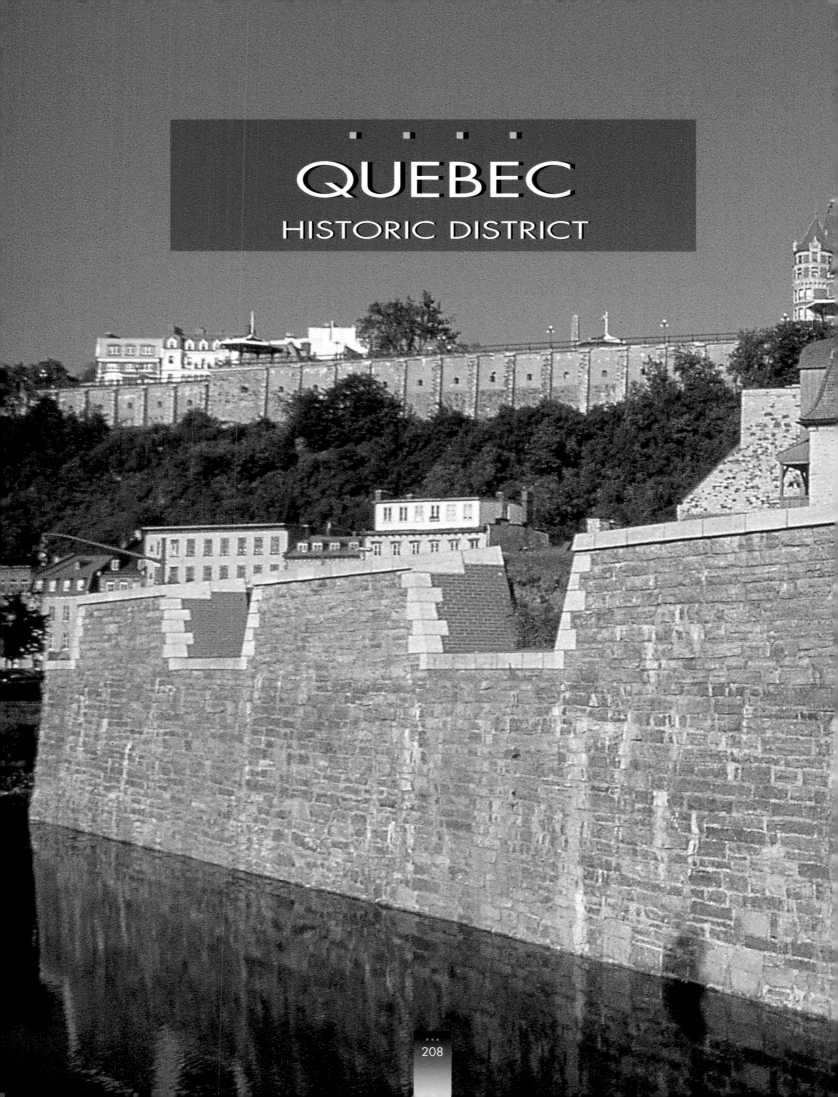

# QUEBEC
## HISTORIC DISTRICT

REFLECTING ON HIS VISIT TO THE HISTORIC CITY OF QUEBEC, Charles Dickens wrote in 1842, 'It is a place not to be forgotten or mixed up in the mind with other places, or altered for a moment in the crowd of scenes a traveller can recall.' Added to the prestigious World Heritage List in 1985, Québec, the oldest continuously settled community in Canada, is imbued with a European air unmatched in North America. Now the present-day capital of the Province of Quebec, it served as the administrative center of New France from 1608 to 1763, and the capital of Canada between 1851 and 1855, and again from 1859 to 1867. As David Ruddel has reminded us, Québec City ' … was once the heart of New France, the bastion of French civilization in the New World.' Within the walls of this picturesque and elegant city, visitors are still able to experience a piece of France in North America.

Each year thousands of visitors wander through Québec's maze of narrow and winding cobblestone streets, admiring the city's beautifully restored architectural treasures. Old Québec boasts dozens of historic institutions and buildings, ranging from 17th century stone houses to impressive fortifications that once protected this much fought-over city. Measuring seven square miles (18 sq km), it is the only remaining fortified city in North America. The city is divided into two distinctive areas: Haute Ville, the upper town, which is filled with fortifications, military barracks, political and religious institutions; and Bass Ville, the lower town, which is the commercial, industrial and transportation center.

PREVIOUS PAGE *Batterie Royale*
ABOVE *Artillery Park*

Although discovered by the French explorer Jacques Cartier in 1535 on his second trip to Canada, it was not until 1608 that another Frenchman, Samuel de Champlain, founded a fur-trading post in the area now known as Québec City. The small settlement was built near the site of the Iroquoian village of Stadacona. In Algonkian, 'Kebec' means 'place where the river narrows.'

One of Champlain's early initiatives was to construct wooden structures, known collectively as the Habitation, along the banks of the St. Lawrence. While functioning principally as a trading post, the Habitation also served a military purpose, for it protected the new settlers against attacks from the Iroquois as well as other trading companies. Place Royale, a collection of restored 17th and 18th century buildings, now stands on the original site of settlement. Within twelve years of settlement, the boundaries of the colony had been extended to the cliff-top. Champlain chose Cap Diamant, or Cape Diamond, to build another fort, Fort St Louis, overlooking the Habitation. This structure was rebuilt on a larger scale the same year.

Flanked by cliffs and built on a promontory overlooking the St Lawrence River, Québec has earned its title as 'the Gibraltar of North America.' Its perfect strategic location made it a much desired prize in British and American eyes. While still a small settlement, the

ABOVE  *National Battlefield*
OPPOSITE  *Old Quebec*

city was taken in 1629, by the Kirke brothers who starved the city's seventy five settlers into submission. In 1632 Québec was restored to the French by the Treaty of Saint-Germain-en-Laye. When Champlain returned in 1633, he found the city in ruins.

In October 1690, Sir William Phips, accompanied by thirty two ships and over 2,000 militiamen, headed up the St Lawrence with the intention of seizing Québec. When he called upon Governor Comte de Frontenac to surrender, he received the following reply: 'I will answer your general only with the mouths of my cannon and the shots of my muskets...' With his troops weakened by the cold weather and illness, Phips left the area ten days after his arrival and returned to Boston. Another unsuccessful attempt to capture the city was made by Sir Hovenden Walker in 1711.

France's rule of Québec ended in the mid-18th century. In September 1759, 4,500 British soldiers, led by a 32 year-old general, James Wolfe, defeated Général Louis-Joseph Montcalm's army of similar size. Before sunrise on 13 September 1759, Wolfe's men landed in a small cove, Anse au Foulon, and worked their way up a steep track to confront the French. Montcalm, who had been expecting an assault from the opposite side, hurriedly prepared his men for battle. The close-range exchange that followed lasted barely twenty minutes, and left 2,000 soldiers dead, including the two commanding generals. When their reinforcements failed to arrive within four days of the start of the battle, the French had little choice but to surrender. By the Treaty of Paris in 1763, Britain gained official possession of the city. The Plains of Abraham, named after Abraham Martin, the original owner of the land where the battle took place, is now part of the 235 acre (98 ha) Parc des Champs de Bataille Nationaux (Battlefields Park).

Following the British victory, the city's defenses were strengthened. After conducting a thorough study of Québec's defenses, British engineer Gother Mann, who arrived in the colony in 1785, proposed an ambitious plan that was implemented entirely by his successors. Between 1786 and 1812, the ramparts were repaired and a masonry wall built along the top of the cliff on the northern and eastern parts of the town. Additions were also made to the French fortifications west of the town and four martello towers were constructed on the Plains of Abraham.

To complete the defensive system, an enormous citadel was constructed between 1820 and 1832 on Cape Diamond, 340 feet (103 m) above the St Lawrence River. A small redoubt in the King's Bastion and a powder magazine in the Cape Diamond Bastion are the only two buildings remaining from the French regime. The Citadel is now home to the so-called 'Vandoos', Canada's Royal 22nd Regiment. It also serves as the residence of the Governor-General of Canada during visits to Québec. In 1871 the original five gates - St. Louis (1757), St Jean (1757), du Palais (1748), Hope (1786) and Prescott (1797) - were demolished. In the late 1870s and early 1880s, three gates were rebuilt as part of a restoration program instigated by the governor-general, Lord Dufferin. Thanks to Dufferin, the wall encircling Québec City was saved from demolition.

In the midst of a blizzard on New Year's Eve 1776, Brigadier General Richard Montgomery and Colonel Benedict Arnold from the American Army, lost 500 of their men trying to defeat the British colonial army in Québec. Montgomery himself died in the battle. American armies from Vermont and New York attacked the city during the War of 1812, prompting the British to rebuild the city's fortifications between 1823 and 1832. No further attempts were made to seize the city.

Québec City is filled with majestic buildings and, as George Leahy has noted, it is far from being '... a quaint tourist town or a sterile museum of plaques and boutiques.' The magnificent hotel Château Frontenac, with its imposing roof and turrets, dominates the city. The opulent hotel, which is reminiscent of a 16th century French castle, was built by the Canadian Pacific Railway Company between 1892 and 1893. Various additions, including a central tower, were constructed between 1897 and 1925. Its designer, the American architect Bruce Price, gained his inspiration from Henry Hobson Richardson's 1871 design for the Lunatic Asylum in Buffalo, New York. At the invitation of Prime Minister Mackenzie King, Winston Churchill and Franklin Roosevelt attended two historic conferences at the hotel in 1943-44. A monument to Wolfe and Montcalm is in the Jardin des Gouverneurs, next to the hotel.

In 1639 the Augustine nuns established Canada's first hospital, Hôtel Dieu, in Québec City; for over 350 years it has provided medical care. In the same year, the Convent des Ursulines was founded by the Ursuline nuns; it is the oldest continuously operating private girls' school in North America. After severe fire damage in 1650 and 1686, it was reconstructed. Ursuline Chapel was built between 1720 and 1722 by master stone-mason François de Lajoue, who emigrated from Paris in 1656. Général Montcalm is buried in the chapel.

Québec's first bishop, Abbé François Xavier de Laval, was appointed in 1674. Twelve years before his appointment, Laval, who had served in the position unofficially for sixteen years, ordered the construction of the Bishop's Palace. Basilique Notre Dame de Québec now stands on the site. In 1663 Laval founded the Séminaire de Québec (Québec Seminary), which later became Université Laval (Laval University), the oldest French-language university in North America. North America's oldest standing chapel was completed in 1678, near the site of Champlain's Habitation. It was renamed Notre Dame de la Victoire, commemorating the defeat of Sir William Phips. Following the defeat of Sir Hovenden Walker in 1711, it was again renamed Notre Dame des Victoires. The church was damaged during Wolfe's assault in 1759 and, on several occasions, has undergone extensive restoration. In response to the influx of tourists who visited Québec City in the late 19th century, Dufferin Terrace (Terrasse Dufferin), a wide 1,400-foot (424 m) boardwalk was erected; work began in 1838 and was completed over forty years later. From here one can see superb views of the lower town and the St Lawrence River. La Promenade des Gouverneurs, named in honor of the governors of the French and British colonies, was constructed in the 1950s to link Dufferin Terrace with Battlefields Park.

# WOOD BUFFALO
## NATIONAL PARK

ONE OF THE WORLD'S TEN LARGEST PROTECTED AREAS, Canada's Wood Buffalo National Park was declared a World Heritage site in 1983, but neither size nor status affords protection.

Straddling the Northwest Territories - Alberta border, Wood Buffalo, at 11,062,222 acres (4,480,200 ha), is an area under threat. Pulp mills on several streams flowing into the park, logging adjacent to it, as well as both proposed and existing hydroelectric dams upstream, are all issues posing multiple threats of degradation. Much has been done to address these issues - the park's streams are cleaner now than they have been in the last few years, and one of the dam proposals has been shelved - but much work remains to ensure that this magnificent wild place will endure.

The park was named for its purpose - the protection of the last remaining herd of wood buffalo (*Bison bison athabascae*). These are the larger, darker, northern relatives of the plains bison (*Bison bison bison*) which are a feature of Yellowstone National Park. When first protected in 1893, there were estimated to be fewer than 500 wood bison remaining. Since then numbers have slowly increased.

By the time of the park's declaration in 1922, there were estimated to be almost 2,000 wood bison. However threats remained, and the federal order creating the park concluded that unless the area was protected, the only remaining wood bison herd in its native habitat could become extinct.

In the 1920s, the plains bison herd at Buffalo National Park in Wainwright, Alberta, became infected with bovine brucellosis and tuberculosis from breeding experiments in livestock. Slaughter of the animals was proposed, but was prevented by a public outcry against such action. Most of the young bison were shipped north to Wood Buffalo National Park in the faint hope that only the older animals were diseased.

Between 1925 and 1928, when the park was increased to its present size, 6,673 plains bison were released in Wood Buffalo. Unfortunately, the infected animals passed on both diseases to the wild wood bison.

For a while however, bison numbers increased. In the mid-1960s the mixed Wood Buffalo bison population reached approximately 12,000, but a decade later it dropped to 9,000, and by 1987 there were only 4,200 left. Present estimates indicate that approximately 2,500 bison live in the park.

PREVIOUS PAGE   *Buffalo*
BELOW AND RIGHT   *Buffalo skulls*

In 1990 Agriculture Canada recommended the destruction of the entire Wood Buffalo herd and its replacement by disease-free animals. Up to 36% of the bison in and around Wood Buffalo are infected with either bovine brucellosis or tuberculosis.

Agriculture Canada advocated the slaughter to maintain Canada's 'brucellosis-free' status and to enable the Canadian cattle herds to be declared 'tuberculosis-free'. Debate continued over the fate of this, the largest free-roaming herd of bison in existence, until April 1995, when the federal government announced it would not pursue eradication, and implemented a five year research program.

The bison herd is not the only part of Wood Buffalo to warrant superlatives. A vast patchwork of muskeg, salt flats, grassy meadows, dense boreal forests and swampy deltas; Wood Buffalo is bordered by the muddy brown Slave River, which flows along the natural boundary between the maze of rock hills and lakes immediately to the east of the park, and the flat expanse of the interior plains on which the park is located.

Three topographical areas of different elevations lead down, like giant steps, from the west across these plains to the Slave River. The most western and southern plains are known as the Caribou and Birch Uplands. They rise 1,400 feet (420 m) above their surroundings. Long, incised, river-eroded gorges cut through the plateau bedrock. Poor drainage and natural fires keep most of the upland in prairie.

The next topographical step, the vast and poorly drained Alberta Plateau, covered with meandering streams, shallow lakes, bogs, sinkholes, and large gypsum cliffs, constitutes most of the park. The world's largest active gypsum karst land in the world occurs in the plateau's eastern portion.

Here, surface water and ground water are dissolving the soft gypsum bedrock, creating underground rivers and caves. Sinkholes form on the surface where water slowly filters underground and dissolves the gypsum below. Cave drains carry the dissolved gypsum away, and the surface soil settles, creating crater-like depressions.

The final topographical step ends in the wide, flat valleys and large flood plains of the park's in-flowing rivers. Combined, the flood plains of the silt-laden Peace, Birch, and Athabasca Rivers, as they flow into the still expanse of the western end of Lake Athabasca, form one of the largest freshwater inland deltas in the world. Enriched by dropped sediment, the 1,185,000 acres (480,000 ha) of meandering channels, shallow lakes, marshes, grasslands, and sedge meadows support bison, muskrat, fish and predators.

LEFT  *Slave River lowlands*
ABOVE  *Wood frog*

The park protects 80% of this delta, which provides nesting, staging and breeding areas for over 400,000 waterfowl during spring migration. Over a million ducks, geese, and swans from the four major North American flyways pass through the area in autumn.

In total, some 227 species of birds frequent the park. The most famous is the endangered whooping crane. First discovered in a remote northern section of the park in 1954, these great white birds are rarely seen. They migrate from the Aransas Refuge in Texas, to nest each spring and leave in October. Wood Buffalo is the only nesting site of wild whooping cranes in the world.

All four species of loon, all seven species of North American grebe, and twenty-five species of duck, as well as bald and golden eagles, have been sighted in the park. The park also contains the only wild breeding population of endangered peregrine falcons in Alberta. The northernmost colony of white pelicans in North America feeds and nests on an island in the Slave River Rapids.

The Slave River lowlands contain approximately 62,000 acres (25,000 ha) of salt plains. Salty water emerges from springs at the base of a low escarpment, flows across flat open areas and deposits the salt in either sheets or mounds. The effect is dramatic. Salt-tolerant plant species, more common in marine environments, grow here, and the grasslands and saline marshes provide habitat for bison, waterfowl and shorebirds.

Flooding and permafrost keep forest out of the delta areas. Bison also keep the prairies open through grazing. Elsewhere, woodlands of white and black spruce, jack pine, tamarack and trembling

TOP  *Peregrine falcon chick*
ABOVE  *Mallard ducks*
RIGHT  *Salt plain*

aspen are common. Bogs, muskegs, and prairies intersperse the forests. All provide habitat for moose, woodland caribou and black bear. Streams and marshes maintain large populations of beaver and muskrat. Fox, lynx, mink, ermine and red squirrel are common in the forest.

Wood Buffalo's wildlife is well adapted to the severe climate. Winters are long, cold and dark, with January daily mean temperatures of -25°C (-13°F). Summers are short and warm, with July daily mean temperatures of 16°C (61°F). Daylight lasts over twenty hours at midsummer.

The park is dry, with an annual precipitation of about 12 inches (310 mm), but an annual evaporation of 16 inches (410 mm). This moisture deficit, coupled with an average forty thunderstorms per season, places the park under extreme threat of forest fires. About 1% of the park burns each year, average for boreal forests in this part of Canada.

Altogether the park contains the largest undisturbed grass and sedge meadows remaining in North America, ideal habitat for bison, which have attracted the largest density of wolves in North America. Wood Buffalo is one of only two places in the world where the predator-prey relationship between wolves and bison still exists - the other being Mackenzie Bison Sanctuary in Yukon.

The World Heritage Committee added Wood Buffalo National Park to its list of World Heritage sites in 1983 because the park protects a large area of salt plains unique to Canada; a magnificent example of the boreal plains ecosystem; one of the world's largest inland deltas, the Peace-Athabasca; North America's best example of gypsum karst terrain; the world's largest free-roaming and self-regulating herd of bison; and habitat for other rare, threatened or endangered species.

In 1990 Canadian conservationists asked the World Heritage Committee to add the park to its List of World Heritage in Danger because of developments outside the park. In 1991 the IUCN concluded that the World Heritage features of the park were in danger of becoming seriously degraded. Both of the major issues which prompted this conclusion have since been dealt with: the proposed slaughter of bison was halted, as was clear-cut logging.

Many concerns for the integrity of Wood Buffalo remain. Owing to the construction of Bennett Dam on the Peace River in British Columbia, the Peace-Athabasca Delta may be drying up, as evidenced by the slow replacement of wetland plants with more woody plants. Almost a dozen pulp mills are being contemplated on the Peace and Athabasca Rivers and logging continues on adjacent land. Fortunately the future is not all bleak - these issues are of great concern to Parks Canada, to conservationists, and to all those people across the globe who recognize the urgent need for identifying vital areas such as these and protecting them for all time. That the World Heritage Convention is an invaluable tool in achieving these goals is exemplified nowhere better than in Wood Buffalo National Park.

BELOW    *Adult beaver on top of lodge*
RIGHT    *Beaver lodge, Gail Lake*
NEXT PAGE    *Buffalo*

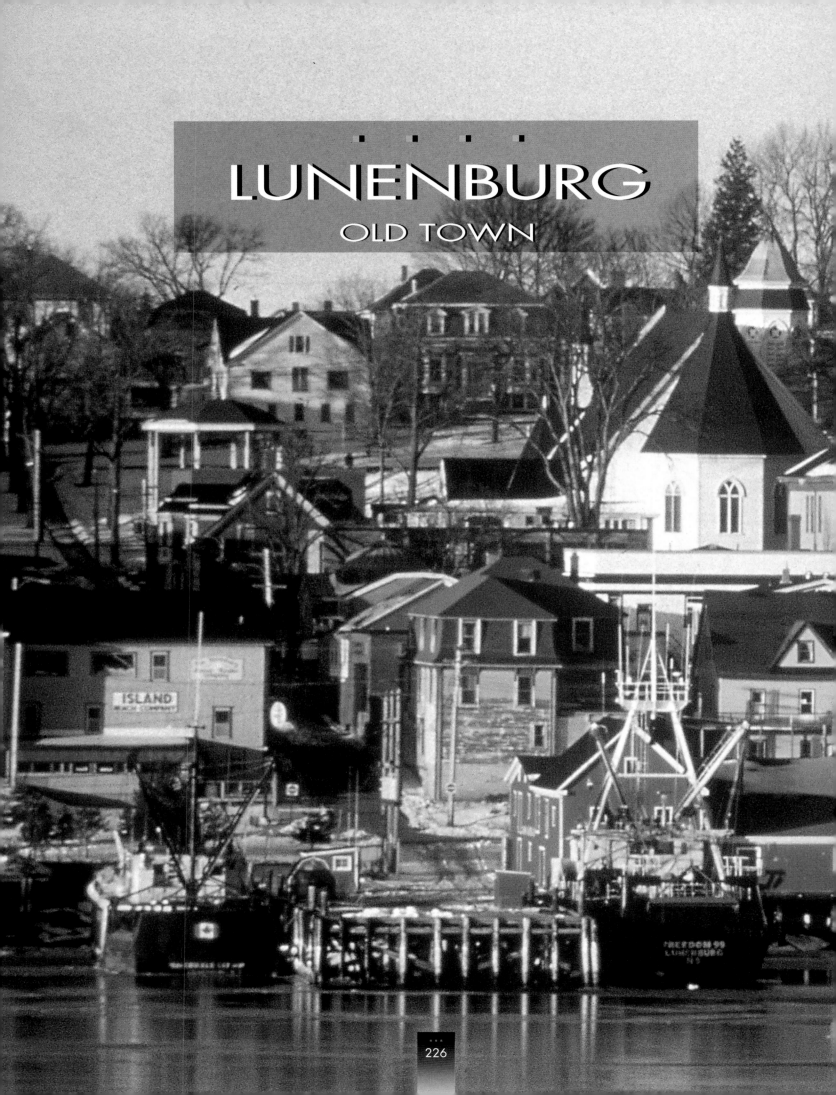

# LUNENBURG

## OLD TOWN

HIDDEN AWAY ON NOVA SCOTIA'S ROCKY AND RUGGED SOUTH SHORE is Lunenburg, one of Canada's most recent additions to the World Heritage List. Apart from providing a well-preserved example of 18th century British colonization and town-planning patterns, this seaport town is home to a remarkable ensemble of architectural styles, spanning 250 years.

At a meeting of the World Heritage Committee in Berlin, Germany, in December 1995, the 'Old Town' portion of Lunenburg (and its harbor front) became North America's second town to be inscribed on the World Heritage List, next to Quebec City.

In 1753 the 'snug little harbor' of Lunenburg became home to 1,453 mostly German-speaking Protestants who were recruited by the British government and sent to Nova Scotia from Germany, Switzerland and the Montbéliard district of France. Equipped with their personal belongings, building tools and little else, the new settlers came to the area aboard two flotilla of ships. The British government's decision to establish the settlement was motivated by its desire to extend the Empire into territory once held by the French. Lunenburg became the first British colonial settlement outside of Halifax, which had been established in 1749, 60 miles (96 km) to the northeast. What prompted the 'foreign Protestants' to leave their homes and move to the New World in the mid-18th century was the promise of land. Indeed on their arrival each new settler was granted farm acreage, a town lot and a garden lot outside the town's boundaries; as well as government rations - all of which they were bound to pay back at some future date. The exercise was supervised by British military forces under the command of Colonel Charles Lawrence, later appointed Governor of Nova Scotia.

Prior to the British government's establishment of the first formal settlement, the French Acadians had inhabited the area, which they named Merleguish; about fifty Acadians lived in Lunenburg as late as 1749. Later it became known as Malagash Bay, Mikmaq for 'milky water'. There seems to be some confusion over how the town came to be called Lunenburg. According to one source, because the majority of its pioneers came from Lunenburg in the Electorate of Hanover in Germany, the town was called Lunenburg to commemorate their home. Though, as Winthrop Pickard Bell noted, ' ... in those days the naming of a town was not a privilege appertaining to the settlers at all.' Furthermore, Lunenburg received its name a month before any settlers arrived. The most widely accepted view is that the town was named in honor of George II (also known as the Duke of Braunschweig-Lüneburg or the Elector of Hanover), who succeeded to the British throne in 1714.

Sandwiched between two harbors, Old Town Lunenburg, which encompasses an area of 74 acres (30 ha), was laid on the 18th century model of a British town. The rigid gridiron plat, the best surviving example of the British model town plan of its kind in North America, was explained by Winthrop Pickard Bell in the following terms: ' ... the streets were laid out with relatively horizontal ones along the hillside more or less parallel with the waterfront, and cross streets running uncompromisingly at right angles straight up the steepest slope.' The grid's six divisions were named after individuals who were prominent at the time of settlement. Each division was subdivided into eight blocks and then labelled with a letter from A through to H. Four blocks in the center of the grid were reserved for public amenities, such as a public parade ground. The remaining forty two blocks, each 280 feet by 120 feet (85 m by 36 m), were divided into fourteen lots, each measuring 40 feet (12 m) across the front and 60 feet (18 m) deep. Here, out of their allocated '700 feet of boards, 500 bricks and nails in proportion', the settlers built what Colonel Lawrence called 'huts' or 'good framed houses'.

Over time, the first settlers shifted their focus from the agricultural to the more lucrative maritime front: they fished for cod, halibut, haddock, lobster and smelt; built ships and engaged in ocean-based trading. Eventually, they succeeded in turning the town into the center of the fishing industry. The tremendous economic growth from the mid-19th century onwards, mainly due to the town's burgeoning ocean-going trade, enabled major renovations to be undertaken on many buildings, as well as the construction of new edifices.

The settlers also succeeded in building the first Grand Bank schooner fleet. Out of this fleet emerged National Sea Products Ltd, one of the world's largest fishing companies. In 1921 Canada's most famous schooner, 'Bluenose', was launched from a shipyard in Lunenburg. This fishing-boat-turned-racer remained the undefeated champion of the North Atlantic fishing fleet, and held four international schooner titles. Sadly, the vessel was wrecked off Haiti in 1946, after being sold to a West Indian trading company four years earlier. Since 1937, a sculptured profile of the schooner has appeared on the Canadian dime. 'Bluenose' II, a replica of the original, was launched in 1963, as a monument to the so-called 'Queen of the Atlantic'. During the winter months when the 'Goodwill Ambassador' takes a break from traveling the Atlantic, visitors to Lunenburg are able to walk its decks.

Apart from being, as Harry Thurston says, ' ... a repository of [Canada's] marine history', the picturesque town of Lunenburg is filled with magnificent and well-preserved architectural treasures. Since the provincial government passed the Heritage Act in 1981, which formed the Heritage Advisory Committee, 26 of the buildings in Old Town have been designated heritage properties. In 1992, the Canadian government acknowledged Old Town Lunenburg, with its narrow streets and several hundred buildings, as a National Historic District - only twelve districts have received this honor. From 1976 to 1992, Old Town Lunenburg was depicted on the back of the Canadian one hundred dollar bill.

Much restoration work has been undertaken on private houses, businesses, churches and public buildings from the 18th and 19th centuries. These buildings are still in use today. The primary material used in the construction of the houses and commercial buildings in the old portion of the town is wood. At least eight buildings in Old Town are representative of the period of colonization. Many are single-story buildings of 'coulisse' construction - this construction technique, which is uncommon in North America, involved using wooden frames infilled with thick horizontal planks. These houses were built close together, usually with their widest elevation facing the harbor.

Of the four hundred or so buildings in Old Town, two-thirds date from the 19th century. While the first half of the 19th century was a conservative period architecturally, more adventurous designs marked the latter half. One of the most distinctive architectural features is the 'Lunenburg bump', an extended and oversized five-sided dormer, which juts out from the second story of around an eighth of the buildings in Old Town. Of the existing buildings in Old Town, less than one third were built in the present century.

Unlike other settlements in North America, the demolition of the older buildings is not a common occurrence in Lunenburg; over the past ten years, only two buildings have been torn down. Instead, the emphasis has been on preserving the town's many heritage buildings. In recent years, Lunenburgers have worked tirelessly to restore their charming homes, painting them in traditional bright colors with accented trim.

The Lunenburg Academy provides one of best examples of Victorian architecture from the 19th century. When the Old Lunenburg Academy was destroyed by fire in 1893, plans were quickly made to build a new school on Gallow's Hill, which, as one contemporary source noted, was ' ... one of the finest and most commanding sites in the Province.' Opened on November 7, 1895, this majestic, wood-framed structure features a mansard roof and frontispiece, which is flanked by two towers. Not surprisingly, the Lunenburg Academy has been designated a municipal, provincial and federal heritage site.

Lunenburg is also home to the second-oldest Protestant church in Canada, St John's Anglican Church, built in 1754. Canada's

PREVIOUS PAGE   *Old Town from the Lunenburg Harbor*
ABOVE   *Montague Streetscape*
RIGHT   *Montague Street looking west*
LEFT   *St. John's Anglican Church*

oldest Protestant church, St Paul's, is in Halifax. The building's oak frame, which still exists within the walls of the present structure, possibly came from the old King's chapel in Boston which was being dismantled at the time. The original church was far different from the structure seen today. For example its original conical tower was replaced in 1840 with a square one which featured Gothic-style pinnacles, and between 1875 and 1877 it was again rebuilt. Other modifications were made in the 1870s and the 1890s: a chancel was added at the eastern end, the nave was extended by 10 feet (3 m), and the flat plastered ceiling was removed to reveal a sloping ceiling. Side aisles were added in the late 1880s. Interior changes, such as marbled columns, stained glass windows, a hammer beam roof and dark wooden pews, have taken place over the years. Another of Lunenburg's churches, St Andrew's, has the longest history of any Presbyterian congregation in Canada.

The layout of the Old Town plat and the physical limitations of the setting (a harbor to the south, and steep slopes to the north, east and west), has meant that the old town has never faced a population explosion or over-development; factors that have assisted in maintaining the Old Town's traditional layout. To facilitate expansion between 1862 and 1878, sections of the surrounding Common Land were subdivided, and New Town created. Today, Lunenburg's population hovers around the 3,000 mark.

# NAHANNI
## NATIONAL PARK

IN FEBRUARY 1972 the then Canadian Minister of Indian Affairs and Northern Development, Jean Chretien, announced the creation of three new national parks in the Canadian North with a total area of 11,579,496 acres (4,824,790 ha).

These lands, in the Kluane area in the Yukon Territory along the South Nahanni River, and on the Cumberland Peninsula of Baffin Island in the Northwest Territories, became Canada's first national parks north of the sixtieth parallel.

Nahanni National Park Reserve is the smallest of the three parks. Its ribbon-like shape of 1,176,543 acres (476,500 ha) protects 186 miles (300 km) of the South Nahanni River, four canyons along its length, and part of the Flat River. Nahanni is situated in the south-west corner of the Northwest Territories in a region of turbulent rivers, rugged mountains, caves, canyons and hot sulfur springs. There are no roads to the park. Access is by air or water.

Two nomadic Athapaskan tribes - the Slavey Indians and the Nahanni, meaning 'people over there far away' - lived here as late as the 18th century. In the 19th century the pelts of fur-bearing animals drew trappers and traders into the Canadian Northwest Territories. Early in the 1800s the Northwest Company, and later the Hudson's Bay Company, established trading posts along the Mackenzie River to support the fur trade. The nomadic ways of the Indians came to an end.

In the 20th century, myths and legends have surrounded the land of Nahanni. Tales of rich gold deposits drew prospectors to the area, and the later discovery of the headless bodies of some of these adventurers gave rise to legends of fierce natives and mythical mountain men.

The South Nahanni watershed drains a rocky wilderness of around 8.9 million acres (3.6 million ha), half the size of Scotland. The slow upper reaches of the South Nahanni meander through the tundra-capped mountains of the Ragged Range, at the northern edge of the park.

Here lie Hole-in-the-Wall Lake and a 106°F (41°C) hot spring. In the valley below, 68°F (20°C) water from Rabbitkettle Hotsprings has formed a succession of terraces more than 88 feet (27 m) high.

Throughout the chill sub-arctic year, the warm, mineral-laden Rabbitkettle Hotsprings bubble up. They create mounds of fragile stone called tufa, on which grow mosses, butterworts and other flowers. Ten thousand years in the making, the spring's wide,

PREVIOUS PAGE  *Nahanni River*
BELOW  *Beaver*
RIGHT  *Virginia Falls*

233

spreading terraces cover an area of 250 square feet (23 sq m). Each terrace dams a mirror-like pool of steaming water, with fringes of emerald-green moss and tiny flowers.

Below Rabbit-kettle Hotsprings, the South Nahanni swirls around a spruce-capped rocky tower to plunge down twin cataracts. The thunderous drop - 294 feet (90 m) - known as Virginia Falls, is almost twice as high as Niagara Falls.

The fall can be calculated at 426 feet (130 m) if the rapid drop of the 'sluice-box' immediately above the main cascades is included. In either case, the volume of water falling over the falls in the summer is only slightly less than the average at Victoria Falls in Africa. In winter the volume decreases as most water in the region freezes. Temperatures often reach -58°F (-50°C).

Once proposed as a site for a dam, Virginia Falls is the most spectacular undeveloped waterfall in Canada, showing more than 3.7 vertical acres (1.5 ha) of water-face shrouded in mist.

Just below Virginia Falls the river turns to rapids and whirlpools and quickly passes through Fourth Canyon. A few miles below the waterfall, more tumultuous rapids and whirlpools mark the river's journey through a tortuous constriction known as Hell's Gate.

At Hell's Gate, or Figure Eight Rapids, the river turns a ninety-degree bend with large standing waves, and back eddies between tall cliffs. Six miles (10 km) below Hell's Gate, the Nahanni is joined by its largest tributary, the Flat River.

Below this confluence lies Third Canyon, 11 miles (19 km) long and from 3,000 to 4,000 feet (900 to 1,200 m) deep. Here at The Gate, a hairpin turn, the river narrows against Pulpit Rock below 700 feet high (213 m) vertical cliffs.

A short distance beyond Pulpit Rock the South Nahanni enters the narrow, steep-walled Second Canyon, which cuts through the Headless Range. Dall mountain sheep graze here, black bears turn over rocks at the water's edge, and moose browse in the shallows.

Between Second and First Canyons lies the wide gravel delta of Deadman Valley.

At the mouth of First Canyon, pools of 97°F (36°C) water have collected below a sulfur hot spring. The immediate area supports a luxuriant growth of grasses, balsam poplar, and spruce. In First Canyon, precipitous limestone walls striped yellow, brown, and

TOP   *Rabbit-kettle Hotsprings*
RIGHT   *Pulpit Rock, Third Canyon*

orange climb to some 4,000 feet (1,200 m) on either side. One of the caves lining these cliffs, Valerie Grotto, contains the bones of more than one hundred Dall sheep which at various times over the past two thousand years sought winter shelter in its depths and starved to death.

Formed by percolating water in limestone, Valerie Grotto is 1.2 miles (2 km) long and is believed to be over 350,000 years old. It contains hundreds of small but still-growing stalagmites and stalactites.

Beyond First Canyon between Yohin Ridge and the Twisted Mountain, the South Nahanni passes near Yohin Lake, a shallow, marshy lake supporting an unusual growth of plants and large numbers of waterfowl.

Seven miles (11 km) southeast of Yohin Lake, on the slopes of the Liard Range, wind and water erosion have sculpted spectacular sandstone arches, pedestals and shallow caves. Powder-like sand from these formations covers the ground.

Both the park's major rivers, the Flat and the South Nahanni, are older than most of the mountain ranges that they dissect. The South Nahanni's four canyons cut through the park at right angles to the major mountain ranges. The cut exposes rock of different ages, types and origins.

The steep-walled gorges of First Canyon preserve traces of ancient river meanders. Two old meanders are raised high above the current river level - 1,600 feet (480 m) in one case.

Boreal forests grow in the lowlands. White spruce and balsam poplar dominate the dense growth along the valley bottoms. At higher altitudes and on northern slopes, black spruce becomes more prominent. Sedges, lichens, grasses and shrubs cover the alpine tundra on the higher mountains in the Tlogotsho, Headless, and Funeral Ranges. Dall sheep inhabit these mountains and the steep cliffs of First Canyon.

Wild mint, golden-rod, violets, yellow monkey-flower, aster, and many other flowering plants grow in small lush meadows near warm mineral springs along the Flat River. Large numbers of orchids grow near Virginia Falls.

Nahanni contains more than forty species of mammals, several of which are considered vulnerable, including the gray wolf and grizzly bear. Moose and beaver live in the forested river valleys. Woodland caribou live in the upper valleys.

At least thirteen species of fish, including arctic grayling and Dolly Varden trout, are found in the streams that flow into the Nahanni and Flat Rivers.

More than 120 species of birds, including Canada goose, American coot, wandering tattler, violet green swallow and song sparrow, have been recorded in Nahanni. Two highly endangered bird species, peregrine falcon and golden eagle, nest in the park. The endangered bald eagle and trumpeter swan also nest here. The area of trumpeter swan nesting activity is one of the three remaining such areas for the species in North America.

Restricted access has not lessened the park's vulnerability. The potential development of a lead/zinc mine on Prairie Creek, a tributary of the South Nahanni River, threatens water quality. The potential redevelopment of an inactive tungsten mine on the headwaters of the Flat River also poses threats.

Nahanni National Park Reserve was among the first twelve sites designated to the World Heritage List in 1978. The first World Heritage plaque in the world was posted at Virginia Falls in 1979. Nahanni was recognized for its extensive canyon system - the longest river canyons in the world north of sixty degrees latitude; Virginia Falls, one of the most spectacular karst landscapes in the western hemisphere; and its geologically significant hot springs.

The inaccessibility of this wild and rugged park attracts visitors who enjoy the outdoors and adventure. There are no roads within the park, but some 1,200 to 1,500 people canoe the river each year. Jim Thorsell, the IUCN's Senior Advisor on Natural Heritage - a man who has visited possibly more protected areas than anyone on the planet - has described this as, '... one of the greatest wild river trips on earth for scenery and wildlife.'

RIGHT   *Nahanni River, Five Mile Canyon*

*'one of the greatest wild river trips on earth for scenery and wildlife.'*

Jim Thorsell,
IUCN

# ANTHONY ISLAND

## SGAN GWAII

'A FEW FRAGMENTS OF MEMORY, a few bright glimpses in the writings of the past, some old and weathered totem poles in a storage shed, and the moldering remnants of once-magnificent carved posts and houses on the site of the old village - these are all that survive of the tribe and village of Chiefs Koyah and Ninstints', wrote the anthropologist Wilson Duff, in a report on Anthony Island he co-authored with Michael Kew for the Provincial Museum in 1957. The report, entitled 'Anthony Island, a Home of the Haidas', continued, 'What was destroyed here was not just a few hundred individual human lives...[but] a vigorous and functioning society, the project of just as long an evolution as our own, well suited to its environment and vital enough to participate in human cultural achievements not duplicated anywhere else. What was destroyed was one more bright tile in the complicated and wonderful mosaic of Man's achievement on Earth. Mankind is the loser. We are the losers.'

As a result of the Kew-Duff report, a major salvage operation was launched in the late 1950s, leading to the removal of several poles. In 1958 the site was declared a Provincial Park, and in 1980 it became a Provincial Archaeological and Heritage Site. UNESCO's decision in 1981 to award Anthony Island World Heritage status led not only to a review of the earlier practices used to save the site, but to increased interest in ensuring the long-term preservation of this haunting and mysterious outpost of Indian civilization. Today, the island is part of Gwaii Haanas National Park Reserve-Haida Heritage Site and is co-managed by Parks Canada and the Council of the Haida Nation.

Situated on the southern end of the Queen Charlotte Islands off the coast of British Columbia, Anthony Island, or Sgan Gwaii ('red cod island') as the Haida Indians called it, is only 1.5 miles (2.4 km) long and little more than half a mile (0.8 km) at its widest point. The English named the tiny island after the Venerable Anthony Denny, whose son served as a midshipman on board the HMS Virago, which chartered the area in the 1850s. For centuries Anthony Island's village of Ninstints was inhabited by the Kunghit, a tribe of Haida Indians. War and disease forced its abandonment in the late 1800s.

Of the two dozen sizeable permanent villages occupied by the Kunghit, Ninstints was the largest. This once-thriving village is tucked away in a sheltered bay on the island's eastern side. Facing the isolated village, and protecting it from the open sea, is a 40 foot high (12 m) rocky islet. Apart from being used as a burial site, this islet served as a refuge for women and children in the event of war. Duff accurately described the secluded site as '... a tiny miracle of sheltered micro-environment.' Ninstints' resourceful and independent inhabitants spent much of spring and summer outside the village. While the men fished for halibut, trout, salmon and cod, and hunted black bear, seals and sea lions, the women collected berries, bird eggs and edible roots. As the Haida carver George Reid once stated, with food being so abundant '... only a stupid man could starve on this coast.' The Kunghit spent winter partaking in ritual and ceremony, and feasting on the food they had collected during the warmer months.

Although the Kunghit were reputed to be the fiercest fighters on the coast, initially at least, their bellicose behavior did not extend to the Europeans, who came to the area to purchase sea-otter skins in the last quarter of the 18th century. The first recorded contact between the two groups came in 1787, when about one hundred and eighty Kunghit, aboard eleven canoes, paddled out to meet with George Dixon, the captain of the 'Queen Charlotte'. It did not take long for other traders to discover the fur-filled Queen Charlotte Islands. An entry from 1789 in the log of the 'Lady Washington', a trading ship captained by Robert Gray, noted, 'A brisk trade was soon set on foot by Coya (Koyah) the chief, who bartered for all his subjects...' The log stated that dealings between the Kunghit and Gray's crew, were based '... on the strictest friendship.'

Unfortunately though, such amicable relations with fur traders were short-lived. What should have been an easily resolved dispute over a petty issue, erupted into a bloody battle in 1789 between the Kunghit chief Koyah ('raven'), and American John Kendrick, who had assumed the command of the 'Lady Washington' from Robert Gray. Triggering the dispute was the theft of some of Kendrick's laundry, which he had hung out on the deck to dry. Kendrick, a known alcoholic, ordered his men to arrest the two chiefs, Koyah and Skulkinants, and demanded not only the return of his pilfered personal washing but all the furs in the Indians' possession. According to a version of the story based on native accounts, Kendrick 'took [Koyah], tied a rope around his neck, whipped him, painted his face, cut off his hair, took away from him a great many skins, and then turned him ashore.' Koyah had been reduced to an 'Ahlike', or member of the lower class in the eyes of his people.

Shortly after the incident, Kendrick returned to the area and continued to trade with the Kunghit. Koyah, along with fifty Indians, managed to board his vessel, forcing most of the crew below deck. Unfortunately for Koyah, some of Kendrick's men slipped below the deck and accessed the arms chest. Wielding firearms, the crew easily overcame the Kunghit whose only weapons were daggers. The ensuing battle resulted in the deaths of between forty and sixty Indians, with many more wounded, making it one of the worst massacres in the history of the Northwest Pacific. While Kendrick lost none of his crew, it is believed that Koyah's two brothers, wife, and two children were killed in the battle.

Koyah set about planning ways of regaining his former prestige. His revenge took two forms: he went to war against his sworn enemy, Chief Skidegate; and took part in the capture of three more trading ships. In 1794 he participated in an attack on an American brig, the 'Eleanora', at Cumshewa. Only one member of the crew survived the attack. Soon after, Koyah became involved in an offensive on an English ship, which had stopped nearby to repair a broken mast. Koyah holds the dubious distinction of being involved in more attacks on ships than any other Northwest Coast chief. His quest for revenge ended on June 21, 1795, when he was killed leading an attack on the 'Union', captained by John Boit. Up to seventy Haida died in the skirmish. As Carolyn Smyly pointed out, ' ... no other coastal village suffered so heavily from clashes with white men.'

European traders paid for sea-otter furs with metal axes, chisels and other tools, which assisted the Kunghit greatly in the construction of their large, planked homes. They built their dwellings on the natural terrace bordering the bay, and later, as the population grew, additional houses were built at the southern and northern ends of the village in front of the terrace. Timber was acquired from areas beyond Ninstints. The chief for whom a particular house was being erected would choose which western red cedar trees he wished to be cut, and would direct the logging. The wood would then be towed back to the village by sturdy canoes. Positioned in front of the completed edifice was a hollowed-out and painted pole carved with the crests earned or inherited by the house family. As George MacDonald has explained, 'The crests carved on the frontal poles ... represented animals, both natural and supernatural, natural phenomena, such as cumulus and cirrus clouds or rainbows, as well as celestial bodies, like the moon and the stars.' In some respects, the crest was the Kunghit idea of a family coat of arms.

House poles are not the only examples of Haida sculpture left behind at Ninstints. Intricately carved memorial and mortuary poles were also found. Mortuary poles, which were shorter than house poles, contained the remains of powerful chiefs. The chief's body was placed in a cedar box in an enclosure at the top of the pole, and a crest representing his supernatural ancestors was attached. In total, the Kunghit left behind twenty five mortuary and twenty carved house and memorial poles. It is believed that many of the poles were carved during the rule of Naostins ('he who is two'), after whom the village is named.

Even with the mysterious disappearance of some poles, and the removal of several others for conservation purposes, Ninstints houses the largest collection of ancient totem poles in the Pacific Northwest still to occupy their original location. Today, these remaining weather-beaten monuments either stand upright or lean at odd angles on the sandy beach. Reflecting on his visit to Ninstints, Aldona Jonaitis noted these ' ... remnants of the town's past glories ... almost seemed to be seeking their creators.'

Because of its remoteness, wild and unpredictable weather, and relative obscurity, the eerie island has not been inundated with as many visitors as some World Heritage sites. Its designation as a Class A provincial park in 1957 afforded it a degree of protection, though not enough to shield it from determined vandals who have, among other things, badly burned one of the poles and carved initials on others. In 1981, as the number of visitors began to increase, the Haida Nation established the Gwaii Watchmen program. Throughout the summer months Watchmen serve as site guardians and hosts at Sgan Gwaii and other important cultural sites in the area.

Five of the poles from Ninstints were removed and taken to Prince Rupert in 1938. Nine years later, an expedition from the National Museum of Man visited Ninstints and other Haida villages of the Queen Charlotte Islands. Apart from photographing the poles to determine which of them could be salvaged, members of the expedition entered into discussions with Haida descendants regarding the possibility of removing pieces from ancestral house sites.

Representatives from the Provincial Museum, the University of British Columbia, the provincial government and the Skidegate Haida band came to Anthony Island and its village of Ninstints in 1957, in an effort to save some of its totem poles. This expedition marked the first serious examination of the island since 1901, when C F Newcombe, a Provincial Museum anthropologist, undertook field research on the island. Despite the damage caused by the lush vegetation and years of wild winter storms, members of the team were surprised and relieved to find several of the poles in surprisingly good condition. Others, however, were in an advanced state of deterioration. The poles, some of which were about 50 feet high (15 m), were cut off at the base and then sliced into large pieces. After being boxed, they were shipped to their new homes. Of the eleven poles removed from the island, most were taken to the Museum of Anthropology at the University of British Columbia and the British Columbia Provincial Museum. Together with three poles from the 1957 expedition, two poles were relocated from Prince

ABOVE   *Long house remains*

Rupert and transferred to the Queen Charlotte Islands Museum at Second Beach. Sadly these poles were lost when a fire broke out in one of the museum's sheds.

Deciding what action to take over the poles and other cultural remains has not been easy for the Haida people. The desire to preserve the material structures has been balanced against preserving the essential spirit of the place and showing traditional respect for the human remains associated with the structures. Nature will be allowed to return the structures to the land, but their natural life will be extended by a few years through some generally 'low tech' conservation efforts. The trees that had grown up since the last of the Kunghit Haida left the village have been removed, and new growth is periodically cut back. This permits better air circulation and slows down decay by keeping the poles drier.

In the spring of 1995 it was apparent that the previous winter's storms had taken their toll. There was concern that several poles were leaning so badly that they would not remain standing another winter unless something was done. Over the summer, Gwaii Haanas staff worked with the Haida community and with Parks Canada and other experts to develop a strategy for straightening the endangered poles. In September three poles were successfully straightened. Artifacts that were excavated in the process were carefully documented and, with prayer and ceremony and respect, human remains were reburied in new cedar boxes.

Scholars have been unable to determine exactly when Ninstints was abandoned, though it is known that by 1875 it was used purely as a camp. In the early 1860s, a third of the 60,000 Indians living throughout the province had died from smallpox. In the early 1840s Ninstints had approximately three hundred inhabitants. Yet when Newton Chittenden explored the area in 1884 for the provincial government, he recorded only thirty inhabitants. Those Kunghit who survived the smallpox epidemic joined their former adversaries in Skidegate, on Graham Island, the largest of the 150 islands that form the Queen Charlottes. No known descendants of the Kunghit tribe are alive today.

*Further Information: Visitors must make a reservation and register with Parks Canada: Gwaii Haanas National Park Reserve-Haida Heritage Site, PO Box 37 Queen Charlotte BC VOT 1SO, tel 604 559 8818.*

# GROS MORNE
## NATIONAL PARK

Gros Morne National Park preserves part of the landscape and sea in the area Canadians know as the Atlantic Provinces. Here, the Appalachian Mountains, anchored in the Smoky Mountains of Tennessee and North Carolina, reach their northernmost extremity. Here also the four Atlantic provinces - New Brunswick, Nova Scotia, Prince Edward Island and Newfoundland-Labrador - as well as Quebec, enclose the Gulf of St Lawrence. The ocean dominates and nurtures much of the life in this part of Canada.

Centuries of European occupation and development have altered much of the land and the sea. Logging and agriculture have stripped away many of the original forests. Hunting and habitat loss have extirpated the wolf, Pine marten, and caribou in a number of places and have greatly reduced wildlife elsewhere. Over-fishing has depleted the cod fishery and produced an ecological and economic disaster.

Located on the western shore of the Great Northern Peninsula on the island of Newfoundland, in the province of Newfoundland-Labrador; Gros Morne's 445,679 acres (180,500 ha) include part of the Long Range Mountains and face the Gulf of St Lawrence and the mainland, 93 miles (150 km) to the west.

The climate is cool, wet maritime at sea level and sub-arctic at higher altitudes. Strong prevailing southwesterly winds from the Gulf of St Lawrence provide a mean annual precipitation of 55 inches (1,400 mm); some coastal areas have snowfalls up to 15 feet (4.5 m). Sea ice forms in winter.

Embracing the dramatic transition from the sea through to the vertical rock walls of towering land-locked fjords, and including coastal plain and alpine plateau that rises to a maximum height of 2,644 feet (806 m) above sea level; it was Gros Morne's spectacular scenery which first prompted calls for protection. The area became a national park in 1973.

Gros Morne was nominated and accepted for World Heritage listing in 1987, but not only for its great natural beauty. The park's World Heritage significance lies in its exceptional geological features which illustrate key concepts in earth science.

Geologists consider Gros Morne 'a Galapagos for plate tectonics.' The park's rocks reveal the story of the evolution of the northern Appalachian Mountains and the ancient continental margin of eastern North America. Rock structures and landforms created by plate tectonics are exposed in near pristine condition in the park.

The earth's surface, or lithosphere, is broken up into more than twenty plates, similar to the cracked shell around a hard-boiled egg. These plates, from 10 to 100 miles thick (16 to 160 km), float and move like rafts on softer, more pliable rocks below them in the earth's mantle. The plates, carrying the continents and oceans on them, shift and collide with one another owing to convective currents within the hot, pliable mantle.

When plates collide, buckling and uplifting frequently occur, creating many of the world's mountain ranges. Normally the oceanic plate slides under the continental plate. This is called subduction. In Newfoundland a rare reverse process, obduction, took place. In obduction ocean crust slides on top of continental margins.

The moonscape atop the 2,300 foot (700 m) high Tablelands on the south shore of Bonne Bay provides the most impressive evidence of massive geological events. The barren, reddish brown rock, peridotite, is more reminiscent of Arizona than Newfoundland.

Plant life is adapted to soil conditions derived from crustal rocks. Peridotite, a dense rock, comes from the upper mantle and is foreign material for most plants. Specifically the rock is very low in calcium, very high in magnesium, and contains a toxic mixture of heavy metals.

Peridotite on the earth's surface is rare. Normally the boundary between gabbro (dark igneous rock) of the ocean crust and peridotite of the ocean mantle, called the Mohorovicic discontinuity, or simply Moho, is many miles below the earth's surface. In Gros Morne, the two layers are exposed.

Glaciers helped mold Gros Morne too. Ice crept from the Long Range Mountains and from Central Newfoundland, scoured the upland plateau, gouged out steep canyons, and created two major fjords and Bonne Bay.

When the ice retreated, the land rebounded and cut off some fjords from the sea, making them very unusual landlocked, freshwater fjords. The most spectacular, Western Brook Pond, one of Newfoundland's most photographed features, slices through the Western Newfoundland Highlands. Its 2,300 foot (700 m) high cliffs plunge to a depth of 540 feet (165 m) and extend for 10 miles (16 km) inland.

All the glacier-carved, freshwater and saltwater fjords lie perpendicular to the coast. All occupy narrow, sheer-sided ravines. Bonne Bay, the only true fjord in the park, is deep; at 776 feet (236.5 m) it is the deepest coastal water in the Gulf of St Lawrence.

Marine areas of the park include the inner portion of St Paul's Inlet, intertidal zones, and estuaries. The shoreline features beaches and steep cliffs. Dune formations extend inland in a number of places.

The gently sloping coastal plain, bordered to the east by the Long Range Mountains, extends inland for 2.5 to 8 miles (4 to 13 km) and along the coast for about 34 miles (55 km). The largely limestone plain slopes gently seaward in a series of steps. Meandering creeks, eutrophic bog lakes and moraine deposits are found on the lowlands. Eight rivers, all less than 21 miles (34 km) long, flow east to west.

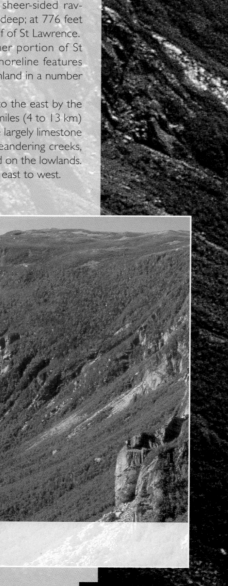

ABOVE   *Western Brook Pond*
RIGHT   *Ten Mile Pond*

An upland alpine plateau with perched lakes, bare rock knobs and valleys covers a large proportion of the eastern central park.

The park's southern boundary ends in cliffs overlooking the Gulf of St Lawrence, where sea stacks rise from the ocean. At the northern boundary rocky beaches and salt flats give way to white sand beaches backed by sand dunes. Park boundaries were drawn to accommodate nine long-established coastal settlements.

Locals use the excluded area for gravel supplies, fishing, firewood and livestock grazing. Hare snaring, wood cutting and harvesting bakeapple berries are also allowed within the park. All of these activities are restricted to adults who were residing within the park at the time of its establishment, and their children.

The park is dominated by a boreal forest of balsam fir, black and white spruce and white birch. Temperate forests of birch, red maple and eastern white pine grow in the low elevation valleys in the south of the park. On exposed ridges, spruce and balsam fir form a twisted mat stunted by wind, spray and ice, called 'tuckamore' or 'krummholz'.

Logging took place within the park boundaries early in the century. Most species are regenerating except for the eastern white pine.

Several plant species reach the northern limit of their distribution at Bonne Bay, such as yellow birch, black ash, eastern white pine, red maple and chokecherry. Others reach the southern limit of their range in the Long Range Mountains, such as alpine bearberry.

Although reduced in diversity compared to the mainland, park fauna include a number of species scarce in Canada, such as lynx, the woodland caribou and arctic hare. The park is also home to moose, black bear, beaver, mink, weasel and red squirrel. Pine marten have occasionally been spotted in isolated areas, but are considered very rare.

Fifteen marine mammals occur in waters near the park. Those that can be observed from the park include pilot whale, minke whale, finback whale, white-sided dolphins and harbor seals.

Two hundred and thirty arctic, boreal and pelagic species of birds frequent the park, which provides breeding sites for harlequin duck and half a million pairs of blackpoll warbler. Populations of common tern and arctic tern may be declining - the colony has moved from a traditional nesting island to a series of nearby islands, probably due to competition and predation from gulls. Bald eagle, osprey, rock ptarmigan, and American tree sparrow also nest in the park.

High visitation levels at Gros Morne Mountain has resulted in damage to some of the alpine plant communities. Over-fishing has put Atlantic salmon populations at risk. Logging on lands adjacent to park boundaries has made the backcountry more accessible and more liable to disturbance.

Seven species of mammals were introduced to the Island of Newfoundland before the park was established. These mammals - moose, snowshoe hare, red squirrel, eastern chipmunk, masked shrew, mink, house mouse and Norway rat - although not endemic, are typical of the boreal ecosystem. Along with the exotic coyote and deer mouse, these introduced species have competed with endemic fauna and disturbed ecological relationships typical of insular settings.

Gros Morne National Park was nominated and accepted on the World Heritage List for its superlative examples of landforms created by plate tectonic activity. In addition, the park protects a landscape of exceptional beauty and provides habitat for many species including black bears and woodland caribou.

RIGHT AND INSET  *Caribou*
NEXT PAGE  *Gros Morne in Fall*

Geologists consider Gros Morne 'a Galapagos for plate tectonics.' The park's rocks reveal the story of the evolution of the northern Appalachian Mountains and the ancient continental margin of eastern North America. Rock structures and landforms created by plate tectonics are exposed in near pristine condition in the park.

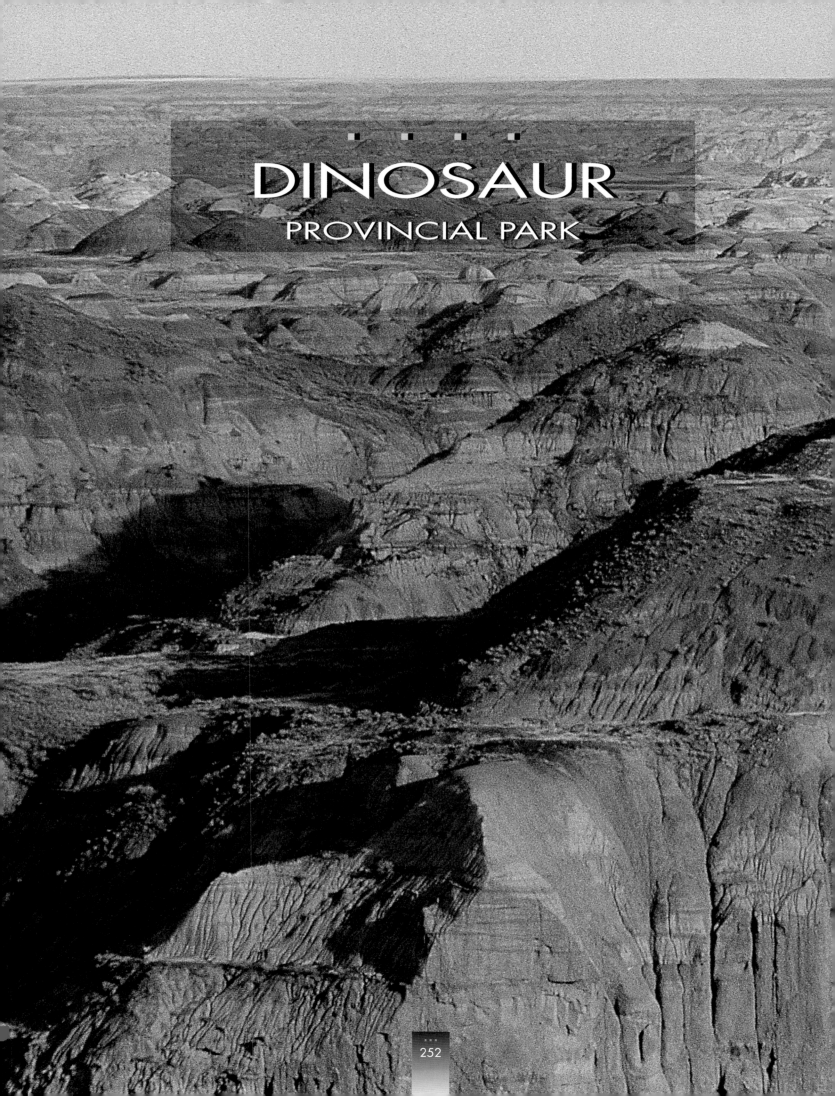

# DINOSAUR
## PROVINCIAL PARK

ABOUT FIFTEEN THOUSAND YEARS AGO, the 2,000 feet thick (600 m) continental glacier that covered Alberta began to melt. As the waning glacier retreated in a northeasterly direction, huge volumes of meltwater spewed out.

Laden with sediments - gravel, sand and clay - the water cut deeply into the soft bedrock sandstones, siltstones and shales of southern Alberta, carving steep-sided channels as well as the Red Deer River.

When all the ice had melted and all the water had drained away, the exposed bedrock was left scoured and sculpted. Similar rugged topography flanks the White River in South Dakota and stretches along many other rivers in the prairie regions of Saskatchewan and Alberta.

Early French settlers coined the term 'badlands' ('les mauvaises terres') to describe these areas, perhaps out of the frustration they felt when they found these rocky lands impossible to travel across. However, badlands are bad only from a human point of view. Since they lie within the great prairie ecosystem of North America, the badlands are rich in life.

The most spectacular badlands are those that shoulder the shores of the Red Deer River, as it curves for 17 miles (27 km) through what is now Dinosaur Provincial Park in southern Alberta. These badlands extend as much as 2 miles (3 km) on either side of the river.

The 18,116 acres (7,332 ha) of Dinosaur Provincial Park were originally part of a much larger Steveville Dinosaur Provincial

PREVIOUS PAGE AND OPPOSITE   *The naked moonscape of Dinosaur Provincial Park*
TOP   *Dinosaur leg bone*
ABOVE   *A complete skeleton reconstructed and on display*

Park created in 1955. Boundaries were redrawn in 1974, and park status was limited to Crown-owned or leased land. Some 7,300 acres (2,959 ha) of private land was excluded from the park.

Within the present park the flatness and grass of the surrounding prairies disappear, replaced by a moonscape of gullies, pinnacles, mounds, flat-topped mesas and naked bedrock; sculpted

and worked not only by glacial melt but also by subsequent millennia of hot, dry summers and long, cold winters.

Although initially carved by glacial meltwater, erosion by other means continues. Chemical dissolution, wind-driven ice and grit, and repeated freezing and thawing, chip away at even the most resilient rock surface. Rain and run-off remain the most erosive agents in Dinosaur Park.

The park receives only 9 to 12 inches (225 to 300 mm) of precipitation a year, most of which falls during a few intense summer thunderstorms that can drop several inches of rain in an hour. Dry stream beds can fill with 2 feet (0.6 m) of water ten minutes after a rainstorm. Flash floods that follow accentuate the erosion and carry away tons of soil and rock.

Harder rocks resist erosion longer, and where they overlie softer rocks, mushroom-shaped pinnacles, or 'hoodoos', form. Hoodoos typify the badlands. In Dinosaur, resistant red ironstones cap the tops of many hoodoos, which are largely composed of softer sandstones and siltstones.

Erosion continues at a rate of one-sixth of an inch (4 mm) a year - an unusually rapid rate by geological standards. By contrast, the erosion rate of the harder bedrock of the Rocky Mountains is one-sixth of an inch (4 mm) every five hundred years.

Every rainfall peels another layer from the badlands and uncovers dinosaur fossils. The park is a seventy five million year old bone bed of tremendous proportions. So far, the park has yielded the fossils of some thirty-five species from eleven families of dinosaurs, including specimens from every known group of Cretaceous dinosaurs.

The park is rich not only in the number of species unearthed but in the amount of fossils for each species. This abundance makes the park one of the two most important dinosaur fossil locations in the world (the other is the Nemegt Valley in southern Mongolia).

The fossils of almost eighty species of other vertebrates, including fish, frogs, lizards, turtles, marsupials, mammals, and birds have also been recovered. Such a complete fossil record enables paleontologists to reconstruct the dinosaur world with greater accuracy.

The high erosion rates on the slopes prevent plants from securing a foothold. As a consequence, most slopes are bare or covered with scanty vegetation. The hoodoos and buttes allow only tenacious species, such as pincushion cactus, to thrive. Nevertheless, remnant and recently created grasslands occur on some buttes and large pediments. Some scarce or threatened species, or those near the edge of their biogeographical range, grow here.

In flatter areas, where run-off accumulates, silver sagebrush, thorny buffalo berry and some grasses grow. Greasewood, Colorado rubber weed and cactus grow here and there.

Caves and crevices permeate the bedrock. Extensive subterranean, water-eroded channels lie beneath the smooth contours of the slopes. When the ceilings of these channels collapse, as they frequently do, sinkholes result.

Cottontails use the cavities and channels as hideaways and nesting chambers, as do spiders. The black widow spider is commonly found in the park. Snakes, especially rattlesnakes, den in cavities deep below the frost line, sometimes in groups of ten or more adults and twenty young.

About 6% of Dinosaur Park is covered by significant, and for the most part undisturbed, riparian habitat - shaped by the meandering channel of the Red Deer River and characterized by point bars, wide terraces, fans, and cutbacks. The river terraces support lush and diverse vegetation, ranging from pioneer willow stands, tall shrub thickets, wetlands and dense sagebrush flats to cottonwood forest containing stands of trees 70 feet (21 m) tall and two hundred years old. Plains cottonwood riparian communities are among the most threatened habitats in semi-arid regions of North America.

Birds of prey find the combination of badlands and riverside communities attractive. Dinosaur Park has one of the highest densities of nesting raptors in Canada.

Golden eagles and the threatened ferruginous hawks build large stick nests on remote badlands slopes or inaccessible cliff ledges. Merlins - medium-sized falcons - nest in the groves of cottonwoods that grow along the Red Deer River. Prairie falcons, kestrels and great horned owls nest in cavities and caves eroded high up in the bedrock.

Nighthawks lay their eggs on bare ground. The female protects the eggs during the day by covering them with her body. If the eggs heat up, the bird pants, reducing body temperature and cooling the eggs.

Different nest sites and divergent hunting practices reduce competition between the raptors. The eagles and large hawks hunt cottontails and jackrabbits during the day; owls hunt them at night. Falcons seek small rodents and songbirds.

In all, over one hundred and fifty bird species frequent the park, a large number for any area on the prairies. Perching birds include the meadowlark, mountain bluebird and rock wren.

The climate is extreme. Winter blizzards can blast the valley and temperatures often dip to -40°F (-40°C). Summers can be searing with temperatures often above 90°F (33°C). Nevertheless, mild respites from winter - when the warm 'chinook' winds sweep down from the Rockies - coupled with an abundant food supply, provide winter range for native ungulates such as pronghorn, mule deer and white-tailed deer.

Much of the life in the park depends on the plains cottonwoods that stretch along the Red Deer River. These trees support many of the park birds and shelter other wildlife. Seventy-five per cent of the birds that use the riverside cottonwood areas use them exclusively, and if the trees were to disappear, three-quarters of the bird species would also disappear.

Cottonwoods depend on river floods to reproduce. Floods deposit rich sediments along river banks in which cottonwood seedlings take root. Without these moist, fertile sediments, the young trees wither and die. Throughout Western Canada and the United States, prairie rivers are being dammed. Dams trap sediments and prevent spring flooding and renewal. The result is fewer young cottonwoods. Eventually these trees will disappear completely.

In 1983 the Dickson dam was built upstream from Dinosaur Park. The resultant cessation of spring flooding and sediment deposition threatens the park's cottonwoods. Already, small islets in the middle of the river, which formerly were barren, have begun to support permanent vegetation. This is one indication that spring flood conditions have changed.

The park is also threatened by the fact that sub-surface mineral rights within the park, south of the Red Deer River, are privately owned. However no new direct land access for extraction purposes is allowed within World Heritage boundaries which protect 94.2% of the park. In the portion of land that is inside the park but outside the World Heritage zone, oil and gas extraction is taking place.

Dinosaur Provincial Park was inscribed on the World Heritage List in 1979. It earned listing primarily because it is one of the most important locations of dinosaur fossils in the world, but also for its stands of rare cottonwood forest and its spectacular badlands.

LEFT   *Golden eagle in flight - the park is a haven for many raptors*

# L'ANSE AUX MEADOWS

PERCHED ON THE NORTHERN TIP of Newfoundland's Great North Peninsula are the remnants of the oldest settlement of European origin in North America. The archaeological site known as L'Anse aux Meadows takes its name from a small fishing village located nearby on Medée Bay. A small river, Black Duck Brook, cuts through the terrace where Norse buildings once stood, and empties into the bay. According to Farley Mowat, L'Anse aux Méduse (Jellyfish Creek) was the site's original name - locally it is known as 'Lancy Meadows'. Following the publication of the Norse sagas in the United States in 1837, researchers set about locating a Norse settlement site in North America. In 1914 the Newfoundlander William A. Munn suggested that L'Anse aux Meadows was the place where the Norse first landed. It was not until the 1960s, however, that ruins of unmistakably Viking origin were discovered in Newfoundland.

In 1960 Helge Ingstad, a Norwegian-born explorer, writer and former Governor of Spitzbergen, came upon the overgrown Norse house-sites near L'Anse aux Meadows with the help of George Decker, a local fisherman and descendent of the community's founder. Between 1961 and 1968 Ingstad's wife, archaeologist Anne Stine, together with assistants from the United States, Canada, Iceland, Norway and Sweden, and the support of local villagers, excavated the site. At L'Anse aux Meadows they found the remains of eight turf-walled structures similar to Norse buildings found in Greenland and Iceland. They also found dozens of items made of iron, as well as one of bone and one of bronze. Their findings appeared in 'The discovery of a Norse settlement in America', published in 1977. This book was later republished as part of a two-volume set, entitled 'The Norse discovery of America'.

Between 1973 and 1976, excavations were continued on the remote and isolated site by an international team headed by Swedish archaeologist Bengt Schönbäck and later by Birgitta Linderoth Wallace, who has written extensively on L'Anse aux Meadows. The archaeological digs undertaken in the 1960s concentrated mainly on the buildings and other visible features, and yielded approximately one hundred and twenty five artifacts, most of which were nails or nail fragments. When the area of excavation was extended in the mid-1970s to cover the areas between the buildings as well as the bog, an additional 650 Norse items were unearthed, including a bow for a carpenter's auger, a barrel lid, rope strands made from fine spruce roots, wooden skewers and chips and slivers from shaping wood.

The hundreds of artifacts found at the site reveal a great deal about the kinds of activities undertaken by the Norse at L'Anse aux Meadows. For example it is known that the main male activities were hunting, fishing, carpentry, iron smelting and smithing. The presence of a soap-stone spindle whorl and sewing tools, suggests that women too resided at the site. Also, the construction of such substantial buildings suggests that the site was inhabited all year round, and not simply used as a temporary residence.

At the same time, it is interesting to consider what archaeologists have not found at the site. There is, for instance, no evidence to suggest that L'Anse aux Meadows was a port of trade. Additionally, as Birgitta Linderoth Wallace has explained, 'in spite of the common house types, the site was definitely not a normal settlement. There are no traces of barns or byres, fences or enclosures usually associated with livestock...normal farming was certainly not an activity on the site.' The Norse food supply came from fishing, hunting and gathering local resources. It is thought that this site was used as a base camp for further explorations as far south as the mouth of the St Lawrence River. The absence of burials, the paucity of middens and the one building phase, has led scholars to conclude that the Norse resided at L'Anse aux Meadows for a short period, possibly only a few years, sometime between AD 990 and 1100.

Facing the Strait of Belle Isle, the mounds, which the locals called 'Indian Camps', were the remains of turf-houses of a distinctly Norse type. The Norse built eight structures on a raised and slightly curved beach terrace about 328 feet (100 m) inland. Seven of the eight structures were organized into three clusters; each cluster contained a large, multi-roomed dwelling known as a hall, featuring straight end walls with bowed side walls, and at least one small outhouse. Long, smoothed tree trunks were used to construct the peaked roofs of the large houses. The wooden frames were covered with turf: both the walls and the roofs were constructed of sod. Floors were simply the bare ground and fireplaces were made of stone. As many as ninety people could be accommodated in these dwellings. Similar building techniques were used by the Vikings in Iceland and Greenland.

The Ingstads used letters of the alphabet to identify the clusters of buildings: the A-B-C complex consisted of a large hall, a small house, which was used as living quarters and workshop, and a small rounded building, which most likely served as accommodation for slaves. The D-E and F-G complexes were made up of a large hall and a hut, used as a workshop. The northernmost hall, House F, was the largest structure: it measured 70 by 55 feet (21 by 17 m) and contained six rooms. The largest of its rooms had a long hearth down its center, around which the Vikings would gather to eat, work and exchange stories. The house also contained a separate kitchen with a stone oven. It is thought that this room also may have been used as a sauna.

On the far side of Black Duck Brook, and separate from the other structures, the Norse built a one-room furnace hut. Originally referred to as the smithy, the furnace hut was used for iron smelting, the first such site in the New World. The furnace hut was built in a hollow in a sandbank, and was the same style of hut used at iron production centers in Norway. In addition to hundreds of lumps of slag, the remains of a stone furnace were found inside the hut.

Why the Norse abandoned the site within years of their arrival is unknown. The site's great distance from Greenland is one likely explanation. In the end, according to Wallace, ' ... the risks involved in maintaining L'Anse aux Meadows and the continued exploitation of its hinterland far outweighed the gain.' The evidence suggests that when the Norse left the site, they set fire to the large halls. What happened to the pit buildings is unclear.

It is known that other groups inhabited L'Anse aux Meadows apart from the Norse. There is evidence of occupation by Maritime Archaic, Groswater, Dorset and unidentified Indians prior to the Vikings' arrival, as well as Indian occupation following their departure. While the latter Indians were also unidentifiable, it is believed that Jacques Cartier, on his 1534 voyage, encountered Beothuks, supposedly belonging to the Algonquin tribe, in the Strait of Belle Isle. It was most likely the hunting of harp seals that brought these aboriginal peoples to the region. Before the English became interested in the area in the mid-18th century, French migratory fishermen used the Strait of Belle Isle. Forty-six people lived in the isolated village of L'Anse aux Meadows in 1874. Ten years later the population stood at fifty seven, dropping to twenty seven in 1891. Today, under one hundred people live near the former Norse settlement.

According to the Norse sagas, in AD 1000 Leif Eiriksson, the son of Eric the Red, along with others, set sail for Vinland - the Land of Wine - in search of new resources and possible settlement sites. The exact location of Vinland has been an issue of contention between scholars for years. In the Ingstads' view 'it appears to be almost certain' that the Norse settlement site at L'Anse aux Meadows is Vinland; others are not so sure. Some experts maintain that Vinland must have been further south, possibly as far as the Carolinas, for the sagas mention wild grapes - such fruit has never been grown at L'Anse aux Meadows. The Ingstads have responded by saying that the 'vin' in Vinland means pasture or meadow and not wine.

After a thorough examination of the evidence, Birgitta Linderoth Wallace has drawn the following conclusion: 'L'Anse aux Meadows is not Vinland itself, but it is at the northern entrance to Vinland.' The site served as ' ... a base camp for further exploration

OPENING PAGE   *Reconstruction of Viking boat and sod house*
ABOVE AND LEFT   *Reconstruction of sod house and interior*

and exploitation of the Vinland resources.' Most recent evidence indicates that L'Anse aux Meadows is the 'Leifsbúoir-Straumfjördr', (Leif's Camp-Current Fjord) of the sagas.

A plaque unveiled at the site in July 1980 reminds visitors that:

'L'Anse aux Meadows is the first authenticated Norse site in North America. Its sod buildings are thus the earliest known European structures on this continent; its smithy, the site of the first known iron working in the New World; the site itself is the scene of the first contacts between native Americans and Europeans.'

In 1968 the archaeological work undertaken by the Ingstads resulted in the Canadian government declaring the L'Anse aux Meadows settlement site to be of national historical significance. Since 1977 it has been a National Historic Site administered by Parks Canada, and in 1978 it became Canada's first cultural site to be placed on the World Heritage List. With the Ingstads in attendance, a $3.5 million Visitor Reception Center was officially opened in July 1985. The Canadian Parks Service has built three full-scale replicas of the sod houses near the original site of settlement.

# HEAD SMASHED-IN
# BISON JUMP

THE REMARKABLY WELL-PRESERVED and rich archaeological site commonly known as Head Smashed-In Buffalo Jump (but officially known as Head Smashed-In Bison Jump), is located in the middle of a rolling prairie on the southern end of the Porcupine Hills, near Fort Macleod in southwest Alberta, Canada. The site covers 1,470 acres (612 ha). For nearly 6,000 years, aboriginal Plains People used this traditional Peigan 'buffalo jump' or 'pis'kun' (Blackfoot for 'deep-blood-kettle') as a trap to kill tremendous numbers of buffalo. Approaching the site from the west, the massive, hump-backed creatures had no idea of the vertical drop that awaited them. The buffalo-jump method of hunting was used at Head Smashed-In from 3600 BC to 2600 BC, and then on and off from 900 BC to as recently as the mid 19th century. Large-scale hunting continued from AD 300 to as recently as the mid-19th century. According to one estimate, the remains of over 120,000 buffalo (male and female, young and old) lie in the area below the jump-off point at Head Smashed-In. The fact that it constitutes one of the largest and oldest surviving examples of a buffalo jump secured Head Smashed-In a place on the World Heritage List in 1981; making it the third Canadian archaeological site, next to L'Anse aux Meadows and Anthony Island, to be included on the List.

The complex at Head Smashed-In is composed of three parts: the Olsen Creek Basin, which served as the 'gathering area'; the exposed escarpment known as 'the kill site'; and the 'processing campsite'. The four-to-five day hunt, which involved the entire tribe, would take place in fall or early winter. Needless to say, hunting buffalo on foot using unsophisticated weapons was far from easy. Though there are no records of unsuccessful hunts, it would be wrong to assume that buffalo jumping was a foolproof exercise.

The native peoples of the Northwest plains used various methods to entice the herd onto the 15 square miles (38 sq km) of grazing pastures and then maneuver the powerful beasts over the cliff into the butchering area below. This required an excellent understanding of the hunting territory and the day-to-day habits of the buffalo. In an attempt to lure the female buffalo toward the cliff, a hunter (buffalo runner), dressed in a robe made of buffalo fur, would mimic the sound of a sick calf or would wear coyote hides and threaten the calves. It was important for the hunters to keep downwind as buffalo have a highly developed sense of smell. When sensing danger, the buffalo face into the wind to pick up any unusual scents to help them identify the direction of possible danger. To disguise their human smell, the buffalo runners would rub their bodies with grease and sage.

The buffalo were forced onto one of several long drive lanes, lined with small clusters of stone markers or rock cairns, which stretched from the hills to the precipice. Thousands of the stone markers are still in place. Some scholars argue that the rock cairns served as 'traffic markers' to assist the hunters who could hide behind them while they waited for the buffalo to pass. Others believe the piles, around three feet (one meter) in diameter and one foot high (0.3 m), were too small to serve such a purpose and were used instead to remind the hunters where to place larger cairns which would guarantee the success of future hunts. Once the buffalo were on the drive lanes the people would wave blankets, shout and shoot arrows to keep them moving.

Traveling at up to 35 miles per hour (56 kph), the mighty buffalo thundered toward the bluff in a state of blind panic. By the time the shaggy beasts reached the edge of the cliff, there was no turning back and they tumbled over the edge. Originally it was believed that a V-shaped drive lane led to the main cliff at Head Smashed-In. However, based on their study of drive lane stone markers at the site, Jack Brink and Maureen Rollans maintain that these stone markers may have led to a multitude of different jump-offs.

Today, the sandstone promontory is about 40 feet high (12 m), however, it may once have been 70 feet high (21 m). At the foot of the cliff lies a large, flat prairie where the buffalo plunged to their

ABOVE   *Excavation site*
OPPOSITE   *Buffalo skulls*

death. Here the butchering and processing of the buffalo was undertaken. It is believed that the hunters may have built a fence to cordon off the area to prevent the carcasses from rolling down into the campsite. Those buffalo not killed in the fall were killed with bow and arrow, spears or atlatls (spear-throwers). Some of the animals suffocated under the weight of the buffalo sprawled on top of them. A male buffalo, the largest land animal on the North American continent, can weigh over 2,000 pounds (900 kg), and measures between 9 and 12 feet in length (2.7 to 3.6 m); it stands at about 6 feet (1.8 m) in height from the ground to its highest point, the hump. There could be no survivors, for the people believed that an escapee could warn other buffalo of their fate, thus depriving them of massive quantities of meat, hide, bone and other material.

The midden is filled with thousands of buffalo bones, reaching a depth of nearly 38 feet (11 m) in places. The butchered bones at the deepest layer are 5,700 years old. Apart from countless buffalo bones, the midden contains other animal remains, such as hair, sheaths and intestinal matter. Bone boiling pits, hearths, baking ovens, pottery and other artifacts also have been found in the processing area.

Archaeologist Brian Fagan believes that the butchery was ' ... a highly efficient, relatively standardized process, which operated almost on an assembly line basis.' The animals on the top of the pile would be dragged one by one away from the base of the cliff to be butchered. In the event of a particularly large hunt, it was not unusual for the buffalo at the bottom of the pile to be left partially butchered.

The buffalo was pivotal to the Plains Peoples' way of life. There was little waste as buffalo carcasses served several purposes. Meat from one successful jump provided the Indians with more than enough food for the coming winter. Some of the meat, especially the bluish-purple tongue which was considered a great delicacy, was eaten soon after the hunt. The rest was hung out in strips and dried; it was then pounded into a paste with melted fat, to make pemmican, which could be eaten cold or cooked. It is known that the Plains People traded surplus dried meat and hides to places as far south as present-day Montana and Wyoming.

Some of the bones were used to make tools. The raw hide was turned into shields, buckets and parfleche bags amongst other things, whilst the tanned hide was used for tepee coverings, robes, moccasins, ropes and many other items. The thick, dark buffalo hair was used for ornamental purposes or braided into rope. Internal parts, such as the stomach and bladder, were used to make containers for storing pemmican, berries or nuts. The carcasses had many other uses: sinew was turned into thread and bowstrings; the hollow horns were made into drinking containers; glue was made out of hooves; fat became an effective hair grease. When water was scarce, the Indians would drink the juices from the stomachs of dead buffalo. Dried manure ('buffalo chips') was used for fuel.

Within a few days of the hunt, the area would be abandoned. Eventually fine earth would cover the remains and other native peoples would return to undertake another buffalo jump. Those who hunted the buffalo were constantly on the move.

In the early 1880s, George Dawson from the Geological Survey of Canada became the first person to record the current name for the site. Interestingly, the proper name of the site, 'estipah-sikikini-kots' (translated from Blackfoot to mean 'where we got our heads smashed in'), refers not to the shattering of buffalo heads, but the crushing of a human skull. According to legend, an eager young man from a Peigan camp on Willow Creek positioned himself on a ledge under the cliff to witness the large mammals careering over the sandstone cliff from the gathering basin. On that day, the hunt was unusually large, resulting in a massive pile of carcasses. Unable to reposition himself in time, the young observer, according to the legend, was crushed against the cliff, and had his head smashed in by the weight of the beasts; hence the name Head Smashed-In. According to another legend, Napi, the creator of the Blackfoot nation, taught his people how to lure large numbers of buffalo to their death. This was his way of revenging the deaths of those of his people who had been eaten by buffalo when buffalo were the hunters.

The first exploration of Head Smashed-In was undertaken by Julius Bird of the American Museum of Natural History in 1938. Unfortunately the results of his research were not published. Eleven years later, archaeologist Boyd Wettlaufer from the University of New Mexico excavated a butchering site close to the main jump site, where he unearthed a profusion of buffalo bones and artifacts. Soon after Wettlaufer finished his work at the site, looters removed thousands of bones and artifacts. The looting at Head Smashed-In did not end until 1979 when the site was made a Provincial Historical Site and placed under the protection of the Province of Alberta. Systematic excavations have been undertaken at the site since 1965 by archaeologists from the University of Calgary and the Archaeological Survey of Canada.

The site houses an excellent, award-winning Interpretative Center which is set in the cliff at a place where few buffalo bones have been found. Exhibits and film presentations provide an insight into the culture and lifestyle of the aboriginal peoples who inhabited the Great Plains from ancient times to the arrival of the Europeans. The immensity of the buffalo drives is explained through film presentations, dioramas, text panels and other means. Information on archaeological techniques employed at the site is also provided. The museum is open seven days a week except on Christmas Eve, Christmas Day, New Year's Day and Easter Sunday. During summer it is open from 9 am to 8 pm, and in winter from 9 am to 5 pm. An admission fee is charged. Other buffalo jumps, such as Pincher Creek and Boneyard Creek, are located southwest and northwest of the site, respectively.

# MEXICO

# EL VIZCAINO
## RESERVE

THE ARID AND NARROW BAJA CALIFORNIA PENINSULA, separated from the mainland of Mexico some five million years ago by movement along the San Andreas Fault system, lies between the Sea of Cortés and the Pacific Ocean. It is divided into two parts at the 28th parallel, forming the two States of Baja California and Baja California Sur. The northern border of the southern State forms one boundary of the area known as the El Vizcaíno Reserve.

The two areas of inestimable natural value included in the Reserve, Laguna Ojo de Liebre and Laguna San Ignacio, shelter some twenty endangered species of marine and bird life in an environment of extraordinary beauty.

These lagoons form indentations on the Pacific edge of the Vizcaíno Desert, an area of shallow sandy bays and inlets and three low mountain ranges (the Sierra Vizcaíno). The Sierra de San Francisco, an adjoining World Heritage rock art site, runs parallel with - but 75 miles (120 km) inland from - the coast of the Sea of Cortés, also known as the Gulf of California. The elevation of these areas ranges up to 5,182 feet (1,580 m) above sea level.

Laguna Ojo de Liebre (also known as Scammon's or Hare's Eye Lagoon) and Laguna San Ignacio are breeding grounds for gray whales, which return to these waters in January each year to calve or mate. The whales spend the intervening months making their way up the western coast of the United States and Canada and feeding in the waters of the Bering Straits, before heading back to Baja California, a distance of some 8,000 miles (12,880 km). Twenty-six marine mammal species are found in these secluded inlets of the east coast, including northern elephant seals and California sea lions, as well as four threatened species of marine turtle - the leatherback, green, hawksbill and olive ridley. Migratory birds find refuge also; of the migratory wildfowl wintering along Mexico's western coast 10% do so in the Reserve. This includes, most notably, 63% of Mexico's annual brent geese migration, some 71,000 birds.

The waters of Laguna Ojo de Liebre open into San Sebastián Vizcaíno Bay, named after a Spanish conquistador and navigator who explored the Mexican Pacific coast and who died in 1606. Whaling along the Pacific coast became very profitable in the 1840s

OPENING PAGE    Chac-mool & Castle of Kukulcan
                Chichen Itza
PREVIOUS PAGE    *California sea lion*
BELOW    *Olive ridley turtle*
RIGHT    *Gray whale, San Ignatio Lagoon*

ABOVE    *Blue whale breaching*
RIGHT    *Looking down at a blue whale*
BELOW RIGHT    *California sea lion*

and the Laguna Ojo de Liebre was famous for the numbers of gray whale found there. The gray, which grows to about 40 feet and 35 tons (12 m and 32 tonnes), is smaller than the right and sperm whales, but still yielded good profits. In the 1850s Captain Scammon and others went there yearly to hunt the whales in such numbers that they were brought to the edge of extinction along the Pacific coasts.

Dotted by mangrove-covered islets, chains of which protect it from the full force of the Pacific rollers, the lagoon is estimated to cover 250 square miles (640 sq km). Its maze of waters provides ample protection for whales and young calves. Although some tides are as high as 8 feet (2.4 m) and many of the passages are narrow, whales seem to know the depths of each section and very rarely become stranded in shallows. The shallow waters of this great lagoon system are highly saline, which lends a special quality to the beautiful turquoise color of the water.

When about to calve, gray whale cows will sometimes seek out the shallowest corners of the lagoons - some of which stretch 30 miles (48 km) into the desert - in search of the most desirable and peaceful situation. Here the extra salinity of the lagoon aids the calves' buoyancy and there is plenty of food such as crabs, shrimps and clams available for the cow as she suckles her young. However, most cows calve at the entrances to the lagoons and some calve at sea. Thanks to an international protection agreement, signed in 1946, these huge creatures are steadily increasing in numbers. In 1972 Laguna Ojo de Liebre and its closely linked neighbor, Laguna Guerrero Negro, were declared gray whale refuges by the Mexican government. Here half of the world's gray whales are born every year. The Reserve's lagoons thus provide locations for the propagation of the majority of the species.

San Ignacio Lagoon lies further south and provides most of the advantages which Laguna Ojo de Liebre offers, to not only the gray whale but also to the harbor seal, Californian sea lion, northern elephant seal and the blue whale. As at Ojo de Liebre, many gray whale cows calve in the higher reaches of the lagoon where the sheltered water averages 15 feet (4.5 m) in depth. Here they can also find peace from males. When the time arrives to migrate north the calves will gain strength for their swim by 'training' in the main channels at the entrance to the lagoons where the tides run particularly strongly. Laguna San Ignacio was declared a gray whale refuge by the Government of Mexico in 1979.

The plains and desert regions in the western and central areas are formed from sedimentary rock, with some evidence of

andesites, rhyolithic lavas and pinoclasts. The Pacific coast contains a series of inlets with shallow, sandy bays and salt water lagoons. The eastern zone is dominated by the high mountains which form part of the chain running right down the Peninsula. Soils in the area are predominantly limestone. The climate is dry with many areas receiving much less than 4 inches (100 mm) of rain per annum and the majority of rivers and streams, many of them underground, run only intermittently. Temperatures reach 113°F (45°C) in the desert in summer, but cold winds in January and February make the median winter temperature of 59°F (15°C) seem much colder. The area is one of the earth's most marginal regions for survival.

The vegetation in this subsection of the Sonora desert is typical of an arid or hyper-arid zone and there are ten plant communities, dominated by many types of cacti. Mangroves are found at the lagoons, which are surrounded by dune communities, bushes and halophytic vegetation. Some gnarled conifers are also found here. After rain the desert flowers in such colors as to completely alter its arid image.

Many animals find their home in the desert, including coyotes, two species of fox, rats and mice, hares, pronghorn antelope, mule deer, bighorn sheep, the Baja Californian rock squirrel, as well as insects, spiders, chameleons and snakes. In all 299 vertebrate species have been recorded of which four are amphibian. There are 43 reptiles, 182 birds and 35 mammals.

Birds found here which are under threat of extinction include the American white pelican, sand hill crane, bald eagle, golden eagle, osprey, peregrine falcon, common caracara and the burrowing owl. The lagoons in the Reserve are major areas for the dispersion of ospreys, with over 200 breeding pairs. The yellow throat and the black-fronted hummingbirds are endemic to the peninsula.

The El Vizcaíno Reserve encompasses unique natural and cultural areas. However these riches are located in an extremely delicate and vulnerable environment. Animal species are being threatened by the activities of man; concern is felt for the vulnerability of the gray whales during their yearly migration. The natural environment is being modified for man's purposes, for example a salt mine that has been operating in the area for some time may soon be expanded. An independent inquiry has been commissioned to review the impact of this on the environment, particularly with regard to the lagoons. Oil drilling is also conducted in the region. The exploitation of fish and turtle stocks and the setting of fishing nets at the mouths of lagoons are of great concern. Almost half of the land in the Reserve is not under government control. Scarce water resources are rapidly being exhausted as areas under irrigation are extended. Water courses have dried up.

El Vizcaíno Reserve was inscribed on the World Heritage List in 1993 primarily because half of the world's population of gray whales is born in and around the area's lagoons.

The town of Guerrero Negro on the Trans-peninsula Highway (Federal 1) is the nearest access point to Laguna Ojo de Liebre. It can be reached by bus or car from Tijuana in the north, Loreto via La Paz in the south, or from Santa Rosalia where the ferry from Guaymas, Sonora, terminates. There is also an airport at Santa Rosalia. Access to Laguna San Ignacio by land is probably best made by taking the dirt road which branches from the Trans-peninsula Highway (Federal 1) between Guerrero Negro and San Ignacio. Careful enquiries should be made of the Mexican authorities regarding travel in the area.

TOP LEFT   *Northern elephant seal*
CENTER LEFT   *Sandhill crane*
LEFT   *Mangrove*

# SIERRA DE SAN FRANCISCO

THIS REGION IS THE HOME OF BAJA CALIFORNIA'S most important pre-Hispanic rock art, remarkable for the quality and diversity of its representations and their excellent state of preservation. They form one of the largest groupings of rock art in the world. The paintings in this central area bear little relationship to those found to the south and north of the Peninsula.

The San Francisco Mountains, covering an area of almost 441,600 acres (184,000 ha), are part of the Sierra de la Giganta (Giant's Mountains), formed by large volcanic rocks of the tertiary age. Because of their geomorphological composition they are very steep and broken; the area being characterized by deep 'arroyos' or canyons which descend from the highest mountains, eroded by intermittently flowing streams. The climate is extremely diverse due to the area's peninsular character, its location between the Gulf of California and the Pacific Ocean (where cyclones originate), and the influence of continental air masses. There is great yearly variation in temperature.

The erosive action of fast-flowing streams, together with the atmospheric environment and the complex natural geology, has produced a landscape in which caves, rock shelters and protecting walls abound. A great part of the area's archaeological heritage is represented by countless examples of rock art and/or petroglyphs on the walls and roofs of these natural hollows, which also contain clues to their occupation by the various peoples which inhabited the area.

Access to the rock art sites is, fortunately for their preservation, difficult. The San Francisco area contains four main areas: Guadalupe, Santa Teresa, San Gregorio and Cerritos. The most important sites are Cueva del Batequi, Cueva de la Natividad, Cerro de Santa Marta, Cueva de la Soledad, Cueva de las Flechas and Grutas del Brinco.

The painting and carving of images on cave walls and other rock surfaces has been a tradition of peoples worldwide. In the ensemble at Sierra de San Francisco, the painted areas display a great variety in size, number and superimposition of figures painted and

ABOVE *Sierra de San Francisco, Baja California*
OPPOSITE *La Pintada cave painting of human figure, deer and desert bighorn sheep*

forms represented. Images clearly identifiable include human figures (men, women and children); land animals such as rabbits, deer, goats, horned sheep, puma and lynx; sea creatures including whales, turtles, sardines, octopi and tuna; and birds such as pelicans and eagles - all creatures familiar to the painters, many of them still found in the area. Abstract elements also appear. Many figures, human and animal, seem to be pierced with arrows and spears, and other elements of hunting and warfare are recognizable.

The animal figures, mostly in silhouette, seem dynamic, often appearing to be in motion and jumping, an impression created by the placement of the front and back legs, the set of the head and the angle of the body. In contrast, the human figures are static, front-on, with feet a little apart and arms raised to form a right-angle at neck level, and hands open. Faces are not depicted, and many appear to wear headdresses such as those reported by the early missionaries in the area. Both human and animal figures are sometimes painted a solid red or black, but most appear two-colored with a longitudinal or horizontal dividing line.

There is a great deal of superimposition of figures and techniques of shading and silhouette are employed. Many of the figures are thinly outlined in white. In some caves the representations are of a super-human size and the location of many have led to much speculation as to the means used to apply paint to such inaccessible areas.

There appear to be two distinct types of painting: in the first the male human figure is dominant and there is a high incidence of superimposition; in the second the figures of animals are of primary importance and the whole reflects a more harmonious spatial relationship.

Colors used are mostly reds, black, whites and yellows. The painters extracted minerals from the colored volcanic rocks around them by grinding them on stones or in mortars. They then added glue until the mixture reached a consistency which allowed its application and retention on the rock surfaces. The skilful use of this recipe allowed the paintings to survive and, in many cases, to retain their color.

The good or bad state of preservation of the paintings and petroglyphs depends largely on two variables: the geological composition of the rock on which they were painted and the level of their exposure to sudden changes of climate.

Petroglyphs probably represent the earliest phase in the development of the rock painting tradition in this area. Here also, two types can be distinguished. The earliest form includes intriguing abstract images produced on isolated rock surfaces in many locations, while examples of a later development are found on the walls of caves and are often covered by paintings.

Most archaeological interest in Mexico has, perhaps understandably, been concentrated on the magnificent monumental sites of Mesoamerica. It is only in recent years that attention has been focussed on the riches hidden in the Sierra de San Francisco caves. Before accurate and systematic exploration and recording of the paintings and petroglyphs was undertaken by Mexican authorities in the early 1980s, research had been fragmented and not integrated. Now some 250 sites have been located and registered, together with 700 archaeological sites. Archaeological excavations are continuing, to attempt a better understanding of the social and religious organization of the hunter-gatherers living in the area in prehistoric times. Some similarities have been observed with the rock art from southwestern areas of the United States of America.

Excavated objects have so far been dated covering a span of 4,000 years to 1655, and most derive from the Late Comondú culture. Some of the most valuable of the archaeological artifacts found are stones bearing fragments of paint. From them the paint 'recipe' can be learnt and the fragments of paint can be used for dating purposes, making the taking of samples from the walls unnecessary.

At the time of first contact with Europeans, the people inhabiting the Sierra de San Francisco area were bands of the

Cochimí, whose territory extended from San Xavier in the south of the Reserve, to the far north of the Baja California Peninsula. They lived a semi-nomadic lifestyle, satisfying their needs by hunting, fishing and collecting seeds, fruit, roots, insects and shellfish. They maintained an harmonious relationship with their environment and a deep understanding of the behavior of plants and animals, which allowed them to survive in very precarious physical conditions.

The first missionary contact was made in 1716 by Father Francisco María Píccolo and the first mission was founded in 1728. In a few decades introduced disease had almost eliminated the local native population and the missions were abandoned. Since that time the isolation of the area, the overall aridity of the climate, and the lack of interest shown in the rock paintings have assisted in the preservation of a corpus of art of outstanding universal significance. Sierra de San Francisco was inscribed on the World Heritage List in 1993.

The rock paintings and petroglyphs of the Sierra de San Francisco constitute some of the most fragile archaeological materials imaginable, and present very serious problems for their protection and preservation.

Although there is no special buffer zone designated, the fact that the area lies within the larger national Biosphere Reserve provides protection sufficient to meet World Heritage requirements. However there is an urgent need for increased management control and for education of the local residents and also of the tourists who visit the area.

Access to the Sierra de San Francisco is from San Ignacio, which can be reached by bus or car along the Trans-peninsula Highway (Federal 1). If traveling by car, it is recommended that four-wheel drive vehicles be used - they can be hired at San Ignacio. Access to the mountains is strictly controlled by Mexican authorities and arrangements for visits should be made with them.

# SIAN KA'AN
## BIOSPHERE RESERVE

S IAN KA'AN IS MAYAN FOR 'BIRTH OF THE SKY'; where the turquoise waters of the Caribbean meet the azure of the tropical sky; where the centuries-old ruins of the Mayan civilization remain in counterpoint to the high-rise hotels and white-sand beaches of Cancún; where paved roads end and the barrier reefs, jaguar, tapir and thousands upon thousands of birds still thrive. This is the Biosphere Reserve of Sian Ka'an.

One-third tropical forest, one-third wetlands and one-third coastal and marine environments, Sian Ka'an is a 1.3 million acre (542,000 ha) reserve in which environmental conservation and sustainable development go hand in hand. Eighty per cent of the land area is part of the core zones which are being preserved in their natural state. The remainder comprise buffer zones: where appropriate, low-impact development will support local inhabitants.

Sian Ka'an lies on a huge limestone flat on the Caribbean coast of Mexico's Yucatán Peninsula, in the state of Quintana Roo. In the reserve, terrestrial and marine environments merge. The landscape includes coral reefs, beaches, dunes, mangrove forests, marshes, wet savannas, lagoons and large tracts of lowland tropical forests. The highest elevation is less than 60 feet (18 m) above sea level.

Sian Ka'an's barrier reef forms part of the second longest such reef in the world. Its great, shallow bays are important spiny lobster nurseries. In these bays, scattered keys provide nesting sites for thousands of water birds such as the roseate spoonbill, woodstork, magnificent frigate bird and boat-billed heron. The rare jabiru stork nests in the reserve and the beaches are nesting grounds for four species of endangered sea turtles.

PREVIOUS PAGE   *Tamandua (anteater)*
ABOVE   *Flamingos*
OPPOSITE   *Geoffroy's spider monkey*

The reserve also serves as habitat for wild cats such as jaguar, margay, jaguarundi and cougar. Two species of crocodiles, howler and spider monkeys, tapir and west Indian manatee are among other species, as well as forest birds such as the ocellated turkey and great curassow.

Plant diversity is high with approximately 1,200 species found in the reserve. Hardwood hummocks, called 'petenes' occur like islands among the wetlands, some of them with sinkholes - huge natural wells more than 150 feet (45 m) in diameter at their centers.

The human population of the area is about 35,000, primarily of Mayan descent; with fewer than one thousand people, mostly fishermen, actually inhabiting the buffer zones of the reserve. The management plan for the reserve includes scientific research and field projects focused on developing and promoting sustainable use of natural resources that will support the residents' livelihood.

The Sian Ka'an Biosphere Reserve was established by Presidential Decree on January 20, 1986. It is integrated in the International Network of Biosphere Reserves and in 1987 was included on the World Heritage List.

The management of the reserve is based on a partnership between the Federal, State and Municipal Governments, who integrate a committee that delegates everyday operations to the reserve's director.

ABOVE *Crocodile*
OPPOSITE *Mangrove roots*
INSET *A juvenile Yucatan Jay*

Various experiments to integrate the local population in the reserve's decision-making process have taken place and are still in progress. A local research center carries out basic research in Sian Ka'an. Amigos de Sian Ka'an, a private Mexican conservation organization, channels national and international support into the reserve and executes applied research projects for sustainable development, community outreach and public information projects, to support and promote the conservation and wise use of the Sian Ka'an Biosphere Reserve.

Mexico's conservation efforts have to be made compatible with its growing social needs. Biosphere reserves are the arena where a new relationship between man and nature should become a reality. Amigos de Sian Ka'an doesn't perceive conservation as prohibiting use, but rather as encouraging wise use, of our natural resources.

The success of this reserve depends on several factors. Firstly, the people of Quintana Roo, and indeed of all Mexico, must come to value the benefits of reserves such as Sian Ka'an as an economic, cultural and ecological resource. Secondly, the agencies charged with daily management of the reserve must acquire the resources to conduct activities such as gathering baseline biological information and implementing a management plan. Thirdly, the various institutions with roles to play in research, management, development and regulations must cooperate and work together.

Finally, the people living in and around the reserve must have clear economic incentives and technical know-how to preserve the natural resource base upon which their livelihood depends. The hotel and resort industry developing along the coast must be managed as it approaches the reserve so that its impact can be controlled.

Fortunately, Sian Ka'an is not so imminently threatened that any one of these challenges is insurmountable. Thus, the reserve is blessed with a somewhat unique resource: time to establish a working model of a Mexican Biosphere Reserve that can show the way for other similar reserves throughout the region.

# CHICHEN ITZA

CHICHEN ITZA LIES IN THE CENTER of the flat northern plain of the Yucatán Peninsula. Its position in this inhospitable region is generally attributed to the presence of twenty or so natural wells (cenotes) and caves which gave access to vital sources of sub-surface water. Cenotes are formed from water trapped in the limestone shelf - the predominant geological characteristic of the Peninsula - and are revealed when the thin top layer of karst collapses to expose a well-like formation. One translation of 'Chichén Itzá' - 'At the Mouth of the Well of the Itzá' - indicates the importance of the water sources.

The proximity of Chichén Itzá to north coast deposits of salt, so valuable as an item of trade, and to agricultural areas to the south, were no doubt also major factors in determining the site of this once great city.

This major complex covers 6 square miles (15 sq km) and its great archaeological significance derives from its representation of two major pre-Colombian civilizations in Mesoamerica, the Maya and the Toltec. It was also the most important regional capital in the Maya area between AD 750 and 1200, thus bridging the Classic and post-Classic eras.

Probably first settled in AD 415-455, and having received numerous influxes of immigrants (including the Itzá whose name is preserved here), Chichén Itzá benefitted from the magnificent attributes of the Mayan civilization before receiving a very important wave of settlement towards the end of the 10th century. The new arrivals were Toltec people, at the end of a long migration from their homeland in Central Mexico (Tula in the Hidalgo State of modern times). Scholars differ concerning these new settlers and exactly how they arrived in northern Yucatán. There is no doubt however, that elements of Toltec culture profoundly influenced the architecture and decoration of many of the buildings and spaces at this site. There is much mixing of styles, rebuilding and addition to pre-existing edifices. A blending of cultures is clearly manifest.

The artificial platforms used by the Maya as bases for their monumental buildings required huge quantities of material, to be assembled by a large labor force without the use of wheeled vehicles or pack animals. At this site there was no shortage of the limestone needed for quicklime, nor of the rubble which, when mixed with mortar, formed a kind of concrete. The building techniques of the Maya were so sound that a remarkable number of their structures withstood the battering of the elements for centuries. Their buildings were also so solid that they provided cool

PREVIOUS PAGE   The Caracol, a Mayan observatory
BELOW   The Castillo, which dominates the Great Plaza
OPPOSITE   Temple of the Jaguars

spaces and shelter for a population living in an area renowned for its intense heat and tropical rain.

This style of building did, however, require the expending of great amounts of energy, the transportation of weighty materials and the burning of quantities of wood for the extraction of the lime.

The wide, flat area over which structures were built at Chichén Itzá was covered naturally by a coarse scrub. There is a central core of monumental buildings on extensive terraces and around large plazas. Spaces beyond were taken up by fields used for agriculture and by thatched houses built on low stone foundations.

While many buildings differ overall and in decoration and facade designs, it is possible to distinguish two major styles, the earlier of which is the Late Classic Maya Puuc. This developed in the southern Yucatán and northern Campeche regions in the 7th and 8th centuries; the name derives from the area of its greatest concentration in the Puuc Hills, where Uxmal is a famous site. The later style introduced elements from other parts of Mesoamerica, predominantly from the Toltec culture, and buildings showing this influence predominate at Chichén Itzá.

The Puuc-style buildings include, among others, the Monjas group and the Caracol ('snail' or 'spiral' in Spanish). They stand on an enormous terrace plaza which also contains the Akabdzib ('dark writing', a reference to the reliefs on one of the doorways) to the east and the Casa Colorada ('Red House'), with its two roof combs, to the west. The High Priest's Grave stands on a small platform further to the north.

Topped with a round tower and containing a spiral staircase, the Caracol is a somewhat perplexing structure of a style almost completely unknown at other Classic Maya sites. Believed since its discovery by Europeans to have been an observatory, astronomers have now proved it to be so (observations taken by the Maya are of a quite remarkable accuracy). Parts of this building underwent reconstruction and none of its different sections aligns with another. It does contain some Toltec links.

The recently excavated Grupo del Osario (Ossuary), situated between the Castillo and the Caracol, has been dated to the 9th century AD. The exterior walls of the Osario itself contain some 3,000 stones sculptured in relief, and friezes depicting eight serpents adorned with jewels whose heads appear at the four corners of the building.

Representations of about eighty birds with the face of the god Itzamná and anthropomorphic torsos cover the walls, together with jewels and fruit, especially of the cocoa plant. The facade is carved with figures of bird-man-serpents and at the corners are Puuc-style masks. The interior floor is painted blue. There are indications that several cults at different times held sway here. The large number of incense burners and bones suggest that this building was used for the performance of rituals until the Spanish conquest.

The synthesis of styles at Chichén Itzá which occurred after the arrival of the Toltec introduced an air of spaciousness to the interior of buildings when columns instead of walls were used to divide rooms. Square, open platforms with stairs on all sides, sweat baths and ball courts with narrow benches along the sides are other innovations. Colonnades were built in the Central Mexican style and decoration included processions of Toltec warriors and feathered serpents. Mayan monster-masks and Toltec mural bands adorn facades. Paint was used to decorate all types of exterior and interior surfaces. Feathered serpents, jaguars, eagles, mythical beasts and warriors were depicted in color, so that the brilliant appearance of the complex in pre-Colombian times would have borne no resemblance to the uniform grey of the present day. Wooden lintels were carved in relief and sculptures of many types adorned the buildings. The blending of architectural elements extended, it seems, to religious and social spheres: Mayan gods mix with Toltec ones and Jaguar and Eagle knights with Mayan men.

To the northeast of the complex and on a huge terrace is the Great Plaza. It is surrounded by a wall and here stands a group of structures showing Toltec influence: the Castillo (Castle) is flanked by the Great Ball Court with its Temple of the Jaguars, the Tzompantli (Skull Rack) and other structures. The Temple of the Warriors, The Court of the Thousand Columns and the Mercado (Market) are to the east.

The Great Plaza is dominated by the Castillo, built as late as the 11th century in the pyramid-temple style and possibly dedicated to Kukulcán (the Mayan version of the Quetzalcóatl of Central Mexico), the Toltec deity. Its base covers more than 32,700 square feet (3,000 sq m) and supports nine levels, with staircases on all four sides leading to a temple at the summit whose roof is 100 feet (30 m) above the ground. It was built with two central columns surrounded by a gallery. Here is found a mixture of monster masks and Toltec soldiers carved in relief on door jambs. Two feathered serpents, always associated with Quetzalcóatl, flank the staircase which leads to the temple entrance. An earlier pyramid has been discovered beneath the Castillo, and within it a stone throne painted red and in the shape of a jaguar with fangs of shell and eyes and spots of jade. Here too is found one of the figures representative of Chichén Itzá - the chacmool (chacmul). This is a reclining figure with legs flexed and head turned at right-angles to the chest. It holds a flat plate-like object across its stomach, and waits at doorways for offerings.

Due to the Castillo's orientation, at the autumn and spring equinoxes a series of images appears on the principal facade. This is produced by a play of natural light and shadow and resembles the body of a serpent, which appears to glide down the building. Its appearance is still celebrated today.

The Great Ball Court is the largest in Mesoamerica and some judge it the finest. Its upright parallel walls are 99 feet (30 m) apart, 272 feet (82.6 m) long and stand 27 feet (8.2 m) high. A stone ring is set high in each wall; seats are carved in low relief. Along the east wall of the Court is the Temple of the Jaguars, in the back section of which is a chamber totally filled with polychrome sculptured representations of warriors, priests and a host of animals and aquatic plants. It shows that the ball game was a religious as well as sporting event. Nearby is a long platform carved all around with human skulls: the Tzompantli. It is Maya-Toltec in style.

The Temple of the Warriors stands on one stepped platform, built above another, with colonnaded halls leading from it. It forms part of the Complex of the Thousand Columns. While many of these columns are round, there are also square columns with figures of Toltec warriors carved in relief, chacmool statues, feathered serpents flanking the entrance and an altar supported by 'Atlantean' Toltec warriors.

Causeways (Sacbe-ob) connect the various clusters of buildings around the central groupings, the most notable being that which joins the Great Plaza to the Sacred Cenote, one of two cenotes of particular importance to the central complex. The Cenote Xtoloc ('iguana') was the main water source and is found to the east of the cluster of Puuc-style buildings.

The Sacred Cenote alone would set Chichén Itzá apart from other sites. The Maya believed that the gods of rain died there, and pilgrimages and offerings were made to them. Sacrificial offerings were thrown into the Cenote, many of which have been recovered. They include gold, jade, ceramic, wooden, textile and other objects; all have added much to the store of knowledge about this remarkable Maya and Toltec site. Much has been made of the human sacrifices performed here but they seem very few when set against the length of time the cult operated.

The cultural model developed at Chichén Itzá was successful and flexible enough to retain power in the region over a long period. The military control (depicted in various artistic ways), the control of trade routes (to Guatemala in the south and Michoacán in the west) and the exploitation of salt and agriculture, were the material bases. These were supported ideologically by possession of the Sacred Cenote - the entrance to the spirit world of the Maya.

The abandoning of Chichén Itzá during the 13th century was related to the rise of Mayapán as a new center of power in Yucatán. It never again attained real significance.

Processions were still made in the 16th century to the Sacred Cenote but the buildings were not maintained. When the Spaniards sought to establish a colonial presence at Chichén Itzá, fully realizing the symbolic value to be gained from such an action, they were repulsed by the people of a neighboring settlement, possibly from Pisté, who still exist in the western part of the ancient city.

Restoration and preservation are continuing at Chichén Itzá. This magnificent archaeological site on the Yucatán Peninsula was inscribed on the World Heritage List in 1988 because it shows the genius of the vanished Maya and Toltec civilizations and represents the legacy of their profound influence on the world of art and architecture.

Chichén Itzá can be reached by road: it is 75 miles (120 km) from Mérida, Yucatán; 27 miles (44 km) from Valladolid; and 128 miles (205 km) from Cancún along Federal Highway Number 180. Cancún and Mérida are served by international airlines, and there is a local airstrip at Chichén Itzá.

# TEOTIHUACAN
## PRE-HISPANIC CITY

ON THE FLOOR OF THE VALLEY OF TEOTIHUACÁN-OTUMBA, 31 miles (50 km) north-east of Mexico City and some 7,590 feet (2,300 m) above sea level, lie the remains of a city, named by the Aztecs when they beheld it in the 16th century, 'The City of the Gods'. It seemed that only the gods could be responsible for constructing a place so awesomely and wondrously perfect. Within its boundaries rose the first of the great classic cultures of Mesoamerica.

Since 600 BC, small groups of Teotihuacán peoples had occupied the valley, settling where springs supplied water. They began in about 200 BC to gather together around a religious center situated in an area now known as the Old City, to the northeast of the Pyramid of the Moon. It developed into a center of great complexity which became the model of a civilized city. In its most flourishing period it covered more than 8 square miles (20 sq km) and had a population of about 100,000 inhabitants.

PREVIOUS PAGE   *Pyramid of the Sun*
BELOW   *Representation of a Quetzal, facing head on, Complex Tetitla*
BOTTOM   *Representation of a priest. He wears a headress similar to a helmet adorned with feathers. In one hand he has an object from which emanate symbols related to that which is precious, and in the other he has a coipal bag. Complex of Tepantitla*
RIGHT   *Pyramid of the Moon*

It became the most urbanized center in the New World and the focus of political, religious and economic power for hundreds of thousands of people. Its pyramid temples reflected the importance of the priests, the intermediaries between man and the gods, who controlled all activities. Their political power enabled them to establish a social order and control natural resources.

Individuals were removed from agricultural activities and allowed to devote themselves to pursuits such as architecture, sculpture, mural painting, ceramics, mathematics, astronomy and the calculation of time (using both the solar and the ritual calendars).

By the period 200 BC to AD 100 (known as Teotihuacán I) the villagers in the Valley were under the control of Teotihuacán. Part of their agricultural production was paid as tribute and they provided labor for the building of the city temples.

As the settlement spread, its population grew to exceed 25,000. Construction began on the two largest structures built at Teotihuacán, the Pyramids of the Sun and Moon, and on other temples and buildings.

The Pyramid of the Sun was built over the site of a cave fed by water from one of the several springs in the valley. It is thought that the position of the Pyramid was calculated according to the sun's position at its zenith.

Astronomy and cosmology determined the layout of the ceremonial area, harmonious within itself and within the surrounding landscape and its fringe of mountains. The city was built on a north-south axis some sixteen degrees east of north; an angle, some suggest, related to the coming of the rains at the beginning of May. The main thoroughfare (which the Aztecs named the Avenue of the Dead) followed this line, at right angles to the axis of the Pyramid of the Sun. It is 132 feet (40 m) wide and 3 miles (5 km) long. It rises steadily but imperceptibly from south to north towards the foot of the Pyramid of the Moon, which faces down its length and whose backdrop is the distant volcano, Cerro Gordo. To the south, a bridge takes the road over the channelled course of the San Juan River before it reaches the 'Citadel' (Ciudadela) and the Temple of Quetzalcóatl, which are set along the same orientation and to the southeast. Major thoroughfares enter here from east and west, dividing the city into four sectors. Opposite the Ciudadela was the largest marketplace in the city.

The Pyramid of the Sun is a monument of exceptional importance and extraordinary grandeur. It originally towered some 248 feet (75 m) above the square terrace, measuring 743 by 733 feet (225 by 222 m) at its base. Its total volume is an impressive 35.2 million cubic feet (one million cubic meters) as befits a structure built according to cosmic considerations. Adobe bricks, stones and mortar formed the interior. It was faced with volcanic stones set in clay and then smoothly plastered with lime. There were four stepped tiers, faced in the taludtablero style, characteristic of Teotihuacán. A staircase led to two sacred temples at the top of the pyramid on the western side. All building work was achieved without benefit of the wheel, draft animals or metal tools.

Beginning in the 2nd century AD, the second Teotihuacán period lasted two centuries. The population exploded to some 50,000 and building continued. The Temple of Quetzalcóatl began construction as the top sections of the Pyramids of the Sun and Moon neared completion.

The Temple of Quetzalcóatl stands in complete contrast to the somber, geometrical Pyramids. It was built on a terrace 1,320 feet (400 m) square, surrounded by platforms with fifteen small pyramids. The eastern side is occupied by the Temple, the third largest in the city. It was dedicated to the Plumed, or Feathered, Serpent - 'Quetzalcóatl', one of Teotihuacán's principal deities. It is one of the city's most fascinating buildings and is composed of structures from two different periods. The earlier and highly ornate temple is constructed in seven stepped sections. It is built of huge blocks of stone decorated with gigantic sculptures of serpents, whose heads protrude from collar-like rings of petals. They alternate with representations of the rain god, Tlaloc, the city's other main deity, with his 'goggle' eyes, moustache and fangs. Feathered serpents undulate around the building and their heads adorn the balustrade of the stairway. Bordering these major elements are bivalves and conch shells which still show traces of the red, blue, yellow and green paint which, in the 4th century, would have made the temple a spectacular sight.

Recent excavations beneath the Temple have uncovered burial pits, laid out symmetrically and containing skeletons of some two hundred individuals, many with their hands tied behind their backs. Scholars believe they belonged to sacrificial victims killed in homage to the deity. If true it destroys the former belief that Teotihuacán was a theocracy of pacifist priests. Archaeological investigations continue in an effort to learn more about these and many other aspects of this remarkable place.

From AD 350 to 650 (Teotihuacán III) was the period of the city's greatest splendor. It saw the final period of great construction and the consolidation of all its achievements. The population reached its peak and it became a center for painters who produced magnificent murals and frescoes. New techniques were developed for decorating palaces, temples and pottery. The use of molds allowed the production of figurines in great numbers. Obsidian continued to be processed into spear and dart points in some three hundred and fifty workshops, where small human effigies were also made. The raw material was extracted from nearby sources and its distribution carefully controlled. Stones like turquoise from Zacatecas were cut for adornment and materials were brought from the Gulf of Mexico and the Pacific Ocean to add to the sophistication of the lives of the Teotihuacános.

It was during this period that the cultural and artistic achievements of Teotihuacán were spread throughout Mesoamerica. Long-distance trade became an important element in its prosperity and this, combined with conquests possibly inspired by religious motives, spread its influence far and wide.

Teotihuacán was a planned city - for example, it boasted a system of underground drainage - and it contained many groups of notable buildings. These include the Palaces of Quetzalpapalotl (the 'butterfly'), Caracoles Enplumados ('Feathered Snails'), Jaguars, Yayahuala and several others.

In the residential areas of Atetlco, Tetitla and Zacuala are found vestiges of mural paintings of exceptional importance and executed in glorious colors. Almost all surfaces were painted, indoors and out, with images of gods, mythical beings, priests, and real and fantastic animals, flowers and plants. At Tepantitla is the 'Paradise of Tlaloc' (the rain god), a mural which depicts a number of men playing instruments, singing and dancing in an idyllic rural setting.

The palaces were generally located close to the ceremonial center and set in large compounds with high walls which formed streets between them. A single doorway gave entrance to each compound.

Beyond the ceremonial center and the areas occupied by the upper classes were the enclaves set aside for merchants and artisans. There were special zones set aside where foreigners such as those from Oaxaca and the Maya lands came to live; for traders; and the houses of laborers and peasants. All contributed to the splendor of the place where a later myth relates that men were transformed into gods.

Teotihuacán's decline occurred between AD 650 and 750 and it was finally abandoned in the 9th century. There is evidence of destruction of buildings by fire. Environmental reasons have been among those postulated for the fires, while some suggest that the huge area under the city's sway had become too large to control. Many of its people probably migrated to other centers, taking their skills with them and helping to spread further the cultural influence of the great city.

In about AD 1000 Teotihuacán became the home of Toltec people from Tula and, following many political changes, the Aztecs took control a century before the Spanish conquest.

Teotihuacán was inscribed on the World Heritage List in 1987 for five of the six cultural criteria - a testament in itself to the unique and important nature of this ancient city.

The site is open daily from 8 am to 5 pm and is served by buses from Mexico City, which depart from the Terminal Central de Autobuses del Norte. The journey takes about one hour. There is a toll road for those with their own transport. It is suggested that visitors avoid the middle of the day when it is uncomfortably hot and the effects of altitude can be felt most keenly.

ABOVE & INSERT
*Temple of Quetzalcoatl featuring the Serpent and Tlaloc gods*

# PALENQUE

## MAYAN CITY AND NATIONAL PARK

THE MAYAN CEREMONIAL CENTER OF PALENQUE is one of the gems of Mesoamerica, an area encompassing parts of Mexico, Guatemala, Honduras, El Salvador and Belize. Here the Maya held sway, dominating a part of the region politically through a number of religious or ceremonial centers. At these centers Mayan cultural achievements were made manifest, displaying an astonishing level of sophistication.

The highest point of Mayan development, termed the Classic period, was attained during the 4th to the 10th centuries AD. Significant Mayan centers, including that of Palenque, emerged in lowland areas covered with tropical jungle in the southern Yucatán Peninsula. A characteristic of Mayan settlements, noticeably different from the central Mexican Teotihuacán pattern of concentrated settlement, is their relatively loose and scattered nature.

The scientific achievements of the Mayans are among their greatest. A remarkable knowledge of astronomy and mathematics -

PREVIOUS PAGE   *The Palace and Temple of the Inscriptions*

they were, for example, familiar with the concept of zero - was used by them for divination and the regulation of religious ritual. It enabled them to use astronomical calculations together with ritual cycles to develop a calendar which was the most complex in Mesoamerica.

It was in their monumental architecture, achieved without the aid of the wheel or of metal tools, that their amazing talents found greatest expression. In ceremonial centers pyramids, some of truly vast proportions, temples and ball courts were constructed. These magnificent buildings were decorated with painting, sculpture and mosaic which, especially in the case of Palenque, anointed them with an air of great beauty.

Palenque's highest achievements were expressed artistically in the complexity of its architecture, ceramics, stone bas-reliefs and

inscriptions; socially in its dynastic history; and diplomatically in its contacts with peoples far and wide. These attributes set it apart from other Mayan sites of the period.

The ruins of Palenque are set deep in the tropical monsoon forest of Mexico's Chiapas State, in the region of the mighty Usamacinta River. The area receives some of the heaviest rainfall in Mexico and is hot and humid. Set within a national park of the same name, this is a region of towering trees and often impenetrable undergrowth, of screeching monkeys, distant echoing birds and thundering waterfalls.

Palenque takes its name from the nearby community of Santo Domingo de Palenque, probably established in the 17th century. It is considered by many to be the most beautiful of all archaeological locations in Mexico, yet it lay hidden for nearly eight hundred years until rediscovered in the late 18th century. As the early morning mist rises to reveal the whitish-colored ruins, the site exerts a powerful response in those privileged to witness it. How much more exhilarating it would have been to have seen the buildings in their prime; painted a beautiful vermilion in contrast to the deep emerald of the forest background.

The ruins, set in the foothills on the north slope of the Chiapas Mountains at an elevation of some 500 feet (150 m), command a view over the low coastal plain of Tabasco which extends to the Gulf of Mexico. Evolving from an agricultural village, possibly as early as the 1st century BC, the city center grew to cover one square mile (2.5 sq km), while the entire city extended out over an area of 3 square miles (8 sq km).

Palenque rested on a natural platform which was modified by the Mayans to form a series of terraces on which buildings were constructed and plazas laid out. The central area was surrounded by other structures, aligned on an east-west axis stretching along the escarpment. Pyramids occupied the higher positions and smaller buildings were at lower levels.

While there was much remodeling of the natural landscape, the city was not forced into a rigidly formal layout. The buildings complement their location and are enhanced by their natural background. They impress because of their proportions and their delicacy of form and decoration. Neither are they dwarfed by the stepped pyramids on which they are built. The many doorways are wide, as are the rooms with their corbelled, vaulted ceilings. Connecting galleries add to an impression of space. The distinguishing roof 'combs' or 'crests' were made lighter by perforations, while the stucco sculptures which decorated them were visible to people

standing in the plaza. It is a lightness and fineness of construction which renders Palenque so elegant.

The designs used in sculpture and the murals employed for their decoration exhibit an elaborate symbolism which changed little during the years of Palenque's greatness. They tell of the mythology of the Maya and vividly demonstrate many of their rituals. They are the manifestation of a stable society dominated by priestly rulers.

Palenque developed from a center of minor importance to one of the great Mayan sites, due mainly to the inspiration and achievements of two remarkable rulers. The club-footed Pacal, represented in hieroglyphs by the sun shield, ascended to power in the 7th century, claiming mythological ancestry. He was succeeded by his son Chan-Bahlum, symbolized by the jaguar and the serpent.

Pacal began the transformation of Palenque into a great Mayan center. The Otulum River, a tributary of the Usumacinta, runs through it and a bridge was built to cross it. A vaulted aqueduct was constructed to channel the water of the Otulum and carry it under the city. Great mounds of earth were removed to form bases for temples and other structures; plazas created space between buildings. The whole created a sense of harmony and balance. Otulum in the Maya dialect means 'fortified houses', which may refer to the ancient city's forgotten name.

Only a few of the many buildings known to form part of Palenque have until recently been excavated. The Palace, raised on an immense artificial platform and built around four courtyards, has as its most distinctive feature a three-storied tower, a structure unique in Maya architecture. This was probably used as a watch-tower or for astronomical observations. It is enriched by painted murals, stucco masks and figures, stucco reliefs and sculptured panels of extraordinary quality.

Even larger is the Temple of the Inscriptions. Set on a stepped pyramid situated to one side of the Palace but rising above it and overlooking the Great Plaza, it is more than 200 feet (60 m) wide at the base and 60 feet (20 m) high. During excavations in 1952 the tomb of Pacal was discovered in a crypt beneath the temple pyramid. It is reached by a narrow internal staircase starting from the temple's rear gallery, and its discovery was of enormous significance. The stone sarcophagus was covered by a huge, magnificently incised slab. The skeleton was adorned with a mask of jade pieces, and many more treasures were interred with it. Nine stucco figures of priests watched over the buried man from the walls of the crypt. Inscriptions have revealed much of the history of the city.

Palenque provides two complementary sources for studying the history and culture of the inhabitants of this site - archaeology and epigraphy. Hieroglyphic inscriptions appearing on many surfaces throughout the complex have gradually yielded the information which makes this site so important as a continuing source of knowledge of the Maya at the middle of the Classic period. The names of the principal rulers and officials, dates of birth, marriage, and death, dates of military contests, alliances, the nature of rituals and the precision of the Mayan calendar, have all been revealed.

The tomb of Pacal was for decades the most wondrous discovery at Palenque. Then, forty-two years later, another tomb of an individual of high rank was found, in Temple XIII. The sarcophagus, which lies north-south, is painted red and covered with a single limestone slab, devoid of decoration. Upon it, in the center, stood a single incense burner and at the foot, a small spindle. Along the east side of the unopened sarcophagus lay the skeleton of a sacrificed adult woman and on the west that of a baby boy. On removing the lid of the sarcophagus the 1,200 year old remains of a tall woman were revealed, surrounded by pieces of jade (including a mask made of 200 pieces), pearls, obsidian knives, bone and shell needles, necklaces, bracelets, hair ornaments and earrings. Pieces of fine pottery stood on the lowest steps of the staircase at the entrance to the crypt. No inscription exists to aid in the identification of this woman, but Mexican archaeologists are certain that the discovery will soon result in answers to some of the questions surrounding the dynastic history of Palenque. For the moment it identifies the Great Plaza structures as the burial places of the city's rulers.

Demonstrating further the magnificence of the Mayan builders' art, and set against a background of luxuriant vegetation, are other temples: the Temple of the Sun, the Temples of the Cross and the Foliated Cross; the Temple of the Count (named after archaeologist Count de Waldeck who used the building while studying the ruins); and Temples XI and XII. These smaller buildings and others provide yet more examples of the artistic accomplishments of the sculptors and artists of Palenque. A small Ball Court, the hallmark of Mayan ceremonial spaces, is found to the north of the Palace.

The city became the center of a vast commercial web, linking it with other parts of Mesoamerica beyond the Maya 'empire', and making it one of the most important in the Maya world. This fact makes Palenque's sudden decline in about AD 900 even more astonishing. Building and carving ceased from about AD 800 and recent

ABOVE *Temple of the Sun*

findings lead to the supposition that the town was not abandoned but was deliberately destroyed. Other peoples appear to have occupied the site until the 10th century when it was finally abandoned and engulfed by luxuriant vegetation.

Recent excavations have revealed many new ordinary tombs, artifacts and inscriptions within the ceremonial center. Such findings serve to heighten the appreciation of the importance of Palenque as a center of great cultural sophistication. Palenque was inscribed on the World Heritage List in 1987 as a masterpiece of human genius and as an outstanding architectural and artistic testimony from a vanished civilization.

The archaeological site is surrounded by a park whose main natural feature is tropical rain forest. A total of 4,250 acres (1,772 ha), two-thirds of which in 1981 was in private hands, was then set aside to form the Palenque National Park.

The park incorporates mountainous areas in the north of Chiapas State and also part of the coastal plain. The mountains were formed in the Mesozoic era and contain many deposits, including the limestone which was of such importance to the stucco decoration of the Mayans.

Two streams, the Otulum and the Michol, run through the park and form waterfalls of great natural beauty, including some readily accessible near the archaeological site. The rainfall is some of the highest in Mexico, with an average of over 80 inches (2,000 mm) per annum. Together with a mean temperature of 26°C (79°F), it produces high humidity and conditions perfect for the growth of a magnificent and diverse flora.

Among the species present in the rain forest are mahogany, cedar and sapote and many species of orchid. An alarming clearance of the forest for cultivation has increased in recent years and added to worldwide decline in this type of vegetation. The forest also shelters important mammal species such as jaguar, puma and peccary. Some of the region's parrots and macaws, as well as other birds and animals, are in danger of extinction, largely due to the pressure put upon the land and its resources by humans.

Palenque is accessible by road. Take Federal Highway 186 from Villahermosa which heads towards Escárcega, Campeche. After 70 miles (114 km). there is a turn to the right which leads to Palenque town. Do not take this turn, but keep going a further 20 miles (30 km) until the road divides; take the right-hand road to the archaeological site. There is an air service to Palenque from Tuxtla-Gutierrez. The site is open daily between 8 am and 6 pm.

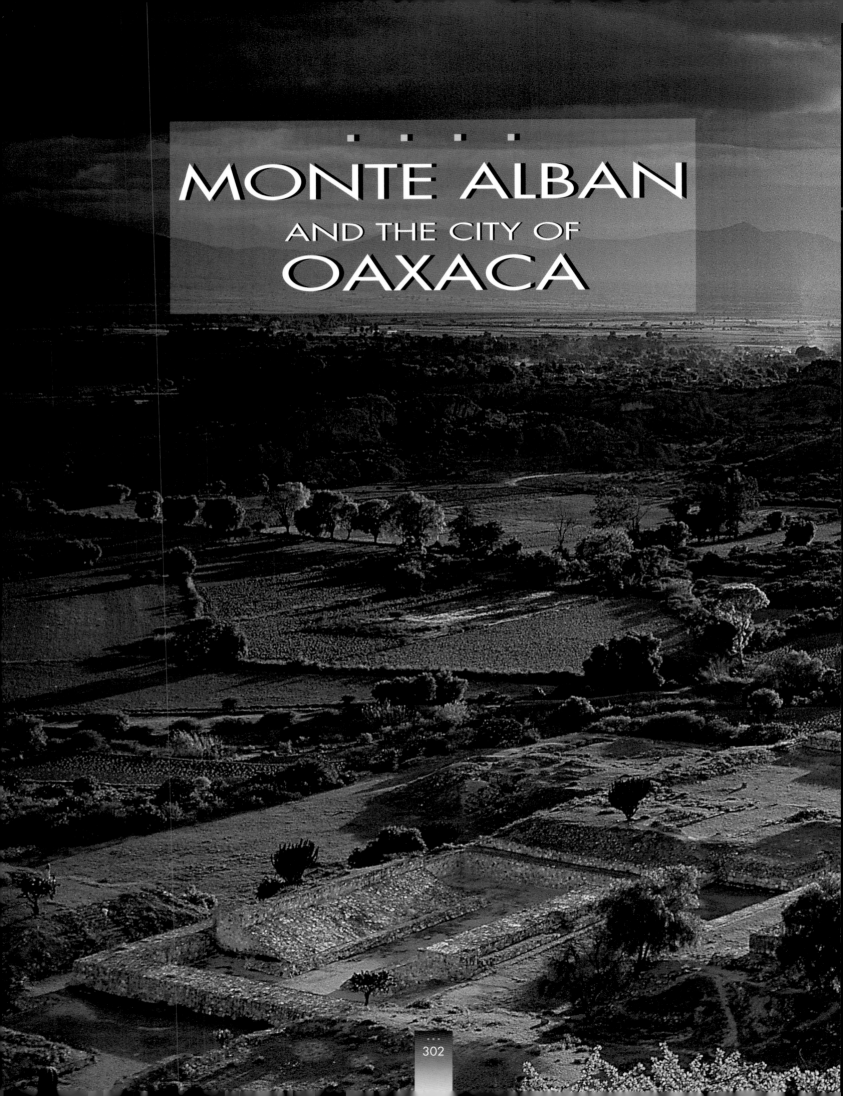

# MONTE ALBAN
## AND THE CITY OF
## OAXACA

PREVIOUS PAGE   *Yagul Ruins*
ABOVE   *Monte Alban*

N AN ELEVATED POSITION IN THE HILLS of the Valley of Oaxaca, 2.5 miles (4 km) across the river to the west of the colonial town of Oaxaca, lies the pre-Hispanic center of Monte Albán - a very large and spectacular archaeological site that once supported the largest urban center in the Oaxaca region. The valley is situated in the southern highlands of Mexico at an average elevation of 5,000 feet (1,500 m). This temperate and semi-arid area boasts one of the longest cultural sequences in Mesoamerica, a region which includes parts of Mexico, Guatemala, Honduras, El Salvador and Belize. Monte Albán was inhabited in succession by Olmec, Zapotec and Mixtec peoples.

The builders of Monte Albán were forebears of the Zapotec people who still inhabit the area today. The city and its sacred center was built on a series of ridge-tops, eventually forming three main areas of settlement - Atzompa, El Gallo and Monte Albán - some 1,650 feet (500 m) above the valley floor. The levelling of the steep hillsides for building sites went on for 1,500 years. Only the area around the Main Plaza of Monte Albán - a very small part of the site - has been excavated to any significant extent.

It was probably in about 500 BC that a decision was taken to build at Monte Albán, a location without arable land or adequate water. It was, however, naturally defensible, close to rich alluvial land in the valley, and centrally situated to the Zapotec communities who had settled in the surrounding valleys. With these attributes, the settlement quickly emerged as the center of political and economic power in the region.

In Monte Alban's earliest phase (to 100 BC) the levelling of the upper parts of the hills began in preparation for erecting the main buildings and the central plaza. The cultural influence of the Olmecs can be seen in a great gallery of low-relief carvings erected along one side of the superimposed 'Building L', a low stone-faced platform. There are 140 slabs showing captives and sacrificed victims arranged in four rows. The lowest of them depicted the so-called 'Danzantes' (dancers), figures of nude men, lifeless, limp and apparently mutilated. Some similar stones were re-used in later buildings at the north-east corner of the central plaza.

During the period 100 BC to AD 250, levelling work continued and 'Building J' - shaped like an arrow-head and aligned differently from all other buildings at Monte Albán - was constructed. It pointed south-west and may have been used as an observatory - the Zapotecs clearly developed both a solar and a ritual calendar. They also devised a system of glyphs to record dates and historical events. These were first carved into the Danzantes' stones and, though still only partly deciphered, are regarded as some of the earliest texts produced in what is now Mexico. Building J displayed more apparent victims on carved slabs, but with many more glyphs than the earlier Building L.

Between AD 250 and 650 - during the so-called Classic period - Monte Albán had developed into a true city, covering 2.5 square miles (6.5 sq km). The population reached 50,000 in AD 800 and expansion beyond the hilltop of Monte Albán led to the construction of some 2,000 terraces on which houses were built.

The majority of structures now visible at the site of the ceremonial center were built in this period. On an artificially levelled area measuring 975 by 660 feet (300 by 200 m), the Main Plaza was laid out along a north - south axis. One great attribute of the Plaza is the manner in which the various structures impart a sense of equilibrium and unity despite the limitations imposed by the topography. A new sacred landscape was created, composed of pyramids, mounds and artificial hillocks.

The huge North and South Platforms stand at each end of the Plaza. Each was topped by a temple, and they were approached by 130 foot wide (40 m) stairways, lending a sense of majesty to the whole area. From both platforms there are breath-taking views over the Oaxaca Valley below. Sandstone and limestone were locally available for construction and low, earthquake resistant stone platforms predominate, some of them constructed on rock outcrops which remained after the levelling of the area. The core of the platforms

ABOVE  *Monte Alban*
RIGHT  *'Dancer'*

was a mixture of earth and rock faced with smooth stone and finished with beautifully painted, white stucco plaster.

Some twenty buildings of different styles and uses were constructed in and around the Main Plaza. The overall style is distinctive while owing much to the influence of Teotihuacán, particularly in the massive monumental architecture allied with large open spaces. Temples, palace-residences built around patios and a small but magnificent I-shaped ball court defined the space. The harmony of the whole complex and the play of light as the seasons alter has impressed many visitors to this place of ritual and ceremony.

Further evidence of the existence of strong links with Teotihuacán - where a considerable group of Oaxacans resided in the foreigners' quarter - can be seen in the great South Platform. Set into the four corners are stellae depicting the arrival of an ambassador from Teotihuacán and his reception by a Zapotec official.

It is Monte Alban's tombs which help to set it apart from other cultural sites. More than one hundred have been discovered all over the site, and the more elaborate are decorated with fine murals on their plastered walls. Sculptures in stucco, carved and painted bones and carved stone slabs were features. Funerary urns were placed around a corpse together with precious objects and jewelry in gold, silver and jade. New paintings covered the old and depicted historical and religious themes with important individuals represented as deities. The jaguar was the symbol of power for the Zapotec and rulers were often depicted wearing jaguar costumes.

Tomb number seven, built under the floor of a typical Zapotec temple, and with walls decorated with paintings, was excavated in 1932. The original burial objects had been removed and nine exhumed individuals were re-buried there, surrounded by offerings. A wonderful collection of five hundred objects - 'The Treasure of Monte Alban' - was found, testament to the practice of re-use. Among the objects were those made of silver and gold, mosaics of turquoise, pearls by the thousands, coral, amber, rock crystal and jet necklaces and carved jaguar bones. This bounty is now kept in the State Museum of Oaxaca.

THE TWO CENTERS OF MONTE ALBAN AND OAXACA are separated across the Atoyac River by only 2.5 miles (4 km), but there is an extraordinary contrast between their physical locations. Each is exceptionally well-integrated in its own setting while also complementing the other.

Shortly before the arrival of the Spaniards, the Aztecs established a stronghold at Huaxyacac ('near the acacia grove') and took control of the Oaxaca Valley. The conquistadors built a fort there in 1521, retaining a version of the name by calling it Antequera de Oaxaca.

Charles V of Germany (also Charles I of Spain), decreed the foundation of the city here on September 14, 1526, but it was not laid out until three years later. The rectangular grid pattern of Mexico City was followed, a characteristic that has been maintained without alteration in Oaxaca.

The principal plaza - the Zocolo - was soon lined with grand edifices. Construction of the Cathedral to the north side was begun in 1544 and supervised by the Dominicans. It is one of twenty or so important historic religious monuments in the city. Erected from the 16th century onwards by the religious orders who evangelized the country, they form a group which has had a powerful regional influence, particularly after the 17th century. Frequent earthquakes have jeopardized the existence of these old buildings.

In central Oaxaca, an area of 172 blocks is surrounded by a buffer zone of 55 blocks. Within this zone are 1,200 listed properties of which 242 are of great significance. Of special mention are the splendid patrician town residences, including that of Hernan Cortés which now houses the Historical Museum. The Rufino Tamayo Museum contains a large collection of pre-Hispanic art. Other fine dwellings line the streets and create an impression of a colonial city which has integrated buildings of later centuries into a pleasurable whole. Oaxaca has now grown into a city of 150,000 people.

The two sites described here are individually of outstanding universal heritage value; geographically proximate, they are also culturally complementary. Together they were inscribed on the World Heritage List in 1987.

Internal airlines fly to Oaxaca from Mexico City and there are also services from several other locations. Oaxaca is some 300 miles (500 km) by road from Mexico City via several routes. It is 260 miles (400 km) from Puebla; 150 miles (250 km) from Tehuantepec; and 500 miles (800 km) from Ciudad Cuauhtemoc on the Guatemalan border. Buses serve the city from every direction. Trains run from Mexico City, Puebla and Tehuacan. The archaeological zone of Monte Albán is 5 miles (8 km) to the west of the city of Oaxaca de Juarez.

RIGHT  *Church of Santo Domingo*

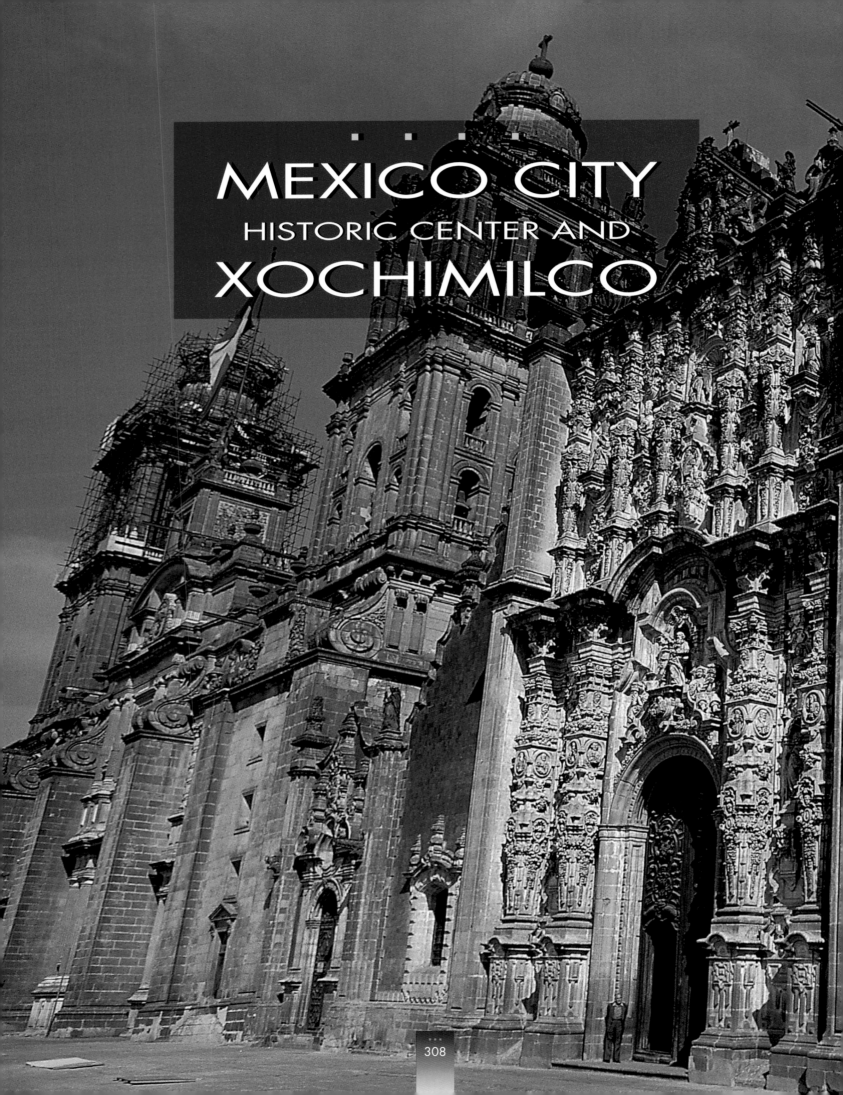

# MEXICO CITY
## HISTORIC CENTER AND
# XOCHIMILCO

At the southern end of the Mexican Mesa Central (the Meseta de Anáhuac), at an altitude of 7,349 feet (2,240 m) and surrounded by volcanoes and mountains, lies a basin which was once a great lake. In it lies one of the world's largest cities - Mexico City. The historic center, the famed Tenochtitlan of the Aztecs, was made the capital of the Spanish colony of New Spain four centuries ago.

The Nahuatl-speaking Aztec people developed probably the best-known of all the civilizations of Mexico. After the political dominance of the Toltecs had waned, these people, also known as the Mexica, moved into the rich Mexico Valley Basin.

An Aztec legend relates how they gained a foothold in the densely settled Valley. In 1325 a prophecy which said that they should settle where they saw an eagle perching on a cactus with a snake in its beak, was fulfilled. In return for the right to live on an unoccupied island off the swampy western shore of lake Texcoco, they became

ABOVE   *Carving from Mayor Temple*
OPPOSITE   *Temple of Tenochtitlan*

tributaries to the possessors of that land. It was there that they built the first temple to their principal gods.

By acting as mercenaries the Aztec fortunes improved. They came under the cultural influence of allies who had learned a ruthless form of statecraft and empire-building from the Toltecs; a system that was to reach its most sophisticated form under the Aztecs.

By successive victories, they not only acquired territory, but also became the guardians of the sun and were responsible for the sacrifices necessary to ensure its appearance each day. Continued military conquests confirmed their grand destiny, and commerce followed the sword. Lands as distant as the present-day Guatemalan border came under their control, and much of central Mexico was unified to form a single empire. By 1428 the Aztecs and their allies

ABOVE    *Serpent carving, Mayor Temple*

seized control of the valley, and by the time of the arrival of Europeans in Central America they had progressed from being subject tributaries to being recipients of massive tributes.

The three cities built in and around the lake (Tenochtitlan, Texcoco and Tlacopan) astonished Hernan Cortés and his colleagues when they first looked down on them in 1519 from the mountains which ring the basin. The conquistador and chronicler Bernal Díaz del Castillo wrote in amazement, '... we were stunned, and we said that it looked like the enchanted things described in the book ... because of the lofty towers and temples and the buildings they had in the water, all in stone and whitewashed. Some of our soldiers even wondered if what they were seeing was not a dream ...' Tenochtitlan covered some 5 square miles of land (13 sq km), built up from a few small islands on the edge of the lake. It was approached by broad causeways and had defenses against any enemy attack. Its various sections were connected by canals, and water was brought into the city by the great Chapultepec aqueduct. Because there were no building materials on the islands everything needed for construction had to be carried in canoes from the mainland. A very light, porous volcanic rock, tezontle, was used to help prevent buildings sinking into the soft and spongy subsoil.

The spiritual heart of the city was the Sacred Precinct. It was dominated by the Great Temple (Templo Mayor), the largest of the pyramids within the city, dedicated in 1487 to the two great Aztec gods Huitzilopochtli, warrior god of the sun and Tlaloc, the rain god. This building was surrounded by temples erected to other deities, as well as a ball court and a skull rack, all painted in glorious colors. Palaces were built around the precinct and beyond them houses and marketplaces, the splendor of the buildings gradually decreasing as the distance from the Great Temple increased.

On the marshy edges of the lake, crops, vegetables and flowers were cultivated in 'chinampas' - fields built up on platforms of loam, reeds and other vegetation and stabilized by tree planting.

The Spanish conquest of Tenochtitlan was completed in 1521 with the aid of disaffected tributaries to the Aztecs. In order to extirpate the old gods and pagan customs, the conquistadors almost totally destroyed the city of some a quarter of a million people. Stones from the great buildings were used to pave the streets and construct the new churches and administrative buildings on the same site. On the ruins rose another capital, that of New Spain. Built to glorify the conquest and the introduction of Christianity to the New World, it was laid out in a grand checkerboard pattern. By making

adequate provision for open plazas the Spaniards emulated the Aztecs' accomplishment in the impressive use of space.

The historic center of present-day Mexico City embraces a huge and majestic open square - the Zócalo or Plaza de la Constitución. Around the Zócalo are several colonial buildings, notably the Metropolitan Cathedral with its baroque facade and reliefs in white marble. The Palacio Nacional, housing many government offices and institutions, was built on the site of a group of Aztec buildings. It fills the whole of one side of the square and has been extensively rebuilt since the 16th century.

Scholars had long believed that the ruins of the Aztec Great Temple were near the colonial Cathedral. In 1790 a huge statue of the Goddess of the Earth and the great round stone known as the 'Aztec Calendar' were found. The statue was 8.43 feet (2.57 m) tall, while the calendar measured 12 feet (3.6 m) in diameter and weighed 26 tons (24 tonnes). It was only in 1978 that chance led to the discovery of a significant relic which prompted the excavations to the northeast of the Cathedral and about 660 feet (200 m) from the earlier finds. An Aztec sculptural masterpiece - a huge stone bearing the representation of the dismembered body of Coyolxauhqui, the sister of the great deity Huitzilopochtli - was then uncovered. This sculpture reinforced an Aztec myth of the struggle for power following the overthrow of the old order.

Excavation during the following three years found that the Temple's final dimensions had been 328 feet (100 m) wide, 262 feet (80 m) deep and 108 feet (33 m) high. Successive reconstructions entombed the preceding ones, burying chambers of offerings, some from distant parts of the empire, and sculptures which glorified the deities of the time. Huge stone serpents writhed along walls, threatening those who had no right to enter the sacred area. Serpent heads flanked staircases. These finds showed that the Aztecs nurtured remarkable sculptors of stone, capable of producing work of great refinement. Pottery offerings, too, impress with their delicacy, as do objects made of gold, precious stones, alabaster, obsidian and shell. Color, as everywhere in Mesoamerica, played its part in decoration - of murals, sculptures and many other objects.

The Temple faced west and was divided in two parts. The construction of the second stage shows that the southern half was dedicated to the elements of sacrifice and war in the worship of the sun god Huitzilopochtli. At its entrance stands the sacrificial stone, a simple piece of tezontle measuring 20 by 18 inches (50 by 45 cm). The northern half, dedicated to Tlaloc the rain god, contained objects linked with water and the sea. Before its door, as at Chichén Itzá, reclined a chacmool, an intercessionary figure. Each sanctuary was approached by its own impressive staircase, flanked by ramps with motifs of serpents. The two gods who ruled the lives of all citizens of Tenochtitlan - whether commoner, noble, artisan, travelling trader or priest - were worshipped side by side.

The wealth and cultural status of the city built by the conquering Spaniards was reflected in its architecture; most notably by the completion of a new Cathedral, and the building of many grand churches and convents - La Santisima, La Profesa and San Francisco among others. These were richly endowed with lavish altars, screens and other forms of religious art in gold, silver and wood, provided by the wealth of Mexico's fabulous silver mines. Civil architecture was not lacking; palaces to house the nobility adorned the city, as well as impressive hospitals and colleges.

Exactly two centuries after the Conquest and following eleven years of armed struggle, Mexican Independence from Spain was proclaimed in 1821. New laws allowed the expropriation of the buildings and land of the Catholic Church. Convents were adapted to other purposes and new public and private buildings of note were constructed outside the now densely built center.

The population of the city rose in the century following Independence from 130,000 to 720,000; it passed its first million in about 1930 and now exceeds 18 million.

ABOVE *El Sagrario Church facade*
RIGHT *Carving from Metropolitan Cathedral*

It is ironic that this city, so well-documented by colonial historians, retains few pre-colonial archaeological remnants. Even colonial buildings of the 16th and 17th centuries are rare, having suffered from the subsidence, earthquakes and flooding so common to this mountain valley. Rapid economic growth since the 18th century has also had detrimental effects on conservation. However, many 18th and 19th century buildings remain, benefiting from early anti-earthquake construction techniques. Twentieth century skyscrapers are now those most at risk and pose a threat to the older buildings around them.

Some later buildings, such as the Palacio des Bellas Artes (Palace of Fine Arts), illustrate the continuity of the architectural and cultural achievements of this remarkable site. This early 20th century building, constructed largely of Carrara marble, stands on the site of a convent and contains external Art Nouveau, as well as internal Art Deco, elements. The decoration includes pre-Hispanic masks of warriors, tigers and eagles and of Maya deities and serpents.

Xochimilco ('place of the fields of flowers') was the site of the first of the seven Nahuatl centers established in the Valley of Mexico. Seventeen miles (28 km) to the south of the city center, almost 3,000 acres (1,250 ha) of the original half-natural, half-artificial, lakeside settlements which grew into present-day Mexico City, remain. On the residual lake of Xochimilco, which was the south arm of the Texcoco lake, and among a system of small canals, are some of the 'floating gardens' so admired by the Spaniards. These gardens consist of solid ground, small islands and artificial islands gained from

the lake by the chinampas system. There are also vestiges of urban and rural habitation dating from the sixteenth century.

This tremendously varied and important cultural site was inscribed on the World Heritage List in 1987 for its exceptional architectural and artistic testimony to the cultural traditions of the Aztecs, the early Spanish colonists and the emergent Mexican Nation.

Mexico City is linked by air with many parts of the United States and South and Central America. Metro Line 2 serves the Zócalo Station. For Xochimilco, take Metro Line 2 to its terminus Taxquena. Buses south to Xochimilco stop outside the station in Calzada Tlalpan.

# PUEBLA
## HISTORIC CENTER

THE LOCATION OF THE COLONIAL CITY OF PUEBLA IS SPECTACULAR. It sits in the center of a broad plain, some 7,128 feet (2,160 m) above sea-level; overlooked by the mountains of the Sierra Madre continental divide which separate it from Mexico City. Within view are four volcanoes, three of them the highest in Mexico: to the west are the peaks of Popocatépetl and Ixtaccituatl, Malinche lies to the northeast and Orizaba, Mexico's highest mountain, is to the east.

Puebla was founded as a strongly fortified Spanish city. In 1530 the group of officials which formed the Government of New Spain (the Audiencia) decided on the need to establish a new settlement. Spaniards who had not previously received land or other privileges would be offered an opportunity to live and prosper, contributing to the growth of Spain's newly conquered possession. There was also a need for a major presence along the road between Veracruz on the coast and the seat of government in Mexico City.

Forty Spanish families took up residence on the south side of the Cerro de San Cristobal, on the eastern side of a valley known as San Francisco, where there was rich soil, abundant water and a temperate climate. Tlaxcala was to the north, and Cholula, or what was left of it after Cortés' bloody massacre in 1519, to the west.

A mass was celebrated on the day of the city's foundation, 16 April 1531. The settlers, who were accompanied by six friars, began to lay out the streets of what would be a city, guided by the principles set out in a decree of Philip II. They were helped by Indians from Tlaxcala, Huejotzingo and Tepeaca (where missions had been established), who put up shelters and carried in tezontle (a porous rock composed of silica and volcanic ash), wood, stones and tools for building. Land was allocated to settlers for the construction of

PREVIOUS PAGE   *Rosary Chapel, Church of Santo Domingo*
BELOW   *An example of Spanish colonial civil architecture*
OPPOSITE   *San Sebastian Square*

houses and for cultivation of crops to provide desperately needed food for the expanding colonial population in the region.

Heavy rain forced a change of location to the western bank of the San Francisco River in 1532, where new houses were built and thirty-four new holdings marked out. New settlers were moved to this location from Mexico City.

A legend states that the Archbishop of Tlaxcala dreamt of angels marking out the boundaries for the city. On waking, he located the place where Puebla was built. In 1532 the Crown authorized the use of the name Puebla de los Angeles, and exempted its inhabitants from some local taxes for thirty years.

As a purely Spanish city, Puebla was attractive to new settlers from Europe. A Moorish element was introduced to the city's architecture. It grew slowly during the 16th century, giving the town an air of dignity. The many Indian workers, without whom the European population would have found life very difficult, lived on the outskirts.

By the end of the 16th century the city comprised 120 rectangular city blocks centered around a main plaza. A period of intense construction began that continued for nearly two hundred years.

Aided by official assistance and the splendid natural advantages of its situation, Puebla began to prosper until it became the second richest city in the Viceroyalty. It became famous for its wheat and was known at one time as the Granary of New Spain. Later, its wool industry prospered and many Spaniards were encouraged to invest in its economic development. Merchants increasingly settled there to take advantage of its location on the main road from the capital to the coast.

It also became a most important religious center. The construction of the first church began in 1536 and churches and monasteries were soon built by Franciscans, Dominicans and Augustinians, who were later joined by Jesuits and Carmelites. The Episcopal See was transferred from Tlaxcala to Puebla, enhancing the importance of the city which, it was said, became the most Catholic

in the country. Apart from the 'fortress' monasteries, almost all churches built near Puebla in the 16th century Gothic or Plateresque styles were replaced by those built under later influences, particularly Baroque.

An exception is the Cathedral, which so influenced the city's architecture that it managed to subdue the normally extravagant Baroque style which prevailed in the city. Puebla, Mexico City and Guadalajara were the most Spanish and the most important cities of New Spain. Here the three largest cathedrals were built. The somber Classic style was employed by the architect Herrera, under the control of Phillip II. Only after their deaths in 1597 and 1598 respectively, did a relaxation in style take place, allowing the Baroque to flourish.

Puebla Cathedral is second in importance only to that of Mexico City. A primitive church had stood on the site before building was begun in 1562. Phillip II's plans were somewhat modified and the cathedral was consecrated in 1649, although the facade was not completed until 1664. It had become a blend of Classic Renaissance and early Baroque styles. Its exterior was built of the local, very hard bluish-grey stone and, while the contrast with the marble of the facade was startling, the overall effect was severe.

The interior was splendid with its marble floor, walls of white, gold, magnificent wood carving and gilded decorations.

The Church of San Francisco also dates from the 16th century, though it too contains many later elements. Built between 1550 and 1580, it was the first religious structure to be completed in Puebla. Its astonishingly colorful facade, with stonework sculptures and brick and multi-colored tiles, was built in the mid-18th century, when such use of brick, mortar and tiles became common.

The remarkable building activity which continued for so many years was made possible largely because of the inordinate riches which were being extracted in Guanajuato and Zacatecas.

The clay of Puebla was found to be especially suitable for the making of pottery and tiles. The city had become famous for both after the Dominican friars brought craftsmen from Toledo to teach the technique to the Indians. The tile and the cupola, both features of Puebla architecture, were legacies of the Moorish influence on Spain. Glazed tiles were used to decorate facades, exterior and interior elements of houses, fountains and even the domes of churches. The Church of San José was the first to experiment with a tile-covered dome. Yellows and blues were the colors most often employed, while orange, red, green and dark brown were also used.

Educational institutions were built in great numbers by the religious orders, particularly by the Jesuits after their arrival in 1571. Not only religious instruction was given; philosophy, the humanities and studies of the local Nahuatl language formed part of the Jesuit instruction. The religious orders also built hospitals.

The population of the city rose to nearly 70,000 at the beginning of the 18th century, but had fallen to 55,000 by its end.

Many of the city's mansions built in the 18th century were decorated with tiles and with wrought iron, another form of artistic embellishment for which the city became famous. It was used especially on balconies, of which those at the corners of buildings are the most notable. Another early 18th century decorative development in Puebla was in the use of stucco, first seen in the vaults of San Ildefonso Church. Its use spread throughout New Spain. In Puebla, it reached its highest expression in the Rosario Chapel of the Church of Santo Domingo.

Silversmiths, potters, painters and furniture-makers produced fine works for religious and secular use in the eighteenth century. However, with the coming of neoclassicism at the very end of the century, much of the glory of the baroque church interiors was destroyed.

Destruction continued into the next century. The rate of development of the city slowed as Puebla suffered from economic ills and political and military upheaval. One of its finest moments

came when troops of the Mexican army withstood the assault on Forts Loreto and Guadalupe by the invading French forces at Puebla, defeating them on the May 5, 1862. It was the first defeat of the forces of Napoleon III anywhere in the world. President Juarez decreed that Puebla should incorporate the name of the General who led the defence and thus was born Puebla de Zaragoza.

Under the Republic, convents and monasteries were disbanded and the buildings converted to public use. Gradually however, new parks and streets were built, and the city grew beyond its colonial boundaries. The area tripled, the city spread in all directions and the population has now reached one million.

The historic center of Puebla covers nearly 4.5 square miles (7 sq km) and corresponds to the city center of the 16th to 18th centuries. The area includes a buffer zone which contains many buildings of historical value, but the great concentration of culturally and historically important structures lies within a zone of just under 4 square miles (6 sq km). The basic pattern of the first settlement can still be seen. In all there are 2,619 buildings in 391 blocks which are listed as of historic importance.

Within the central zone, educational institutions, museums with collections of Pueblan arts, the theater said to be the first in America built in the shape of a horseshoe, the 16th century House of the Dean with its beautiful murals - the oldest civil colonial paintings on the American continent - and the splendid Palafox Library are among the treasures on view. The library is housed in the Tridentine School and was created with a donation made in 1773 by the Bishop of Puebla and former Viceroy of New Spain, Juan de Palafox y Mendoza. It houses 40,000 volumes dealing with theology, philosophy and ancient languages and is the most important library of its type in Latin America.

The city center was inscribed on the World Heritage List in 1987, as an outstanding example of all stages of cultural and historical development in Mexico over four centuries; from colony to independent nation, through reform and revolution.

Puebla is some 78 miles (125 km) and two hours' drive by autopista from Mexico City. Long-distance buses serve the city from many directions. It is 187 miles (301 km) from Veracruz. The city has an airport.

# ZACATECAS

PREVIOUS PAGE   *A view of the Cathedral of Zacatecas*
ABOVE   *Street scene in Zacatecas*
OPPOSITE   *The Guadalupe Museum*

ZACATECAS LIES ON THE SIERRA MADRE OCCIDENTAL, 7,920 feet (2,400 m) above sea level and over 600 miles (960 km) from Mexico City. Both Guanajuato and Zacatecas were the result of the frenetic search by Spaniards for the fabled riches of their newly-conquered land.

In 1546 an Indian showed Captain Juan de Tolosa a piece of rock which proved to contain traces of silver. Told that it had come from up north, Tolosa led a small group which included the Ibarra brothers, Diego and Miguel, to a deep ravine carved out by a small stream. At its head rose a rocky eminence composed of rhyolite quartz, green in color, which he named La Bufa.

Having confirmed the presence of silver, the men set about extracting as much of the metal as they could. They built rough shelters as protection against the intense winter. Warnings of attacks by resentful Chichimec Indians sent many of these prospectors back home.

Tolosa persuaded them to return, more permanent houses were built and the settlement began to grow. Zacatecas was officially founded in January 1548.

Like Guanajuato, the town did not develop on the classic grid pattern but followed the natural contours at the bottom of the ravine. Dwellings were erected along narrow, winding and often precipitous streets which gave access to the mines in the northern part of the valley. The city is surrounded by sparsely wooded mountains which are covered with cacti of different varieties. In the rainy season the water washes off the almost sheer rock faces and rushes down the narrow waterway. This created havoc for the early settlers. In the dry winter, water was often scarce and new houses soon incorporated a tank or cistern.

To support the growing population of miners, haciendas were established for agricultural production. Colonies of Indians were re-settled from the center of New Spain. Africans, mestizos and mulattos also provided labor for the mines and for agriculture. From 1550, herds of cattle began to appear on the surrounding plains and Zacatecas became the economic center of the region. Forts, haciendas and villages provided a system of defence and of supply.

By 1550 there were thirty-four mines in operation. Refineries with attendant buildings took up most of the space along the streams which ran through the town. Houses also grew up along the tracks which connected the refineries with the mines. In 1588 the town became a city.

Zacatecas, together with Potosí in the Viceroyalty of Peru (another World Heritage site), stimulated the economy of the New World and enriched the Spanish Treasury. It was for a time the greatest producer of silver in the world. The first large mine, San Bernabé, was so productive that it is said to have created the age of silver in Mexico - centuries of riches which nourished and sustained Spain's global empire. Before the Zacatecas mint was built, silver was processed in refineries or in smelters, and converted into bars or ingots. From there it was sent to the mint in Mexico City or to Veracruz, where it was taken aboard royal galleons for carriage to Spain. The system changed after 1683 when Mexico, by law, could export only minted coins - mostly the famous 'pieces of eight'.

Zacatecas retained its place at the head of the Mexican mining industry for almost two hundred years. It produced silver worth an average of two million pesos a year. In 1732 there were twenty five amalgamation refineries and twenty smelting furnaces in production. Soon after many were flooded and abandoned, and by 1767 only five refineries and two furnaces were in operation. The fortunes of Zacatecas were restored by the actions of José de la Borda, who demonstrated how abandoned mines could be brought back into production.

Communications were extremely important to Zacatecas, particularly those with Mexico City. The 'silver road' was built which also linked Guanajuato to the capital. Originally it was a narrow path, rough and stony, so difficult that travelers called it 'the road to hell'. It carried missionaries, explorers, mule drivers, troops and caravans of traders from Veracruz and Acapulco. By 1630 it carried more than 60% of all the silver exported from New Spain. During the 17th century the road was continued north from Zacatecas over mountains and desert as far as Santa Fé in present-day New Mexico. Goods were carried on the backs of mules or in wagons, the most important of these being mercury for the amalgamation process. This was particularly difficult to transport and was generally carried in sheepskin bags, placed in wooden frames set on wagons.

The church accompanied the early settlers to Zacatecas. Conversion of the native peoples went hand-in-hand with exploitation of the new territory, and the town was regarded as the frontier of the un-Christianized lands. The first chapel was built in Zacatecas in 1549, quickly followed by one constructed at the foot of La Bufa, where later parish churches and finally the cathedral were sited. This became the focal-point of the settlement, and a plaza laid out on each side allowed for commercial activities and the establishment of a market place.

The first of the religious orders to establish themselves during the sixty years after the foundation of Zacatecas were the Franciscans. By 1600, seventeen Franciscan monasteries had been built in the region and Zacatecas was raised to the level of a province, an acknowledgment of the Franciscans' contribution to the pacification of the Chichimec.

The Augustinians were the next to arrive, followed by the Jesuits, the Dominicans and the Juaninos, or members of the Order of Saint John of God, who devoted themselves to the care of the sick. The last to arrive, in 1702, were the members of the Order of Merced.

Mining changed the life of the church in Mexico. Through its tithe and generous donations, it received much of the wealth extracted from the mines. This was employed in the construction of ecclesiastical buildings and in their decoration. Some of the country's

most famous churches could be found where the silver mines were the richest. Such a building is the Cathedral of Zacatecas.

Built as the parish church from 1612, it was largely reconstructed in the 18th century and raised to the status of a cathedral in 1864. With its carved pink sandstone facade, some regard it as a masterpiece of Mexican Churrigueresque. The stone's fine grain lends itself to carving. Above the door, standing in niches, are life-size figures of Christ and the Apostles. The design incorporates both Indian and Christian motifs: there are plants, flowers and acanthus leaves. A large rose-window is surrounded by sculptures of angels and cherubs. The richly decorated interior of former days, when adornments in silver and gold filled the space, has been replaced by a much simpler design. The riches fell victim to the plundering of the turbulent years after Independence.

Among the fourteen other religious buildings of historical importance within the 264 acre (110 ha) heritage site are the mostly 17th and 18th century churches, convents and monasteries bearing the names of the orders which established them: San Francisco, San Agustin, Santo Domingo and San Juan de Dios. San Agustin is considered one of the most beautiful baroque churches in Northern Mexico. The church of Santo Domingo was taken over by the Dominicans after the expulsion of the Jesuits in 1767, and contains gilded Churrigueresque retables. Its quiet baroque exterior contrasts with the more flamboyant style of the former Jesuit College of San Luis Gonzaga which stands beside it. This is now the Pedro Coronel Museum and it contains, among other exhibits, a library made up of the collections of all the former religious houses. The former convent of San Francisco, once one of the most important monasteries in the region, has also been converted to a museum.

In the city there are 456 buildings of historical importance among which are several secular examples. The Mala Noche Palace, built in the 18th century, is now the Palace of Justice; the Calderon Theater dates from 1834 and the Gonzalez Market from 1886, while the former Governor's Residence (now the Francisco Goitia Museum) was constructed of the local pink stone early this century. Many examples of houses built for ordinary citizens and dating from the 17th century are visible along the steep lanes.

Although Zacatecas surrendered its place as premier silver producer to Guanajuato in the 18th century it remained important because of the continued working of its mint. The struggle for Independence touched Zacatecas deeply and led to the suspension of production. Interruptions during the 1910 Revolution, including the major battle of 1914, had the same effect. Decline continued throughout the 20th century as the city settled down to a more routine existence.

This city, once of such great importance to the economic power of Spain, has retained its original pattern of streets and many of its early buildings. It was inscribed on the World Heritage List in 1993 as an outstandingly well-preserved example of an early settlement of New Spain, developing through all its stages.

First-class bus services are frequent between Mexico City and Zacatecas, and from Guadalajara, Aguascalientes and Durango. The main railway line between Mexico City and Ciudad Juarez on the Mexico-United States border passes through Zacatecas. There is an airport at Zacatecas which receives frequent flights from Mexico City.

# EL TAJIN

## PRE-HISPANIC CITY

THE ARCHITECTURE OF EL TAJIN, an ancient ruined city in the northern region of Veracruz State, displays a tropical vivacity in contrast to the highland austerity of Teotihuacán and Monte Albán, also Mexican World Heritage sites.

El Tajín archaeological site is in the foothills of the Sierra Panteca, at the western edge of the coastal plain. It lies in a steep-sided valley at the headwaters of a tributary of the Tecolutla River, which flows east into the Gulf of Mexico some 25 miles (40 km) away. It is surrounded by humid tropical rain forest. The town of Papantla is some 5 miles (8 km) to the north east in the center of some rich oil fields. The land is fertile; maize, cocoa, tobacco, vanilla and honey are still produced here.

El Tajín is a Totonac name for thunder. This reflects the belief that the god of the thunderstorm once inhabited this, the largest and most important ancient city in northeastern Mesoamerica. It is not certain however, whether this was the name used by those who built the city. The basis for El Tajín's emergence as a political and economic unit larger than those already in existence, was most likely its status as a religious center. Its location between two streams enabled it to dominate the rich plains nearby and to control trade through the area. At its most powerful, it dominated a vast area of the coastal and highland regions. It was sustained economically by the receipt of tribute in the form of goods and services. It also developed as a center of architecture, engineering and art, and was the most important site amongst those which developed a distinct artistic tradition known now as 'Classic Veracruz', one that differs from other Mexican styles.

Recent research has shown that El Tajín enjoyed only a relatively brief flourishing - from AD 800 to 1200 - after the abandonment of Teotihuacán in the central highlands. Opinions differ concerning the influence these two great cities exerted on each other, but it is certain there was a strong connection between them.

The nucleus of El Tajín covers an area of 146 acres (60 ha), but associated sites occur over some 2,000 acres (830 ha). Mounds were constructed to provide level surfaces on sloping ground and walls were built to define certain areas. The location of El Tajín's buildings is a testimony to social stratification: the higher the elevation the more important the occupant. Outside the ceremonial center are traces of four or five 'suburban' areas with housing, workshops and terraces where intensive agriculture was practiced. Beyond was the open country on which mainly maize and beans were extensively cultivated.

The buildings in the ceremonial center were constructed of local sandstone which stands out against the background of hills covered with green vegetation. Those built in the earliest phase were aligned slightly east of north - common in many Mesoamerican centers built between the 4th and 10th centuries. Later groupings in the city's expansion northward were aligned northeast, while the final phase saw apparently haphazard placement of buildings wherever space could be found in the difficult and uneven topography. These buildings fall into the tradition of temple, palace (or elite residence) and ball court.

El Tajín follows the general pattern of most Mesoamerican ceremonial centers of the Classic and post-Classic eras, where groups of monumental buildings are arranged around courtyards or plazas. Its distinction lies in the style of its architecture and decoration, and in particular to its use of the niche. Almost all buildings were stuccoed and then painted in red or blue monochrome or polychrome, depending on the function and period. Low relief sculpture, in a style distinctive to El Tajín, appeared on columns, the walls of ball courts and in religious sanctuaries where ritual scenes were depicted. Polychrome paintings with religious themes showed mythical beings representing deities in the pantheon of El Tajín. Examples of mural painting are regrettably few but those which survive display a pure technique in drawing and the handling of color.

The Central Zone (referred to also as 'Tajín') is on the floor of the valley. Around the rectangular central plaza, monumental buildings are set in pyramid form, the most remarkable and impressive being the Pyramid of the Niches from the final phase of construction. Ceremonial and market plazas are also found here, along with the bulk of the ball courts, both decorated and plain. This was the center of both religious and commercial life and the focus of much of the sculpture.

The Pyramid of the Niches was originally faced with stucco and painted a glorious red. Although only 60 feet (18 m) high and 120 feet (36 m) square, it is a building of beautiful symmetry. It rises in six tiers over a similar, earlier structure and is faced with carved stone blocks. A single staircase rises to a temple, which has balustrades at each side decorated with a step-and-fret motif. Its basic talud-tablero style is modified by the introduction of 365 square niches capped by 'flying' cornices, one for each day of the year. The resultant play of shadow and light lends a degree of tension and drama to this unique structure. The Pyramid has now undergone extensive restoration, while the on-site museum displays murals and friezes from the temple.

Tajín Chico is a huge complex some 1,000 feet (300 m) from the Central Zone. It is built on an artificial terrace measuring 1,000 by 5,000 feet (300 by 1,500 m) and 23 feet (7 m) high. A multi-storied residential palace and administrative buildings for the city's elite dominate the area. Walls separate higher functionaries from lower, and both from the rest of the population. Tunnels providing access to buildings have also been excavated. The buildings were highly decorated with stucco designs and murals of some complexity, as were the surrounding colonnaded buildings and temples.

Innovative techniques were employed for construction, especially in the use of cement. Asphalt was applied to surfaces to render them waterproof, and there is evidence of arched ceilings in Tajín Chico's later buildings. The cement contained sea shells, sand and pumice powder (pozzolana); pottery fragments provided bonding material.

Especially noteworthy is Building A, the most richly decorated of Tajín Chico's structures. Its friezes and vertical bands of sculptures in relief are particularly striking. The building features four smaller buildings, one at each of its corners - an unusual feature in pre-Hispanic architecture.

Building B provides an example of the construction techniques applied to the generally flat roofs of the complex. It is a medium-sized building and the single slab which covered it was 39 inches (1 m) thick and utilized 16,500 cubic feet (350 cubic meters) of concrete.

Above Tajín Chico, on an 'acropolis', is the Group of the Columns named from the magnificent pillars supporting the portico of the Building of the Columns. It also includes an associated Annex in pyramid form, and a large, irregularly-shaped plaza. It is the largest architectural complex of the city and is associated with the dynamic 'Rabbit 13', an incarnation of Quetzalcóatl, who ruled at the city's zenith.

The Building of the Columns dominated the city from all directions. There were originally five or six columns more than 10 feet (3 m) high, formed of limestone blocks shaped to a circle and stacked one on the other. Carvings in low relief showing the ceremonial life of the city were created with the stones in place; only about half of them survive. One shows warriors bringing captives before their ruler, while a disembowelled victim lies at his feet. Writing appears in the sculpture, but there is no evidence that systems as sophisticated as those developed by the Zapotecs or Maya were used at El Tajín.

At least seventeen ball courts have been located at El Tajín, in contrast with other Mesoamerican sites, some of which have only one. Some scholars note an obsession here with the ball game and its elevation to cult status; manifested by the number of courts and the magnificence of the sculptures associated with them, especially the six found in the South Ball Court. These panels depict the mythology and rituals associated with the game; the figure of the God of Death watching the scenes, a player being dressed and armed for war at the same time, part of the game itself, and the apparent sacrifice of the captain of the losing team using a flint knife. Other panels depict the importance of the sacred pulque, an intoxicating drink made from the maguey plant. Others panels in the Central Ball Court depict Tlaloc, Quetzalcóatl and other zoo-anthropomorphic divine beings.

It is not certain exactly why the sacred game was played - except that it was more ritual than sport - or what determined its completion. It was played with a solid rubber ball weighing up to three pounds (1.5 kg) which would indicate that it had its origin in an area where rubber grows naturally. It is possible that the Olmecs, whose cultural influence was exerted more than 1,000 years before El Tajín was constructed, were its originators. The search for a full explanation of the game continues.

This ancient city, with its aura of splendor, was abandoned in the 13th century when the forces of Mexico-Tenochtitlan overran and took control of the area. The Totonac people now preside over ruins which lay undisturbed for 500 years, reminders of the most important ceremonial center in north eastern Mesoamerica after the fall of Teotihuacán. El Tajín was inscribed on the World Heritage List in 1992 as a unique testimony to the architectural and cultural heritage of a vanished civilization.

Poza Rica can be reached by air from Mexico City. Long-distance buses serve Poza Rica from several directions. There is a local bus service to the El Tajín Archaeological Site entrance. Long-distance buses also serve Papantla from many locations. Local buses take passengers to the entrance road of the archaeological site and run more frequently than those from Poza Rica. Drivers can take Federal Highway 180, which follows the coast from Veracruz to Nautla via Cardel, and then to Poza Rica; or Highway 129 between Teziutlán to Nautla. From Poza Rica take the State Highway which leads to San Andrés. There are signs in Poza Rica indicating the way to the Archaeological Site.

# MORELIA

M ORELIA IS THE CAPITAL OF MICHOACAN STATE in the beautiful western Sierra Madre region. Originally named Valladolid by the Spaniards, it is set on a hill in the Guayangareo Valley, itself formed by a volcanic eruption, and at an altitude of 6,440 feet (1,951 m). The climate is pleasant and the soil rich.

At the time of the arrival of the Spanish conquistadors the area was occupied by the Tarascan people, agriculturalists and makers of fine pottery. Soon after word of the fall of Tenochtitlan reached them, Spaniards were seen in their territory. The first real disturbance to the established order occurred in July 1522, when Cristobal de Olid, at the head of a considerable force, pushed into the region and proceeded to sack the Tarascan capital Tzintsuntzan. After withstanding nine months of destruction the young Tarascan leader went to Tenochtitlan to deliver up quantities of gold and silver. Cortés ordered his troops to leave the area. Soon after though, he decided that the population should submit to the encomienda system; by which the conquering Spaniards were rewarded with land and control over the Indians living on it, and received tribute from them in return for ensuring their conversion to Christianity. There was resistance from the Tarascans, but in February 1530 their supreme leader was put to death, and the struggle of his people against the imposition of the encomienda system came to an end.

The church - initially in the guise of the Franciscans - had followed the army, and on a rather flat and elongated hill in the Guayangareo Valley, Fray Juan de San Miguel built a small chapel. The

OPPOSITE *Mural by Alfredo Zalce, Gobierno Palace*
ABOVE *Cathedral*

building of a monastery commenced in 1537, the year before the first bishop of Michoacán, Vasco de Quiroga, took up his position. It was on the same small hill that, on the orders of Antonio de Mendoza - the first Spanish Viceroy of New Spain - the city of Valladolid de Michoacán was founded on the May 18, 1541.

The Guayangareo Valley is surrounded by hills including Santeaguito and Santa María de la Asunción. Close by were the quarries where a distinctive pink stone, used for much of the city's construction, was extracted.

Members of sixty Spanish families - often referred to as 'noble' in later accounts - founded Valladolid. The settlement grew very slowly despite Charles V's bestowal on it of the rank of city in 1545. However, when civil powers were transferred from Patzcauro in 1579, and also from the episcopal See in 1580, Valladolid's future was assured. Growth in the region may have been affected by the appalling decline in the Indian population of New Spain. In the first century after the conquest an estimated four-fifths of that population is said to have died from introduced disease, war, intolerable working conditions, starvation, suicide and the effects of volcanic disturbances.

Early in the next century some one thousand Indians were selected from many parts of Michoacán to assist the growth of this,

ABOVE  *College of San Nicholas*

the only formally-designated 'city' in the state at that time. The seventeenth century was one of slow but steady growth. This was due in large part to the continuing benefits obtained from growing food for the mining populations to the north.

The first stone of the cathedral, widely regarded as the finest building among the many architectural treasures in Morelia, was laid in 1640. It is flanked by gardens and stands beside the main plaza at the highest point of the city, facing onto a long boulevard. Begun by Bishop Marcos Ramirez de Prado, it was not completed until the 1740s and, considering the length of time it was under construction, retains an amazing unity of style. This would seem to indicate that the original plans, drawn by Vicente Barroso de la Escayola, were largely followed throughout. Unaffected by the severe classic and the florid baroque, it remains pure plateresque, a name derived from the designs used by those who worked in silver, although the style had by then been superseded in other parts of Mexico. The building's proportions are magnificent, particularly those of the towers. Its lines are delicate and the pinkish stone gives it a warmth that makes it glow.

The facade contains three doors, corresponding to the three naves of the interior. The low relief decoration is continued to the towers, which soar 203 feet (62 m) from massive plain bases. The preference for low relief is reflected in the lack of external columns, although there are 200 pilasters.

Educational and civic buildings, as well as colonial residences built in the 17th century add to the impression of a dignified city. There has however, been considerable reconstruction and alteration made to significant buildings over the centuries; the church of San Francisco, begun in 1541 but not completed until 1610 was greatly modified to allow new construction work.

Morelia is famous for its churches. Those built in the baroque style in the 18th century include San José Capuchinas, with its very tall tower; the Iglesia de las Rosas, with its fine plateresque-inspired stone carving; and La Merced. The monastery of San Diego was also built at this time. The Santuario de Guadalupe, across the city, has an interior decorated in the Moorish style and every surface is brilliantly ornamented.

By the middle of the 18th century Valladolid contained some of the finest buildings in all America. The population was only twelve thousand, ten thousand of whom were the Indians largely responsible for the city's construction. It was a city whose functions had been solely administrative, ecclesiastical and educational. Industries increased rapidly in number, and development of all kinds was encouraged by the increasing production of gold, silver and copper in the Sierra Madre mountains.

Civil architecture also flourished in the 18th century. The Casas Reales (today the Court of Justice), the former Tobacco Factory (now the Town Hall) and the Alhondiga, a public granary, are all examples of the buildings of the time. Luxurious mansions were built in great numbers, one of which is the present Michoacán Museum

A devastating drought in 1785 caused immense suffering throughout Michoacán. In October of that year Archbishop Antonio de San Miguel stimulated the provision of funds sufficient to finance the rebuilding of the city's aqueduct and the paving of its streets, in order to provide work and sustenance for the population. The aqueduct supplied the city with water from springs in the hills and its 253 arches extended over a mile. Today it runs almost into Valladolid's heart and remains a feature of the city.

Valladolid did not escape the turbulence of the struggle for independence which began in earnest in 1810, and in which one of its most famous sons played so large a part. José María Morelos y Pavón was born in Valladolid in 1765, baptized in the cathedral and educated in the city whose name was changed in his honor to Morelia in 1828. Further political struggles caused considerable destruction, but they also produced other heroes, like Augustín de Iturbide, one of the architects of the Plan of Iguala - which finally delivered independence to Mexico - who then declared himself Emperor. Morelia however, continued to develop steadily throughout the 19th and into the 20th century.

Morelia today is a city of nearly half a million people. The 16th century layout of streets is still intact and implies the Renaissance love for order and large open spaces. The orderliness never degenerates into boredom and the streets which spill over the sides of the hill follow the contours of the landscape.

The main plaza sits at the top of the hill surrounded by the main administrative buildings, with the Cathedral at the center. There is a harmony between building and landscape, enhanced by the fact that all buildings are constructed of the pink-brown local stone.

This beautiful material, in the hands of expert craftsmen, allows a lightness of effect in the solution of architectural problems. Bell-towers were made to look more slender by building them open on all sides: a square tower here often has eight and not four openings. Such towers can be seen on the churches of La Compania, Guadalupe, Las Capuchinas, Las Monjas and San Augustín. Gables and pediments atop facades emphasize their vertical nature.

Other buildings show particular aspects of the builders' art: the refinement of the doorways on the main plaza's western side, the main patio of the Michoacán Museum, the arches of the mirador at the former Dominican convent of Las Rosas and the geometric perfection of the domes of many of Morelia's churches, are notable.

Even more remarkable is the treatment of many arches which could be expected to end in corner columns, but in fact find support in the walls. A minimum of support provides a maximum of covered space.

This Spanish colonial city's most striking characteristic is its appearance of architectural harmony, as if it had been built within a period of a very few years. Only after more careful examination can the mixture of many styles be seen.

This city of culture contains a total of 249 historical monuments of which 41, including 20 churches and the cathedral, are deemed of special importance. In 1991 Morelia was inscribed on the World Heritage List as an outstanding example of a Spanish Colonial architectural ensemble.

Morelia is 151 miles (242 km) by road west of Mexico City, a drive of about four hours. There is an air service from Mexico City.

# GUANAJUATO

## CITY AND ITS MINING AREA

Tucked away in a deep, narrow valley at an altitude of 6,836 feet (2,084 m), is the Spanish Colonial city of Guanajuato. From vantage points in the surrounding hills, a magnificent vista unfolds as buildings fill the valley floor and spread up its steep sides along narrow, twisting streets and an occasional small plaza. Running through these hills are not only underground passages serving as roads, but miles of mining tunnels.

'Guanajuato', the Spanish version of the Tarascan name 'Cuanaxhuata' or 'Hill of Frogs', exists because of the silver discovered almost half a millennium ago in this area of mountains, canyons, narrow passes and mile-high plains formed of rich volcanic soil.

After the conquest, Spaniards sought all over their new territory for the riches they had been told existed and for which they had undertaken the hazardous journey to the New World. Cortés said that he and his followers suffered from a disease of the heart 'which can be cured only by gold'.

Apart from the golden artifacts of the conquered peoples, they found little, but after twenty years of searching they discovered the next best thing - silver. The Crown, wishing to reap the benefit of the hidden riches of its new land, gave freedom to Spanish subjects to prospect and extract whatever they might find. The subsequent silver produced by her American mines enabled Spain to achieve a pre-eminent economic position in Europe. It was the crucial factor in trans-Atlantic trade and affected the commerce of the whole known world.

The restless quest for wealth of any kind had taken the conquistadors beyond the settled lands of the Aztecs and their allies. Spaniards started to move north soon after the taking of Tenochtitlan and began to settle in the area in 1529. In 1548 rich outcrops of silver - from the San Bernabé vein - were discovered by accident near the Hill of Frogs and led to the discovery of other deposits; of Rayas in 1550, Mellado in 1558 and the fabulous Veta Madre (Mother Lode) in 1558.

To protect the eager prospectors (and the silver they might produce) from raids by the nomadic Chichimec people resentful of the incursions onto their hunting lands, troops were despatched and fortifications - or encampments - were built: Santiago at Marfil, Tepetapa (now a suburb of Guanajuato), Santa Ana (today a village) and Santa Fé on the slopes of Cerro del Cuarto. Santa Ana was intended to be the principal fort, but it was that of Santa Fé which prospered most and formed the nucleus of the future city. The year 1554 is held to be the date of foundation of the city which was to become the richest in New Spain.

By the 17th century Santa Fé had 4,000 inhabitants, and with each new discovery the population rose. The large Cata mine was in production by 1618. In 1679 Charles II bestowed the title of 'town' on the settlement and land was released for the formation of a town square, today's Plaza de la Paz.

The population reached 16,000 at the beginning of the 18th century. In 1741 the status of a city was granted to the Villa de Santa Fé y Real de Minas de Guanajuato, and in 1790 the inhabitants numbered some 50,000.

Indians and mestizos supplied the basic labor of the mines and lived on the fringes of the settlement. Africans, slave or free (first introduced to New Spain by Cortés), generally worked in the refineries above ground.

Almost all silver deposits in Mexico had been formed at altitudes between 6,000 and 8,000 feet (1,860 and 2,480 m). After surface deposits were exhausted, the cost of mining often became prohibitive, especially when deeper workings were flooded. Production would then cease and new deposits were sought. More efficient means were devised for working the mines when rationalization of mining practices occurred. By the late 18th century,

partners were contributing funds to finance operations which included the sinking of deep shafts.

Technological improvements accompanied such changes and continued to be introduced, spreading throughout the mining regions beyond Guanajuato. Pumps to extract water from the workings and whims - hoists driven by mules for lifting ore to the surface - were early developments. Blasting came later and provided a great impetus to production. The ore was processed near the mines by either smelting or the technique of amalgamation with mercury generally in use by the 1570s. The latter method was particularly appropriate to the largely low-grade Mexican ores. Most mercury was supplied from Spain and a check could be kept on the amount of refined silver delivered for payment of royalties, set originally at a fifth of the value and later reduced to a tenth.

Silver output was high between 1580 and 1640, but then greater technological needs required huge investment. Mercury was also in short supply. Recovery began early in the 18th century, though by the 1760s several of the great mines were flooded and had virtually ceased production. However a new mine, La Valenciana, located along the Veta Madre between the Mellado and Rayas mines where the lode was believed to peter out, had its first bonanza in 1771 and was largely responsible for making Guanajuato the richest city in America. Baron Alexander de Humboldt reported that Guanajuato delivered 20,986,500 pesos worth of silver into the Treasury between 1785 and 1789.

Developed from about 1760 by Antonio de Obregon y Alcocer and operated on new financial principles, La Valenciana employed 3,000 men underground. Between 1780 and 1810, when the struggle for independence halted operations, it produced 60 to 70 per cent of Guanajuato's total output. Three vertical shafts were sunk to allow easier extraction of ore. Then in 1800, another was begun and had reached an astonishing 1,800 feet (545 m) by 1810. The name Boca del Infierno (literally 'Hell's Mouth') referred to the distinct increase in temperature as shaft depths grew.

The symbiotic relationship between the mines and the town continued until the 19th century. As the mines were developed, the scattered settlements around the valley grew closer together as suitable building sites were sought in the difficult terrain. Guanajuato is one colonial town which is not laid out in a grid pattern.

The increasing prosperity of Guanajuato stimulated agricultural production and livestock-raising on the rich plains of the Bajío and in the drier northern regions. Thousands of mules were needed to work the mines and refineries, and the provision of the animals and their fodder stimulated employment. The leather industry prospered. There were also adverse effects, such as extensive logging to procure timber for use in mine shafts and galleries, and for fuel, particularly in smelters.

When production at the mines at Potosí in present-day Bolivia, declined in the 18th century, as it had at near by Zacatecas, Guanajuato became the world's largest source of silver. The wealth generated by mining brought noble titles to mine owners, who sought, and gained, further respect by making generous donations for religious works; prompting the construction of churches literally above the sources of their riches. Baroque churches at Cata, Mellado and La Valenciana mines are examples of such offerings of thanks. The church generally benefitted also from the collection of the tithe.

Some of the most beautiful baroque buildings in the New World are found in and around Guanajuato. Among the churches built in the elaborate Mexican style (also known as churrigueresque) are two masterpieces: La Compañía and San Cayetano. The church of Compañía de Jesus, begun by the Jesuits in 1745 and completed in 1765, is in the center of the city. Built on grand lines, it contained three naves, a tower and a dome (which caved in during 1808). The inverted pyramid column (estípite) was introduced to Guanajuato architecture here. This building, like most others of the period, was much modified over the intervening two centuries.

OPPOSITE  *Spanish colonial architecture*

San Cayetano, at La Valenciana mine, overlooks the city from a hill high above. Contributions from the mine owners and workers paid for the building of the church between 1765 and 1788. Built in churrigueresque style, with a refined pink stone facade, it was mythologized to have been built with mortar containing silver mixed with famous Spanish wines. It continued the style introduced in the building of La Compañía, expanding it with exuberance. The statues of the Trinity over the entrance are surrounded by rococo ornamentation. Estípite columns and pilasters support figures set in niches, while carvings of floral motifs and 'a fear of space' leave an impression of a dense network of foliage, human figures and divine personages. The resplendent interior contains three magnificent gilded wooden altars and the only examples in the mining area of original retables (altar screens containing paintings) in situ. Large sums were offered to allow the removal and rebuilding of San Cayetano when the rumor spread that it stood on a rich mineral deposit; the offer was declined. Blasting underground after the mine re-opened in 1883 has had an effect somewhat worse than removal might have had.

In a central position in town is the former parish church of San Francisco, built between 1671 and 1696 as the Church of San Juan de Dios and now elevated to be the Minor Basilica of Our Lady of Guanajuato. Its baroque exterior contains a neoclassical interior which houses the image of the Virgin of Guanajuato, presented in 1557 to the city by Philip II of Spain. This statue had spent eight centuries hidden in a cave near Granada to save it from desecration by the Moors.

Other civic buildings of note are the former residences of mine owners and those raised to prominence by their good fortune. The 17th century manor house of the Marquis de San Juan de Rayas is now the Guanajuato Museum (Museo del Pueblo de Guanajuato). It is the oldest mansion in the central part of the city and its 18th century chapel is unique of its type although its beautiful gilded retable was sold to the United States in the 1920s. The grand neoclassical Casa Rul, built of pink stone by the famous architect Tresguerras, now houses the Superior Court of Justice.

The owners of the Cata and Mellado mines also built imposing houses in town and at the mine sites. The Casa Mina at La Valenciana was completed in 1788, and served as a residence as well as the administrative center of the mine. A group of houses of a different kind is the 18th century Dos Pares de Casas owned originally by the Countess of Valenciana and still standing in the city. Built at the end of the 18th century and spanning the movement from baroque to neoclassicism, is the house of Manuel Doblado, the present Quijote Iconographic Museum.

The Guanajuato of today includes many 19th century neoclassical buildings, constructed where baroque buildings had formerly stood. Silver is still mined in the valley of Guanajuato, as is gold, which began to be extracted in small amounts in the 1660s. The period of the city's greatest importance and influence, however, ended at the beginning of the 19th century.

This city is a treasure-house in the economic history of Mexico and of the world. The World Heritage listing of 1988 covers the historic monuments of Guanajuato and the adjacent mines.

A train service operates to Guanajuato from Mexico City, but the best means of access is by an excellent bus service. Guanajuato is 269 miles (432 km) north-east of Mexico City and 928 miles (1493 km) from Ciudad Juarez by road. There are airports at Leon and Queretero.

# POPOCATEPETL
## 16TH CENTURY MONASTERIES

Perpetually snow-capped, the volcano of Popocatépetl, at 17,883 feet (5,452 m), is the second-highest of all Mexico's peaks. Part of the Sierra Nevada system, it is some 40 miles (65 km) south-east of Mexico City and 12.5 miles (20 km) east of Puebla. To its north lies Iztaccihuatl 17,444 feet (5,286 m), the third highest volcanic peak in the country. Cortés made his way through the pass which bears his name, between the two volcanoes, on his historic journey from the coast near Veracruz to conquer the Aztec capital Tenochtitlan.

Cortés had urged the need for the conversion of Mexican Indians. When the Aztec forces in the Mexico Basin had been contained, Carlos V ordered the instruction of the people in the Christian doctrine. Cortés favored members of mendicant rather than secular orders. The King agreed, and in 1523 three Franciscans were the first of the new 'troops' to arrive. They were followed in 1524 by twelve more. Twelve Dominicans arrived in 1526 to help in the task, but were quickly reduced to only three, and it took them some time to begin their missionary activities. Meanwhile five Augustinians arrived in 1533, and within six years their number had grown to between thirty and forty.

The achievements of this small band of men were astonishing. All believed in the Millennial philosophy that only by the conversion of all the native peoples would the Second Coming of Christ be made possible; and between 1525 and 1570 they directed the building of more than a hundred monasteries in the region. By the end of the century over three hundred had been established.

The Franciscans chose Cuernavaca as their first center, establishing themselves there in 1525, in a monastery designed and built by Francisco Becerra. The Dominicans selected Oaxtepec in 1528 and the Augustinians began their labors at Ocuituco in 1534. Relations between the different orders were harmonious as each consolidated its own sphere of influence. Contact was maintained between their settlements by routes such as that linking the Dominicans at Hueyapan and the Franciscans at Tochimilco.

While very many more monasteries and churches were built and survive, fourteen of the earliest built, all on the slopes of Popocatépetl, have been chosen for World Heritage listing as representative of them all.

In 1529 the Franciscans began constructing their first monastery on the eastern slopes of Popocatépetl at Huejotzingo. Because of the hostility of the local people, the Dominicans found great difficulty in establishing themselves at Tepoztlan in the Tepozteco valley to the south of Mexico City, and it was only in 1560 that they were successful there. Meanwhile they turned their attention from Oaxtepec southward towards Oaxaca and founded monasteries at Tetela del Volcan and at Hueyapan.

The Augustinians took the middle ground and built the greatest number of monasteries in the region. From Ocuituco, they branched out to Totolapan and Yecapixtla (to the east of Tepoztlan) and Atlatlauhcan, Zacualpan and Tlayacapan towards the 'hot lands' in the south.

These earliest structures have been termed 'fortress' monasteries because of their obvious defensive capabilities. The term 'monastery' here refers to the groups of buildings where people lived and worked and which were contained within perimeter walls.

All the monasteries contained a number of basic common elements which were built in sequence. First came the walls of the atrium, the open chapel and the posas chapels. The nave of the church was next, followed by the ancillary buildings and finally other additions such as an extra courtyard, upper stories to the monastic buildings, towers and side chapels. The core elements were the atrium, the church and the monastic buildings.

The atrium was a large space open to the sky, usually rectangular and at ground level. Some atria were sunken and others raised, occasionally on earlier, pre-Hispanic structures. They served as an outer or entrance court, and were surrounded by colonnades or stone walls 7 to 17 feet (2 to 5 m) high. Access to the atrium was through two or three gateways.

The posas, small vaulted chapels, were built at the corners of the atrium. They were open on two sides to the atrium and were of many different styles. Some were elaborately finished with sculptured decoration while others were plastered and painted. The posas were connected around the walls by a processional way - a place where rituals were conducted during religious processions.

Open chapels, in which mass was celebrated, were built either just inside the church entrance, raised above the entrance, or built to stand independently of the church.

The outer approaches of the monastery featured a cross in the atrium set in line with the monastery entrance, niches to represent Stations of the Cross, and devices both mundane and decorative to assure a supply of water.

The church was always the centerpiece. The friars who built them had to rely on memory, and these early churches were built in the Gothic tradition, with some elements of Renaissance. They featured great buttresses, at least 33 feet (10 m) wide, reaching to the top of the building, and battlements along the roof. Towers were sometimes features. Windows were rare and set high.

The church's size assured its dominant position. It usually had a single barrel or rib-vaulted nave, but rarely transepts or domes. Chancels were usually raised 3 feet (1 m) above the level of the nave and some contained baptisteries and stone fonts.

The monastery was usually built to the south of the church to utilize its shade. The living and working quarters were set around a courtyard or patio, with cloister-like protection on all four sides and often at two levels. This was the center of life in the monastery for recreation and meetings. The ground floor buildings housed the refectory, kitchens and workshops; while the library and dormitories were ordinarily upstairs. Frescoes adorned most inner walls and depicted a wide variety of subjects. They are some of the most-prized features of the monasteries.

The friars were responsible for the construction of the first complexes. The labor of the Mexican Indians was vital in the construction of the many buildings which began to dot the countryside. The friars instructed the people in the useful arts of carpentry, masonry and sculpture, and also in silver and gold-smithing - some of which had been ancient arts of the local people. The blending of the Christian and the Indian elements in the decoration of the buildings makes them particularly interesting. The front facade of the church attracted the greatest decorative attention, and the Augustinians built the most highly-decorated of them all. All the monastery complexes were built in a highly earthquake-prone zone and have suffered damage.

RIGHT    *Monasterio De Atlatlahuacan, Estado De Morelos*

ABOVE   *Zacualpan Monastery*
RIGHT   *Monasterio De Yecapitxtla, Estado De Morelos*
OPPOSITE TOP   *Atlatlauhcan Monastery*
OPPOSITE BELOW   *Monasterio De Topoztlan, Estado De Morelos*

Two decisions made over the centuries had fundamental effects on the clergy. In 1567, following the Council of Trent, many of the monasteries were converted to parish churches and placed in the hands of the secular clergy, while in the Reform period of the 19th century many of the monastic buildings were turned to secular uses.

The churches, however, retained their original function and remained at the center of village life. Although many have post-16th century features, their furnishings remain largely intact and they have been maintained in good repair. Some have had considerable renovation work done on them - for example the building of new roofs.

Evangelizing fervor declined in Mexico as the mendicant orders were replaced by secular priests. However, the legacy of astonishing energy and dedication in the first period of Christianization of the indigenous peoples is forever preserved in these surviving monasteries of Popocatépetl, which were inscribed on the World Heritage List in 1994. The prototype established here accompanied colonizing and evangelizing efforts across Mexico and well into the southern regions of the United States, where they were built on a smaller scale and became known as 'missions'. This special type of architectural structure provided a center for the reorganization of a huge, heavily-populated territory, became the focus for new settlement and was a vehicle for the introduction of new social and cultural concepts.

All of the monasteries are accessible from Mexico City. Cuernavaca is 53 miles (84 km) south of Mexico City on Highway 95D, a toll road, and can be reached in about one and a half hours. All the other centers can be visited from there.

# NEW WORLD HERITAGE NOMINATIONS

EVERY DECEMBER, THE WORLD HERITAGE COMMITTEE MEETS and evaluates any new sites nominated by State Parties for World Heritage Listing. Two sites are being nominated by Mexico for inclusion on the List next year. Neither Canada nor the United States of America have nominated sites this year. Following is an edited version of the text from the two Mexican nominations.

## THE HISTORIC MONUMENTS ZONE OF QUERETARO

LOCATED NEAR A LARGE PRE-HISPANIC ARCHAEOLOGICAL SITE of the Teotihuacan and Toltec periods, which has so far been little studied, the present site of Queretaro was initially settled by an Otoml group fleeing from the Conquistadors into lands controlled by the Chichimecas. Twenty years later, in 1550, Spaniards flocked to the site, attracted by the opening up of the road to the mines at Guanajuato and Zacatecas, and the outlines of the new town were laid down around a center already established by the Franciscans. However, the indigenous people who quickly settled around this center had an influence on the basic urban characteristic of Queretaro.

The extensive archaeological site known as El Puebilto or El Cerrito, which is dominated by a 100 feet (30 m) high pyramid, is situated four miles (7 km) from the center of Queretaro. The limited investigations carried out there indicate that it has experienced two phases of growth: AD 400-600 in the Teotihuacan period and AD 650-1050 in the Toltec period.

At the time of the Spanish Invasion the lands around the abandoned site were the territory of the nomadic Chichimecas; they were occupied by Otoml people from nearer the Aztec capital; around 1520 they settled on the site of the present town. The Otoml leader Kho-nl, who took the name Fernando de Tapia when he adopted the Christian faith, was granted permission in 1532 by the Second Royal audience to establish an indigenous village on the site, along with the Spaniard Juan Sanchez Alanis. Two years later Spanish settlers coming up the Lermer River, accompanied by a large number of Tarasco Indians, arrived at the site, which was given the name 'Querrehtaro,' a Tarasco word meaning 'at the ball-court', a reference to the form of the narrow valley in which the settlement was situated.

From the outset the town had a unique character. The indigenous settlement founded in the name of the Spanish Crown was based on the presence of three indigenous groups - Otomls, Tarascos, and Chichimecas; they shared the area with the Spaniards, who entrusted the laying out of the town to Sanchez Alanis. Thanks to its favorable environmental and geographical conditions it quickly assumed a double pivotal role in the structure and organization of the new lands of the colony. On the one hand it was the link between the mountains of the south-east that had to be crossed in order to reach the capital of New Spain, passing through the rich lowlands (El Bajro) of the north-west, stretching some 400 miles (700 km) almost to the Pacific coast. At the same time it was the boundary between the southern lands, gradually settled by the Spaniards, and the northern region, which was under the control of hostile nomad peoples such as the Chichimecas.

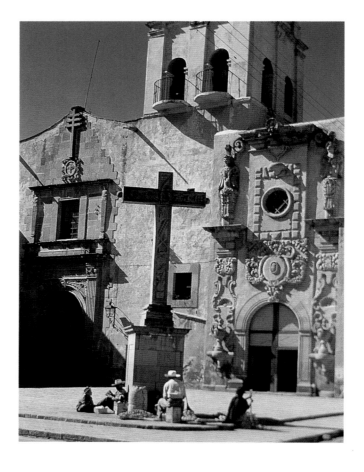

It was also to have an important supply function for the mining towns of Guanajuato and Zacatecas. By 1680 it had become the third city of New Spain, after Mexico and Puebla, with a population of over thirty thousand. The wealth of Queretaro in the mid 18th century is reflected by the important buildings that were built or reconstructed at that time, giving the town its special Baroque appearance. In the early 19th century its prosperity was based on textile manufacture and tobacco production, which provided employment for one-third of its forty thousand inhabitants. Its considerable degree of autonomy, as witnessed by the appointment of a Corregidor in 1770, encouraged exceptional commercial activity.

However, Mexican independence in 1810 spelt the beginning of Queretaro's economic decline. The region saw many military engagements, continuing to the end of the century. It was also the site of important historic events: the peace treaty with the USA was concluded there in 1848, and in 1867 the Emperor Maximillian was imprisoned and later executed there after the defeat of his army nearby. With the beginning of the revolutionary movement in 1910 Queretaro once again assumed a central place in the nation, since it was here that the new National Constitution (which is still in force today) was assigned on 5 February 1917 by all the revolutionary groups after two months of debate in the Teatro de la Republica.

The area nominated for inclusion on the World Heritage List covers 1.5 square miles (4 sq km), with 203 blocks. There are 1,400 designated monuments, of which twenty are religious and fifteen are used for public services. In terms of area Queretaro is in sixth place among the forty Historic Monument Zones in Mexico, but it occupies fourth place (after Merida, Mexico City, and Puebla) in terms of the number of historic buildings.

It was not intended that Queretaro should become an Episcopal See and so no place was allocated in the plan for a cathedral. However, all the monastic orders established themselves there. First came the Franciscans, Augustinians, and Dominicans, who founded large houses, and they were followed by the Jesuits and

Filipenses, as well as female orders. All have left imposing Baroque ensembles, of which the convents of Santa Teresa, El Carmen and, in particular, the convents of Santa Clara and Santa Rosa, are outstanding.

The many non-religious buildings in Queretaro, again mostly Baroque, are not innovative or exceptional in plan. Their special significance lies in the design and construction of a wide range of multi-lobate arches, to be found only in the interiors of the houses and palaces, which give the Baroque architecture of Queretaro an exceptional and original character, which is enhanced by the 'Pink Stone of Queretaro,' eagerly sought and used in other parts of the region.

It is the buildings erected during the economic heyday of the town in the last quarter of the 17th century which gave Queretaro its present-day appearance. The religious houses of San Antonio, El Carmen, and the Jesuit College were rebuilt and expanded and the churches of the Congregation of Guadalupe and Santo Domingo were built, mainly from the financial resources provided by Juan Caballero y Oclo, who was responsible for establishing Jesuit missions in California. The original Franciscan monastery of Santa Cruz was also expanded, and became the first Apostolic College of Propaganda Fide founded by the Holy See in the Americas.

Between 1726 and 1735 the most striking feature of the townscape of Queretaro was built; the 0.8 mile (1.28 km) long aqueduct that brought water to a central distribution point near the church of Santa Cruz. The 18th century saw the construction of a number of high-quality public buildings, such as schools and hospitals.

Queretaro is a well preserved Spanish colonial town which retains its original street layout virtually intact, and also a high proportion of its 17th and 18th ecclesiastical and secular buildings. As a significant group of buildings making up a living urban ensemble its authenticity is of high order. It is an exceptional example of a Spanish colonial town whose layouts symbolizes its multi-ethnic population. It is also endowed with a wealth of outstanding buildings, notably from the 17th and 18th centuries.

TOP   *The 0.8 mile (1.28 km) long aqueduct in Queretaro*
ABOVE   *An example of the 'Pink Stone of Queretaro'*
OPPOSITE   *Church of Santiago*

# THE PRE-HISPANIC TOWN OF UXMAL

UXMAL HAS LONG BEEN RECOGNIZED as one of the most important sites of the Maya culture, along with Chichen Itza, Palenque, Tikal, and Copan, and as the center of the Puuc region of southern Yucatan. It was the urban and ceremonial center for a group of settlements in the southern part of the Yucatan peninsula, the most important of which were Kabah, Labna, Sayll and Xpalak, for four centuries during the Late Classic Period (AD 650-1100).

Recent studies have shown that the layout of the buildings in the ceremonial center was based upon very accurate astronomical observations and alignments. Their facades are arranged in two horizontal elements, the lower plain and the upper richly decorated. These compositions often bring together in a harmonious way many elements from other Mesoamerican styles and cultures.

The 16th century Mayan history known as The Books of Chilam-Balam dates the foundation of Uxmal to the later 10th century, but archaeological investigations and radiocarbon dating suggest that the main structures in the complex were built between AD 700 and 1000. The earliest settlement in the area was around 800 BC (Pre-Classic Maya Period), but its main development and eventual disappearance was in the Late Classic Period (AD 650-1000), notable for the communications and movements between different regions of Mesoamerica.

Unlike most other pre-Hispanic towns, Uxmal is not laid out geometrically. Its space is organized in a more subtle way, seemingly based on two main principles. First, the buildings are orientated in relation to astronomical phenomena, such as the rising and setting of Venus. Secondly, they are adapted to the topography of the site, made up of a series of hills.

### PIRAMIDO DEL ADIVINO (PYRAMID OF THE SOOTHSAYER)

By virtue of its height and bulk, this structure dominates the ensemble, despite its location in a lower-lying part of the site. It is 116 feet (35 m) high and elliptical in plan. It is made up of five superimposed elements, two of them reached by monumental stairways on either side of the structure. It is from the Late Classic Period (AD 700-900) and brings together several artistic traditions, including the Toltec of central Mexico.

The western lower building (Temple I) dates from the earliest phase of the settlement. Within the structure, on the eastern side, is the small Temple II, and on the opposite side is a smaller element, known as Temple III. This was extended to form Temple IV, which stands out from the main pyramid and is richly decorated with masks of Chaac. The final phase in the evolution of the building is Temple V, built around 1000-1050 in the closing years of Uxmal.

### CUADRANGULO DE LAS MONJAS (QUADRANGLE OF THE NUNS)

This group of four buildings arranged round a large trapezoidal courtyard is situated on an artificial platform and reached by means of a stairway on the southern side leading to a monumental gateway. Each of the buildings is at a different level. The principal building, on the north side of the complex, is the only one that is two-storeyed; it is also the highest of the four. The decoration is especially rich, and is recognized to be an outstanding example of Mayan abstract and geometric art.

### PALACIO DEL GOBERNADOR (GOVERNOR'S PALACE)

This elongated building is constructed on a leveled natural feature and consists of three elements joined by covered vaults, the highest in the Mayan region. It is acknowledged to be one of the masterpieces of Mayan art for both its architecture and its decoration. It is severely symmetrical, its long facade being breached by two monumental entrances, and the exterior of the upper story is ornamented with rhythmically ascending masks and frets. Representations of the rain-god again surmount the main doorways and the corners of the building.

### CASA DE LAS TORTUGAS (THE HOUSE OF THE TORTOISES)

This building is located on the same terrace as the Governor's Palace. It is simple in design but the overall effect is harmonious. The

ABOVE    *Pyramid of the Soothsayer*
RIGHT    *The principal building from the Quadrangle of the Nuns*
BELOW RIGHT    *Stonework detail from the Quadrangle of the Nuns*
OPPOSITE    *A view of Uxmal*

upper story is decorated only with a series of slender columns supporting a robust cornice decorated with sculptures of tortoises, each different.

### THE BALL COURT

Despite its smaller dimensions when compared with other pre-Hispanic examples such a those at El Tajin, Xochicalco, or, in particular, Chichen Itza, the Uxmal example is of importance because of its location within the complex in relation to the main structures. In style and construction it can be dated to the same period as the Quadrangle of the Nuns.

### THE SOUTHERN COMPLEX: GRANDE PIRAMIDE (GREAT PYRAMID), PALOMAR (PIGEON HOUSE), AND SOUTHERN GROUP

This part of the site has not been extensively investigated. The nine-component structure known as the Great Pyramid is less striking than the Pyramid of the Soothsayer. Its upper temple, known as the Temple of the Parrots, has a richly decorated lower story, unlike other buildings at Uxmal, and probably dates to the earliest phase of the town. The Pigeon House seems to be one of the components of another quadrangular complex, like the Quadrangle of the Nuns.

Uxmal is an outstanding example of a Mayan ceremonial site. It is of especial interest by virtue of the very high quality of its architecture and ornamental art, which blend elements from other parts of Mexico with those indigenous to Yucatan.

# GLOSSARY

**acropolis** fortified part of an ancient city, it was usually built on an elevated position and housed the temple for the city's patron deity

**adobe** a sun-dried brick used for building; a building constructed from such bricks

**aeolian** (of the wind) produced or blown by the wind

**aestivation** (of animals) to pass the summer or dry season in a dormant condition

**alluvium** a fine-grained fertile soil consisting of mud, silt, and sand deposited by flowing water

**andesite** a type of volcanic rock

**anthropomorphic** resembling the human form

**atlatls** spear-thrower

**auger** a hand tool with a bit shaped like a corkscrew, for boring holes in wood; also a larger tool of the same kind for boring holes in the ground

**Aztecs** a major Indian group of the Americas, they inhabited what is now part of Mexico and rapidly developed a powerful and extensive empire. Their civilization declined in the early 16th century with the arrival of the Spanish.

**azure** sky blue

**badlands** extensive area of highly eroded waste land

**balds** hills with no vegetation cover; 'grass bald' grass cover only

**baroque** 17th century architectural style typified by dramatic lines and the free use of classical motifs

**basilica** a large oblong building with a nave, an apse and aisles, originally a Roman law court, later adapted for use by Christians as a special type of church

**Benedictines** order of monks founded in 529 AD by Saint Benedictine; founders of the herb flavored brandy liqueur of the same name

**biota** animal and plant life found in a particular area

**bog** wet spongy ground consisting of decomposing vegetation; a small marsh or swamp

**boreal** pertaining to the arctic, the north, or the north wind; from 'Boreas', the personification of the north wind in ancient Greek mythology, of or denoting the coniferous forests in the Northern Hemisphere

**brucellosis** a bacterial infection frequently causing abortions in animals and undulant fever in humans

**butte** an isolated hill or mountain rising steeply from a plain

**byre** a shelter for cows

**cenozoic (cainozic)** the third major era of Earth's geological history

**cairn** a stone mound used as a landmark, or to indicate a specific site

**caldera** a large basin-shaped crater at the top of a volcano, formed by the collapse of the volcano cone

**chancel** the part of a church between the altar and the railing that usually encloses it, or the portion where the altar is placed; reserved for the clergy

**chinook** a warm, dry southwesterly wind blowing down the eastern slopes of the Rocky Mountains

**conifer** a tree which bears cone-like fruit

**corbel** a horizontal support, projecting from a wall

**corpus** a complete or comprehensive collection of a specified type

**coulisse** a timber with a channel or groove in it within which a sluice gate slides

**Cretaceous** the third geological period, following the Jurassic, in the Mesozoic Era

**deciduous** (of trees and shrubs) shedding all leaves annually at the end of the growing season

**deity** a god or goddess; the state of being divine; Godhead

**delta** the flat alluvial area at the mouth of some rivers where the main stream splits up

**detritus** in geology, fragments of rock, etc produced by disintegration or wearing away; debris

**diorama** a miniature scene, wholly or partially three-dimensional, depicting figures in a naturalistic setting; a museum display, as of an animal, of a specimen in its natural setting

**dormer** a construction with a gable roof and a window that projects from a sloping roof

**dripstone** calcium carbonate ($CaCO_3$), deposited by dripping water in the form of stalactites or stalagmites

**elliptical** pertaining to an ellipse; as the planets move in elliptical orbits, having the sun in one focus

**endemic** restricted to a given area; used to indicate the strictly local occurrence of flora or fauna

**epigraphy** the study that deals with deciphering, interpreting, and classifying inscriptions, especially ancient inscriptions

**equinox** the precise time when the sun crosses the equator, when day and night are of equal length; the vernal equinox in the Northern Hemisphere occurs about the 21st March, and the autumnal equinox about the 22nd September

**escarpment** the long continuous steep face of a ridge or plateau formed by erosion or faulting; a cliff

**eutrophic** rich in organic and mineral nutrients and supporting an abundant plant life

**fecundity** fertility

**fen** a marsh, bog, fen; low land covered wholly or partially with water by producing sedge, coarse grasses or other aquatic plants; boggy land; a moor or marsh

**fescue** widely cultivated pasture and lawn grass, having stiff narrow leaves

**frieze** a decoration or series of decorations forming an ornamental band around a room; in architecture, a horizontal band, usually decorated with sculpture between the architrave and cornice of a building

**gable** the triangular wall enclosed by the sloping ends of a ridged roof; popularly the whole section, including the wall, roof, and space enclosed; a triangular decorative feature in architecture, such as that over a door or window

**genus (pl genera)** in biology, a classification of plants or animals with common distinguishing characteristics; a genus is the main subdivision of a family and includes one or more species; the genus is capitalized and precedes the species name, which is not capitalized eg Homo sapien - the scientific name for man

**geomorphology** the branch of geology that is concerned with the structure, origin and development of the topographical features of the earth's crust

**glacier** large, moving mass of ice formed by the accumulation of snow

**glyphs** a carved figure, either incised or in relief; carved pictograph; hieroglyph; in architecture, a vertical channel or groove

**guano** the dried excrement of fish-eating birds used as a fertilizer; also of bats

**halophytic** describes plants that grow in salt-impregnated soil

**hieroglyph** a picture or symbol representing a word, syllable or sound

**hoodoo** mushroom shaped rock pinnacles or cones

**hydromagnesite** a white, chalk-like variety of magnesium carbonate

**hydrothermal** of or relating to hot water; especially having to do with the action of hot water in producing geological changes by dissolving mineral substances and redepositing them when cool

**ICOMOS** International Council of Monuments and Sites

**in situ** in the natural, original or appropriate position

**Incas** the people indigenous to that area now known as Peru, before the Spanish conquest

**IUCN** International Union for the Conservation of Nature and Natural Resources - The World Conservation Union

**karst** characteristic of a limestone or dolomite region, featuring underground streams, sinkholes, gorges, etc

**kiva** in a Pueblo Indian dwelling, a large room used for religious and other purposes

**lacustrine** pertaining to a lake or lakes

**lahar** flow of volcanic mud

**leeward** in the direction toward which the wind blows; of the lee part or side; opposite to windward

**lintels** the headpiece of a door or window; in architecture, a horizontal piece of timber or stone over a door, window, or other opening, to support the superincumbent weight

**lithosphere** the rigid outer layer of the earth, comprising the earth's crust and the solid upper part of the mantle

**mansard** a roof having two slopes on both sides and both ends, the lower slopes being steeper than the upper Also known as a mansard roof

**mantle** in geology; the soil, sand and other loose material covering the solid bedrock of the earth

**maravedí** an obsolete Spanish copper coin

**martello** a circular fort of masonry, formerly built on coasts to protect against invaders

**masonry** brickwork or stonework

**Mayans** a large grouping of peoples indigenous to Central America

**Mecca** the birthplace of Mohammed in present day Saudi Arabia; the Holy City to which Moslems make pilgrimages; commonly denotes any place visited by many people

**megalithic** constructed with large stones

**mesa** a small, high plateau or flat tableland with steep sides

**Mesoamerica** The name generally applied to that section of Central America which is considered to have constituted a continuity in pre-Columbian times; corresponding to central and southern Mexico, Guatemala: parts of Honduras, El Salvador and British Honduras.

**mestizo** a person of mixed parentage; specifically, in the western United States and in Latin American countries, the offspring of a Spaniard or Portuguese and an American Indian

**Mesozoic** the second major era of Earth's geological history

**microclimates** the slight differences in climate, as between adjoining terrains, due to slight differences in soil, exposure, etc

**midden** a dunghill or pile of refuse

**mirador** in architecture, a passage; a balcony or gallery commanding a extensive view; also called a belvedere

**moraine** an accumulation of stones, sand or other debris on the surface or side of glaciers or at their foot. The latter are called terminal moraines, the former lateral or medial moraines

**mulatto** a person one of whose parents is Negro and the other Caucasian

**mural** a picture, usually large, painted directly onto a wall

**muskeg** a kind of bog or marsh formed by the deposit of thick layers of decaying vegetable matter, mosses, etc, in a depression or hollow in the earth's surface

**New World** the western hemisphere; particularly used in reference to Spanish colonialism in the Americas

**obduction** the act of drawing over, as a covering

**outliers** in geology, a mass of rock at some distance from the main formation as the result of the wearing away of the intermediate rock

**paleontology** the branch of geology that deals with prehistoric forms of life through the study of plant and animal fossils

**paleontologist** one who studies and is versed in paleontology

**Paleozoic** the first major era of Earth's geological history

**palisades** a fence or fortification consisting of a row of stakes or posts set firmly in the ground and sharpened on top, as a further defense against invasion

**pantheon** a temple or structure in which the gods or great people of a nation are entombed or commemorated; also used to describe the gods of a particular mythology considered collectively

**parfleche** the prepared hide of an animal, as of a buffalo, dried on a frame after the hair has been removed; also anything made of such hide

**pedestal** a base or bottom support, as for a lamp, column, statue or vase; any foundation, base, support, etc

**pediment** in architecture, the low triangular mass resembling a gable, at the end of buildings in the Greek style, and especially over porticos surrounded with a cornice, and often ornamented with sculptures

**pelagic** used to describe those fish which dwell in the upper layers of the open ocean

**pemmican** dried lean meat, pounded into a paste with fat and preserved in the form of pressed cakes

**petroglyphs** any inscription cut into the face of a cliff or rock; especially, a prehistoric carving of this kind

**piazza** an open, public square, especially one surrounded by buildings; a covered gallery or arcade

**pilaster** a rectangular support or pier, treated architecturally as a column, with a base, shaft and capital

**pinnacles** a small turret or spire that rises above the roof of a building, or that caps and terminates the higher parts of buildings or buttresses

**plaques** any thin, flat piece of metal, wood, porcelain, terra-cotta etc, used for ornamentation, as on a wall

**plate tectonics** a theory which attempts to explain seismicity, volcanism and mountain building in terms of the motions of plates (rigid segments of the Earth's outer shell)

**Pleistocene** one of the seven epochs that constitute the Cenozoic era

**podocarps** a large family of conifers

**polychrome** multi-colored

**portico** an open space covered by a roof supported on columns, sometimes detached

**pre-Columbian** Relating to the Americas; that time in history before the explorations of Christopher Columbus

**pulque** a fermented drink, popular in Mexico, made from the juice of an agave plant

**quicklime** calcium oxide; unslaked lime

**ramparts** an embankment of earth surmounted by a parapet and encircling a castle, fort, etc, for defending it from attackers

**relief** carvings on a surface that are raised up against the background; high relief (haut relief) is deeply cut, low relief (bas-relief) is more shallow

**rhyolithic lava** (pertaining to rhyolite) a kind of volcanic rock containing much silica and resembling granite in composition but having a texture that shows flow

**riparian** in zoology and botany, growing or living along a bank of a stream

**sarcophagus** a stone coffin, especially one exposed to view in the open air or in a large or monumental tomb

**sinkhole** a hollow or hole into which surface water drains especially such a hole worn through rock and leading to an underground channel

**solstice** the time at which the sun is at its greatest distance from the equator, and when its diurnal motion in declination ceases; the summer solstice of the Northern Hemisphere is on June 21, the winter on December 22; the summer solstice in the Southern Hemisphere is on December 22, the winter on June 21;

**stalactite** a pendant cone or cylinder of carbonate lime, attached like an icicle, to the roof or side a cavern and formed by the evaporation of dripping water from the rock above holding carbonate of lime in solution

**stalagmite** a cone-shaped deposit of carbonate of lime extending vertically from the floor of a cave, often forming beneath, and becoming continuous with, a stalactite above

**stratigraphic** (relating to stratigraphy) the arrangement of rocks in layers or strata; the branch of geology dealing with such stratification

**stucco** a plaster or cement of any kind used as a coating for walls; especially, a fine plaster composed of lime or gypsum with sand and pounded marble, used for surfacing inside or outside walls, molding relief ornaments, cornices, etc

**subduction** the act of taking away or withdrawing

**talus** slope; the sloping face of a wall, narrow at the top and wide at the base, in a fortification; in geology, a sloping pile of rock fragments at the foot of a cliff

**tectonic** (of landforms) resulting from distortion of the earth's crust due to forces within it; occurring within the earth's crust causing structural deformation

**tithe** the tenth part or any small part; a tenth

**Toltecs** an American Indian tribe which inhabited central Mexico between the 10th and 12th centuries AD

**totem** an image of a natural object, usually animal, which was commonly adopted amongst clans or individuals of northern American Indian tribes as an emblem representing kinship. A totem pole is a pole which totems were hung or carved

**topographical** of pertaining to topography

**topography** the accurate and detailed description of a particular place, city, town, district, estate, parish or tract of land

**tuberculosis** an infectious disease caused by the tubercle bacillus and characterized by the formation of tubercles in various tissues of the body; especially, tuberculosis of the lungs

**UNESCO** United Nations Educational, Scientific and Cultural Organization.

**ungulate** a mammal having hooves

**whorl** a radial arrangement of petals, stamens, leaves, etc, around a stem; a single turn in a spiral shell; anything shaped like a coil

**windlass** an apparatus operated by hand or machine, for hauling or hoisting, consisting of a drum or cylinder upon which is wound the rope, cable or chain which is attached to the object to be lifted

**WWF** World Wide Fund for Nature; in Canada and the USA, World Wildlife Fund.

**yucca** a plant of the lily family having stiff, sword-shaped leaves and white flowers in a single cluster, found in the south-western United States and Latin America

**zenith** the vertical point of the heavens at any place, or the point right above a spectator's head; the upper pole of the celestial horizon; the highest point; culmination; peak; summit

**zoo-anthropomorphic** Pertaining to animal forms; commonly refers to religions which have their gods represented by animal forms.

# INDEX

# PHOTO CREDITS